My Story Was Listening

Recollections of a Retired Psychotherapist

Fairlie Nicodemus

Front cover photograph —the author with her twin brother and her two older sisters in 1923
Back cover photograph by Morli Nicodemus Wilson

To my much-loved nieces and nephews who
are a treasured gift from my three siblings

If the eye could cry
To the measure of our sorrow
Whole days and nights till dawn it would weep.

Jalaluddin Mohammad Rumi
Ode 2893, Divan

Translated from the Persian
by Zahra Partovi

Contents

Acknowledgments

First, love and gratitude to my niece, Morli Wilson, who mastered the challenge of self-publishing and transformed a disorderly manuscript into this comely book. Thanks next to her friend and mine, Dawn McGuire, for believing that the book should be published. And thanks to my great nephew, Blake Wilson, an editor by trade, who encouraged an early manuscript to believe it could become a book, and to yet another dear niece, Anne Kane Holmes, a retired English Professor, for the labor of close editing. And how can I ever thank Carole Sbordone for patiently teaching an old brain how to work with a computer? Finally, forever gratitude to my dear friends, Mary Ambrose, Georgia Couden, Rebecca Dalton, Suzannah Lessard and Hilda Wilcox, who read early drafts and said yes.

INTRODUCTION

This book has been a challenge to write. When I grew up in the first half of the last century, the lid was on just about everything. Furthermore, in the upper class society in which I was raised, social behavior was formal and unspontaneous. There was an unspoken rule in my family that I learned at an early age: *Nothing with emotional voltage should ever be talked about in this family; we should never express anger; we should never reveal our private, deepest selves.*

My mother was a painfully insecure woman and lest her children humiliate her with inappropriate behavior, she raised us strictly and there was much correction of conduct and speech. Fearful of her disapproval, I tried to be her good girl in every way. Thus I became cautious, conforming, and mostly silent —the last person who should be writing a self-revealing memoir. If this were not enough to make honest self-disclosure difficult, my professional training as a psychiatric social worker, modeled in part on psychoanalytic concepts, had warned me to remain anonymous in my role as therapist. I was not to talk about myself, reveal my feelings, or share personal experiences. Why, then, did I decide to write this book?

I had been practicing psychotherapy most of my adult life. After I retired I found myself wishing that I could write about the subtleties and challenges of that work, how psychotherapists learn to do their craft, and about the complexities and depth of psychic pain. I thought first of writing a book of patient stories, but the psychic troubles I understood most profoundly were my own. If I could summon the courage to open the door to my private self, was not mine the patient story I should be telling? The prospect was daunting, but I decided to try.

"My mother taught me to be afraid of the world," I began.

I liked that beginning and proceeded with confidence. Writing about my professional career presented no problem. I could write easily about how I became committed to the work, how and where I was trained to do it, my early failures and successes, my growing expertise, and my increasing restlessness in the harness of professional correctness. But when I tried writing about my own fears, my progress stalled. Writing about fear in the abstract was one thing, but revealing mine, and revealing things I had said or done or not done in my lifetime, which I regretted, or of which I was ashamed, was another. Not that I had a lurid past. Far from it! I had tiptoed through life, fearful of taking risks and full of regrets that I had not taken more.

And so for a time I drifted about, unwilling to abandon my book, but fearful about how it would be received by my family and friends and by other professionals and my ex-clients. When I had been trying to help those clients overcome *their* fears, it had almost become a mantra for me to tell them to "take risks!" So why was I not heeding my own advice? Most of my life was behind me now, so there was not that much more left of it to lose. One of the few advantages of being old is caring less what people think, and with this thought my confidence returned and my writer's block was gone.

There is both fact and fiction in this book, and this needs clarification:

- In order to protect confidentiality, a sine qua non of responsible psychotherapy, all clients and case histories are fictional composites drawn from my practice during the past half century.
- Bernie, my supervising analyst, is also a fictional composite, based on the consultants and supervisors who have guided me over the years. It is also based on myself as a supervisor.
- I have given pseudonyms to my relatives and others close to me, with one exception. My mother's name was Dorothy and I have not changed it. I could not find a pseudonym that did not erase the image

of her in my mind, and to write about her I needed to be able to see her. She and my father are long dead and cannot protest; I could never have written this book were they not. I refer to them as Ma and Pa, as did my eldest sister whom I call Hope in this book, who artfully mined some of this same material in her book of poems, *Ma's Ram.*

- Have I altered facts? Occasionally yes, in order to protect sensitivity, but never at the cost of the truth of my story. I have sometimes altered the sequence of events to tighten the narrative. A more liberal use of fictional devices comes into my chapters about two major characters, Leo and Beth, in which there is a great deal of action and dialogue, for I cannot claim total recall.

- Almost all the dialogue in the book is fiction. Without a tape recorder how can it be otherwise? But I know these characters so well that if they did not speak these exact lines, they might well have. However, throughout this memoir there are sentences that *were* spoken to me at one time or another, words that were either lovely or painful to hear, and for these I do have total recall.

PART I

GENESIS

My mother taught me to be afraid of the world. And since one's mother looms large in the world-view of a small child, my fear of the world began with my fear of her. Struggling to overcome that fear has taken me the better part of my life and I will, no doubt, go to my grave with a few wisps of it still clinging to me. I have lived my life as best I could, and sometimes well, but I have never been able to spread my wings and soar into my possibilities. Always present, attached to one leg, has been the ball and chain of fear.

Psychotherapists often ask their patients to recall their first memory because of its possible value as a diagnostic clue. Mine, a memory of fear, took place sometime between my second and third birthdays in a room in our house called the nursery. This room was half a level below the rest of the second story and was reached by descending a short flight of stairs. My twin brother, a dark-eyed, dark-haired little boy, and I, blue-eyed and very blond, occupied the nursery. We slept in separate cribs constructed of white metal bars. Anna, a woman who worked for my mother and whom I disliked, came into the nursery one morning to get us up and found me in my twin's crib. I had climbed out of mine, crossed the room and climbed into his. That alone was not the crime. Beside me in his crib, presumably deposited by me, was a bowel movement. I remember its dark length lying on his white bedding and Anna's face, looking shocked and revolted. I remember her saying, "I'll have to get your mother," and knowing what that meant: this was serious, major, too big a thing for her to handle. I remember her leaving and me waiting, afraid of what was to come.

Moments later my mother appeared at the top of the nursery stairs, their height adding to her own. She was a tall woman, almost six feet. I waited for her to come down and deal with me, but she didn't. She just stood there, her face clouded with disgust. I do not remember the exact words that finally came out of her. I may not even have known the meaning of some of them, but I had no doubt about what she wanted me to understand: What I had done was so terrible there was no punishment for it. Then she turned and went away.

A few months later my twin would be dead.

Rescue

"Can you take me with you?"

"I don't know, dear child. I'll have to ask your mother."

I had just turned five. Aunt Carrie, Pa's younger sister, had come up from her Maryland farm to hear the Metropolitan Opera's performance of *Parsifal* and she was visiting our family on Long Island. She was forty-one, married but childless, although she had longed for children. In her day, when they didn't come, a woman had to accept that fate as God's will. She was leaving the next day.

Aunt Carrie was beautiful. She was slender and smartly dressed. I can still see a modish black hat perched at an angle on her pile of braided and coiled auburn hair. Although Ma had a pretty face, she was dowdy and overweight, but she also had a nice wit. I remember the two of them laughing a lot when Aunt Carrie was visiting, but when my sisters, Mary and Hope, were at school in our neighbor's house and Ma and I were alone, I had often found her crying.

"Your mother was never the same after your twin died," Aunt Carrie told me years later when I was a young woman visiting her on her farm in Maryland. "Before that she was lively and full of spirit. I'll never forget that day when she was coming down with all of you for a few weeks. I met her at the Baltimore station and saw her walking towards me carrying one of you twins and leading Hope or Mary by the hand. A porter was following carrying the other twin and holding the other child by the hand. Following them was another porter carrying two large suitcases. When she met up with me she said, 'Carrie, I think I'm going to have to stay until the children are older!' You two were so adorable. I remember saying, 'Oh Dorothy, can't I have one of them?'"

I was waiting to hear if I would be allowed to go off with Aunt Carrie. After I asked her, she looked at Ma and Ma looked at her and they walked into the next room.

"Tell me honestly, Carrie, what you think of the portrait," I heard Ma say. "His hair is the wrong color. Do you see what I mean? But Alice was fussy about my wanting her to change things."

Ma's friend Alice had been staying with us, and every day she was making the painting from pictures Ma had given her. Mary and I wanted to watch, but she wouldn't let us. After she left, Ma and Pa hung it over the mantelpiece. They never asked us if we liked it. We never talked about Little Brother.

"I think it's a lovely painting, Dorothy," Aunt Carrie said. "I know you'll be glad to have it, especially as the year's pass. Remember, no one will ever be able to paint the memories you have of him."

Then their voices quieted down and I couldn't hear what they were saying. In a few minutes they came back and Aunt Carrie was smiling.

"Your mother says I can borrow you for a little while."

"What does borrow mean?"

"It means that she is still your mother, but that you can come with me and I can pretend you're mine for a while." She drew me against her.

"I broke my china doll last week," I said. "Ma said she can never be fixed."

"I'm sorry, dear," she said. "But you can play with my old doll when you come down. She doesn't have a beautiful face like your china doll, but I loved her. She's in the house somewhere. We'll look for her when we get home."

I was scared of Aunt Carrie's house. It was so big. And I was scared of Uncle Willie. He smiled more than Pa, but his voice was gruff too. He left early in the mornings like Pa, but at dinner he and Aunt Carrie sat at two ends of a long table and I sat in the middle, feeling very small. It was such a big table for just a few people. Maybe Aunt Carrie had expected to have a large family like ours. Martha, one of Aunt Carrie's servants, would burst through the swinging door with a platter of meat and put it in front of Uncle Willie. He would carve a piece, dangle it on the end of a fork and pointing it at me would growl, "Have some meat, Sitty?" And then he would wave it in the air and pretend to take it away.

"Stop teasing the child, Willie," Aunt Carrie would say, but part of me liked it. Pa rarely spoke to me except to say things like "stop that" or "go away." I liked Uncle Willie calling me "Sitty." Little Brother and I were called Brother and Sister before he died, but after he died, I was still called "Sister." Uncle Willie had made a little nickname out of it.

For the first few days in Aunt Carrie's house, she took me up to my room at night and sat with me for a little while. We had found her doll, Melissa, in one of her closets. I never told Aunt Carrie that I didn't like Melissa. I thought she was ugly. But one day I thought of her lying all that time in the dark in Aunt Carrie's closet and feeling lonely, and after that I was nicer to her. I was even glad later that she was up in my bed waiting for me because after a couple of days Aunt Carrie told me it was time for me to go upstairs by myself and get ready for bed. She would come up later to say goodnight and hear my prayers. I told her I was scared to go up alone. Her stairs were taller than ours and wound around and there was just one tiny light up there when you got to the top. Then I had to walk to the end of a long dark hall to get to my room.

"You're old enough now to go up alone," Aunt Carrie said. "There's nothing to be afraid of."

"How do you know?"

"Because I know, and I know you are brave."

I was still afraid, but I did what I was supposed to do. I almost always did.

In the mornings after Uncle Willie had driven out the long lane, I would go into Aunt Carrie's bedroom, knocking first, of course, and I would usually find her at her dressing table fixing her hair. It came down nearly to her waist. I would stand beside her while she brushed it, then braided it and coiled it on her head. We would have conversations then and sometimes she would show me pretty things in her jewelry box and tell me where they had come from. One day she took out a little gold pendant on a chain that had words on it and she told me it was a music prize that her mother had won in school. Her mother's piano, standing in the parlor, was the first thing in her house that I had seen on that first night when we came in after our long trip on the train and the drive back with Uncle Willie. Even though I did not know what it was —I had never seen a piano before —I was drawn to it and ran my hand along its shiny smooth surface.

"We have to be very careful of the piano," Aunt Carrie said. "It belonged to your grandmother. I'll show it to you in the morning."

The next day when we sat down together at the piano and she made beautiful sounds come out and let me touch the slippery black and white keys, I fell in love with it even though I didn't know what falling in love was. Aunt Carrie told me that her mother had played it beautifully, but that she had died when Aunt Carrie was still a little girl. In Aunt Carrie's dining room there was a beautiful portrait of her mother that was painted when *she* was still a little girl. I loved looking at it when I was sitting at the long table between Aunt Carrie and Uncle Willie. She had long golden curls and blue eyes and her two small hands were folded together on her breast. I have blue eyes and my hair is the same color as hers. I loved knowing that she was mine.

After breakfast Aunt Carrie would be busy and when the weather was nice I would go outside. At home there were houses all along our street, but when I stood on Aunt Carrie's porch and looked out I could see only one house and a barn, far, far away. There were fields all around Aunt Carrie's house that stretched to the edge of the sky. Uncle Willie's cows would be grazing in those fields, first in one and then another, and in the evenings they would walk to the barn to be milked. The man who took care of Uncle Willie's cows was friendly and he would talk to me while he aimed the steaming milk into the glistening pails. Dan and Charlie, the horses that worked on the farm, were in their stalls nearby, contentedly munching their grain. I liked Dan best and he seemed to like me. One day the man lifted me up onto his back. I loved feeling tall up there and my legs loved clinging to his warm flanks.

Sometimes Aunt Carrie needed to go out in her car to do something at her church or to go to the little store, or to visit someone. She would put on her little black hat and we would drive out the lane together. She said it was half a mile long. The man in the store would say, "Good morning, Miss Carrie. What can I do for you today?" The first time we went there he said, "I see you have someone with you today," and he reached into a big jar and gave me a candy. Everyone we saw seemed glad to see us.

I was happy being with Aunt Carrie and one of the things I loved best was going out in the afternoons with her and bringing in the chickens that had been let out earlier to hunt for bugs in the grass. We would call them in, "Here, chick! chick! chick!" and they would come running to get the corn that she was rattling in a pail. While they were feeding in their yard she would send me into their house to collect their eggs in the little boxes. It was like Easter every day.

But one night after I had been at Aunt Carrie's for a while I had a dream that I was back in our house playing with Mary and I woke up crying. When Aunt Carrie came in and asked me what was wrong I said, "I want to go home." "All right, dear," she said. "I'll call your father tonight."

I had expected that *she* would take me home, but a few nights later when Uncle Willie drove in the lane, Pa was with him. "Your father has come to take you home, dear," Aunt Carrie said cheerfully.

"I thought you were going to take me."

"No, dear. It's best for you to go with your father."

But it wasn't best. I had never been with him alone and I was afraid of him. The hardest thing about it was that we got on the train at night and had to sleep together in a little room. I didn't know where the bathroom was and I was almost wetting my pants, but I was afraid to ask him. Then he opened a little door, went in and closed it, and I heard a toilet flush. After he came out I went in. Ma said I should never sit on a strange toilet and she always held me so I could stand over it. I tried standing over this one by myself, but the train kept making me fall, so I had to sit. I decided I just wouldn't tell Ma.

GETTING ON THE COUCH

My mentors at the School for Social Work at Smith had given me such a hard sell about the benefits of psychoanalysis and the wisdom of Freudian theory that I slid onto the couch in the expectation that I could be almost guaranteed a cure. Of course I would have to be a "good" patient, follow the rules, and work hard. There weren't many rules as I understood them, but they were strict. I would have to pay for all contracted sessions whether attended or not; I could be verbally abusive, but not violent or destructive; I was expected to strive for honest self disclosure, dredging up a steady flow of material to work on; and I could not make any major changes in my life during the analysis.

Everyone knew that an analyst sat behind the couch, taking notes, but the more sophisticated of us knew that he (maybe she) was a mostly passive, indistinct, although wise and knowing figure on whom the patient transferred feelings from past relationships. These were then "worked through" to some kind of psychic liberation. The kind of person the analyst was outside his role was supposedly irrelevant, so when Dr. Gautier and I first met in his waiting room and I was immediately disappointed I told myself, "Too bad, but it doesn't matter. He can still do the job." I had put him in an unfair position by falling hard for the consultant Miss Garrett, my adviser at the school, had sent me to and who had found this analyst for me. Of course in his role as consultant he was freer to interact with me and to be himself, more or less —smiling and warm and making me want to make a flying leap into his lap. He was a short man, a little overweight and physically soft, whereas my tall, trim, unsmiling analyst with a manly moustache seemed all testosterone.

Dr. Gautier asked why I was there. I told him that I wanted to overcome my fears and feelings of inadequacy, to liberate myself -- at the advanced age of 28 —from the grip of my parents, to understand normal sexuality and be free of my sexual inhibitions, and to stop being such a needy child. My goal was to become a mature, confident woman and to marry and raise a family.

So the analysis began. I lay back on the couch and stared up at the ceiling and there was Ma reclining comfortably as if stretched out on an invisible bed. I gave a long, deep sigh of resignation. I should have known she would be there. She had been hovering over me all my life, not in the overprotective way she had been with Robert, but more like a coach who can paralyze his team at mid-game by finding too much fault. A major task of the analysis I now realized would be getting her out of my space and it seemed overwhelming. But if I did my analytic work diligently, perhaps I would look up one day and find that she was gone and I would know then that the analysis was ready to end.

Pa presented a different problem. He was nowhere in sight. I had not told my parents that I was in analysis, but if he had known I felt sure he would have scorned it as a waste of time and money. Pa wanted no part of me and I wanted no part of him, but if one of my analytic tasks was to get Ma out of the room, perhaps it was another to get —or let —Pa in. My professional self knew that if I were ever to be free I would have to stop hating my parents and to forgive them and, before this whole thing was over, to forgive myself. Now I just wanted to lie back and revel in hating them for the way they had hurt me, and for a while that's what I did. But when I looked up and saw Ma's injured face and quivering mouth, my guilt swung back like a pendulum and hit me in the face. So instead of hating them, I was hating myself for being a cruel and hurtful person.

I soon discovered that Ma wasn't the only interloper in the room. To my dismay my first psychiatrist, Dr. Porter, kept barging in, finding fault with the process and reprimanding me for having succumbed to the brainwashing at Smith. He was particularly scornful of my wanting to talk with my new analyst about sex. When I had brought up the subject with Dr. Porter he had dismissed it and railed about the emphasis placed on sex by the Freudians. Sex was a natural part of human nature, he had declared, and did not need discussing —it took care of itself. His dismissal had left me feeling that there was something seriously wrong with my sexuality, since it wasn't taking care of itself. I was eager to get on with the analysis and to explore this and other issues, but Dr. Porter kept glowering at me, so that analyzing my relationship with him became a time-consuming issue in itself. I had not realized until he barged in how betrayed I had felt after giving him my trust.

A person in psychic pain who seeks professional help is vulnerable in much the same way that an infant is. So much depends on the hands into which each falls. When I started therapy with Dr. Porter I had been an ideal patient —bright, open-minded, curious, and eager for help. Somehow I knew that I was getting in my own way and I was searching for someone wise and caring who could lead me out of the maze. If I had fallen into the right hands I believe that my therapy would have had a good outcome and readied me for the marriage and family I so much wanted. I was angry with Dr. Porter for those lost years and the time it was taking to get him out of my analysis, but I had painfully mixed feelings about him and I could not dismiss him as easily as Miss Garrett had. She could not know how much his kind listening had meant when I was struggling to understand my confused feelings about Leo. Before our last meeting I had been ready to forgive his therapeutic lapses, harmful though they had been, but his final rejection I could not forgive. He had thrown me out when I was no longer a dutiful daughter, just as Pa had threatened to do when I became engaged to Leo, but anger frightened me, and it would take many more hours of analytic work before I would be ready to throw Dr. Porter out of my space.

As the analysis progressed and Dr. Porter was claiming less of my time, I kept revisiting the question of why Ma disliked me so much. It was clearly related to the death of my twin. If he had lived he would still have been the preferred one, but she would probably have liked me well enough, and I would not have been a depressed child and thus, more likeable. On occasion Ma talked to me about the two of us. She told me that I was the first born and larger, that I was dominant and aggressive while he was passive and gentle, and that he was courageous and willing to try new things while I paradoxically was cautious and, by implication, cowardly. She once told me of an incident that may have sown the seed of my belief that I was a cruel person. He and I were in her bedroom. I had gone over to her dressing table, picked up a razor blade and cut his hand. She implied that I had done this deliberately to hurt him. Possibly I had, for I was certainly jealous of his favored position, but I believe that I was simply curious.

I wanted to bring back sweet memories of the two of us and never could, but I have a faded photograph of our sitting on the running board of our old car holding hands, and I am smiling and looking flirtatious. When he became ill I remember his being taken from the nursery into another room, that the door was always closed, and that I never saw him again. I remember being outside that door and hearing him cry, then wandering alone in the house. Years later Mary told me that she was asked to sit beside his bed and cheer him up, but I feel quite certain that Hope would not have been there and would have escaped to the life she had found on the other side of the hedge. So there is this mix of remembering and of being told and of speculation, but there is one more memory that I will never forget and that is when Little Brother had his accident.

He, Mary, and I are riding our tricycles in the village house, following a course around three rooms and through three doorways. Mary is setting the pace and he and I are hurrying to catch up. At one of the doorways I crowd him to get through first and knock him off his tricycle into a fireplace. He is badly hurt and starts screaming. Ma is out doing errands and Anna rushes in from the kitchen, picks him up and takes him on her lap on a nearby chair. Blood is gushing from his forehead and she tries to stop it with her apron. I stand against her knee trying to get closer, trying to see what has happened to him, but she tells me, "Go away!" Mary is standing at a distance, watching. She is thinking, *"I am the oldest. I should have been looking out for them. I made them ride too fast. It's my fault that he fell"* and I am thinking, *"I tried to get through the doorway first. I bumped into his tricycle. I made him fall. It's my fault that he fell."*

It is morning in our household not long after Little Brother has died and before Robert has arrived. Pa has left early to take the train into the city and Hope is over at the stable with Mr. Carle. Anna is cleaning the house and Ma is in her bedroom, sitting at her sewing machine. A bolt of material and a dress pattern are spread out on her bed. The morning sun is slanting through the window onto the rug and Mary and I are sitting on the floor in the shaft of sunlight, playing with our dolls. As she works Ma talks to us like confidantes, talking about things that are bothering her, and we pay no attention, intent on our play. As it so often does, her mind goes back to those awful days when her little boy was dying and her eyes fill with tears, and then she says these powerful words:

"I am sure he wouldn't have died if he hadn't hurt his head, if he hadn't had that terrible fall."

The two little heads look up from their play. Their mother has said this before and it frightens them. Then she places a length of cloth on her sewing machine and it starts to whir. She has no idea what has been going on in the little heads that are turned down again, attending to their dolls.

"How did your twin die, Miss Nicodemus?" Dr. Gautier wanted to know.

"He had spinal meningitis. It's odd, don't you think, that none of the rest of us got it."

"How did your father react to his son's death?"

"I have no memory of Pa then. I was told that he started coughing up blood. They thought he had tuberculosis and sent him to a sanitarium, but he didn't stay there long. Later, during World War II when Robert was fighting in France and my mother had a nervous breakdown, it happened again —his coughing up blood. This time the doctors found a lesion in his trachea that they believed had ruptured under the stress. The only emotions of his that I remember from my childhood were annoyance and anger, but I've learned since that he makes a little moaning sound when he's upset. I don't think I've ever seen him cry. I don't know how my mother reacted either just after Little Brother died. Maybe we girls were sent away some place. But my aunt told me that my mother lost her religious faith then and stopped going to church. My father never had any use for religion.

I heard Dr. Gautier's chair creak as it did when he got up to signal the end of a session, and I slid my legs off the couch. "I'll see you next week," he said.

Navigating Ma and Pa

Before I left Aunt Carrie's I had dreamed about being home and playing with Mary, but I had forgotten that she and Hope went off through the hedge every morning to school in Mr. Carle's house and I was left alone again with Ma. She would tell me to "go out and play" and I would go out and look for something to do, maybe ride my old tricycle for a while, but I was getting too big for it and Mary's bicycle was too big for me. Other children lived on our street, but they were in school too -- a different school -- and Ma said I couldn't play with them anyway because they were common.

"What does 'common' mean?" I asked.

"Different from us," she said. "From a different class."

I didn't know what that meant either, just that there was something wrong with them and it made me scared of them. So I would wander around looking for something. For anything. I didn't know what. Cars would drive by now and then and I would wave at them and sometimes the person inside would wave back.

Before I went away I used to wait for Hope and Mary to come back from school, and after we had our lunch, Mary and I would play with our dolls and Hope would go off by herself. She said dolls were silly. She was always reading a book and she would hide somewhere so we wouldn't bother her. Ma usually made us all go out for a while in the afternoons and Mary and I would put our dolls in their carriages and take them for a walk. But Hope would hide her book under her coat and climb a tree where Ma couldn't see her and we couldn't reach her. She often didn't do what Ma told her and Ma would be angry. But after Pa brought me back from Aunt Carrie's things were different. Instead of reading, Hope would go back through the hedge to Mr. Carle's. When Mary asked to go with her Hope would be cross. "I told you Mr. Carle only wants me." Whether he did or he didn't, Hope was not about to share what she had found. Mr. Carle's place was bigger than ours. He had enough room in his house for Hope and Mary's school and he also had a stable with horses like Dan that you could ride. Hope had asked him if he would teach her how and after that she was over at his stable every afternoon.

At first Mary didn't want to play with me. "Dolls are silly," she said. But then I saw her playing with her own dolls and after a while she let me play with her again, but never when Hope was around. For a time it was like before. That is before Mary made a friend in school who had a pony. After that she went over to play with her friend as often as Ma would take her, and soon she was learning to ride like Hope. She had left me and dolls behind. And so I took to wandering again.

One day I wandered into the Arthurs' yard. They were our neighbors on the other side from Mr. Carle. Mrs. Arthur was outside kneeling in her flowerbed. She was a friendly lady. I walked over to her and she said hello. I watched her digging around her plants, and after a while she stood up.

"Well, I have go in now," she said. "I guess you should be going home. Your mother must be wondering where you are."

I shook my head. "No, she isn't."

"Oh, I'm sure she is. You'd better run along now."

But when she walked over to her house, I followed her and when she opened her door, she saw me behind her.

"Can I come in with you?" I asked.

She didn't answer at first. Then she said, "Oh, all right. But just for a little while."

When we went into her house, a man was there, sitting in a rocking chair. He was reading a newspaper.

"This is my husband, Mr. Arthur," she said. I had seen him out in his yard sometimes.

He smiled at me. "Hello, little girl. What's your name?"

"Sister."

"Sister? Do you have a brother?"

"No. I have sisters."

"She's our neighbor's little girl, Henry. You remember. They lost the other one."

An orange cat was curled up in his lap and I reached over and touched its soft fur.

"Sometimes she's likes to play," Mr. Arthur said, "but she's sleeping now."

I followed Mrs. Arthur into her kitchen and an old woman was there cooking at the stove.

"This is my mother," Mrs. Arthur said. "This is our neighbor's little girl." The old woman smiled at me.

"I guess your mother's cooking supper too," she said.

"No, she isn't. She doesn't cook. Delphine comes to our house every day to make the food. She doesn't let me in the kitchen. She's grumpy."

Mrs. Arthur looked at her mother and her mother looked at Mrs. Arthur.

Later, while they were all sitting at the table eating, I sat on the floor and played with the cat who had wandered over. When it was time for their dessert, the old woman asked me if I'd like a dish of pudding. I smiled. Mr. Arthur got up and brought another chair to the table and helped me into it.

"It's nice having a little child in our house again," Mrs. Arthur said when we were all finished, "but now I'm going to have to send you home, dear. I don't want your mother worrying."

When I left their house and looked back I saw Mr. Arthur watching at the window until I went into our yard.

I liked the Arthurs and took to wandering over there in the afternoons. If one of them saw me they would invite me in and a chair would be at the table, waiting for me. Once Mr. Arthur opened the window and called out,

"Dessert time!" I don't know how I managed to visit so many times before Ma missed me.

"Is my little girl here?" Ma asked. She knocked at the door and Mr. Arthur let her in. Then she saw me sitting at their table.

"Hope said you might be over here," she said. She was looking very cross.

"But we love having her," Mrs. Arthur said, getting up from the table and shaking Ma's hand." Mr. Arthur stood up too and put out his hand, but Ma didn't take it.

"Has she been over here before?"

"Oh, often."

"I can't tell you how embarrassed I am," Ma said. She got all funny and began smiling too much. She often did that when I went out with her in the car to do errands and she met someone she didn't know very well. I didn't like that face.

"She knows she's not supposed to go out of our yard. Don't you, Sister?"

"But it's been a pleasure to have her," Mrs. Arthur said. "Won't you sit down with us?"

"No, no. Please. I don't want to disturb you. I'm so sorry she's been bothering you. She reached out her hand and grabbed my arm. "Come on now, Sister. Have you thanked the Arthurs for being so kind to you?"

"Thank you, I said."

Then she pulled me towards the door. Mr. Arthur followed us and opened it, letting us out into their yard.

"I'm very angry with you," Ma said as we walked into our yard. "You are never to go over there again, do you understand?" I nodded. "Say, 'Yes Mother.'"

"Yes, Mother."

"I don't know how I'm going to punish you. I think maybe I'll take your dolls away for a while."

"But the Arthurs like me."

Ma stopped walking. "I want you to listen to me. I don't want you in that house ever again. They're common people. Do you hear me?"

"Yes, Ma."

"Now go upstairs to your room. I'll tell you when it's time for supper."

It was what she had said before about not playing with the children who went to that other school. How did you know when someone was common? We could go over to Mr. Carle's. I still didn't know what common was.

I couldn't wait for summer. Ma loved to go to the beach. She took me with her almost every nice day and sometimes Mary came, but Hope never wanted to go. Ma's friends had come back from the city to their summer homes and I was allowed to play with their children. We would be out on the sandbars building castles while Ma and her friends sat under an umbrella on the beach keeping an eye on us and talking and laughing. Ma was happy. She would be knitting and lately she had been knitting little sweaters almost the right size for my dolls. Her stomach had been getting very fat. One day she told me that I was going to have a little brother or a little sister. She took my hand and put it on her stomach. "Maybe you can feel the baby in there," she said. "Kicking." But I couldn't and I took my hand away. I didn't like it touching her stomach.

"That's where you and Little Brother were before you were born," she said. She rarely mentioned him and her mouth looked as if it was going to cry.

"Did *we* kick?"

"You certainly did! I didn't know there were two of you in there."

"Do Hope and Mary know?"

"Yes, they do."

"Are they glad?"

"I think so. They didn't say."

But I was glad. Now that Mary was away most of the time I would have someone to play with. But then after summer was over it was time for school to start and I was old enough to go through the hedge with Mary and Hope.

I was the youngest child in our schoolroom. There were five girls and two boys. I liked our teacher. When I was lonely before I went to school I used to wait outside the hedge for the children to come out for recess and I would run over to be with them. Miss Tyler would be standing there watching, and she would smile and wave to me, and when she went back in with the children she would wave goodbye and wait until I had gone back through the hedge. I loved being in school. I loved learning how to make my letters and then how to make my letters make words. One of the older girls helped me sometimes. She was nice, but I liked one of the boys best. He lived down near our beach and rode his horse all the way to school, even when it rained or snowed. He kept his horse in Mr. Carle's stable and then after school he rode it home. I liked it when he smiled at me.

Ma seemed pleased that I was learning to read. She was a big reader like Hope. If she wasn't sewing or knitting she was reading and she could even knit and read at the same time. I couldn't figure out how she did that. When I came home from school I would show her my papers and sometimes she would help me with my reading. She liked reading aloud and sometimes she would read me stories, but then she went away and when she came back she brought my baby brother with her. After that, everything was about Robert. He was a beautiful little baby and I wanted to hold him, but she was afraid I would hurt him or make him sick, so I would wander around again, looking for something to do.

Ma loved Christmas. One day when she was making a wreath to put on our front door she told me that as children she and her brothers and sister could only have one present. Her father was a minister and he said that Christmas was a time to celebrate the birthday of Jesus in the stable, not to get presents. He didn't want them to have any, but her mother said they had to have at least one. I knew the Jesus story. When I was with Aunt Carrie she had read it to me.

"I think children *should* have presents," Ma said, "particularly when other children have them. All my friends did."

So every Christmas there were lots of presents under our tree, some that Santa Claus had brought and some from her. Pa never gave presents. I guessed that it was just the mothers who did.

Before Christmas that year and not long after Robert was born, Ma had begun talking about needing to lose weight, and one day I heard her talking on the telephone to the mother of Mary's friend.

"Do you still have that book about dieting I lent you? That little orange book? Are you sure? Well then, it's got to be around here somewhere."

Another day I saw her looking in the bookcase in our upstairs hall.

"Darnation!" she said. "I just can't find it anywhere!"

"Find what?"

"A book I'm looking for. A little orange book. I don't know what I did with it." And she went off grumbling to herself.

I remembered that book because she was reading it a lot before Robert was born and she had gotten very fat. I decided I would look for it and several days later I found it, just where she had been looking. She must have missed it. I was going to run and give it to her, but then I had an idea. Christmas was coming and since she wanted that book so much I decided I would wrap it up and give it to her on Christmas day. It would be her best present.

On Christmas morning I was more excited about her opening my present than opening my own. When the moment came and she removed the wrapping I waited for her face to look happy, but it showed nothing. She said nothing, then turned away. I don't remember much more about that Christmas, but I remember Mary handing me a package and telling me it was from Aunt Carrie. When I opened it, lying in a box under a pretty blue blanket was a china doll.

Ma was sitting on the sofa holding Robert. She had heard him crying in the hall and had brought him in.

"Aunt Carrie said she was going to give you one," Ma said. "You'll have to thank her."

I loved my new doll as soon as I saw her, but I loved her so much I was afraid to pick her up. I was too afraid of dropping her. So I left her in her pretty box until I could take her upstairs. After that I mostly kept her in my doll carriage, and at night when I went to bed I moved the carriage so that she would be close by.

A few days later I heard Ma talking again on the telephone to her friend. She was talking about me. "Sister wrapped up that old dieting book of mine that I asked you about and gave it to me for Christmas. I don't know where she found it. Maybe she was hiding it from me. I can't imagine what she was thinking. She's the strangest child."

Why I was failing in my romantic life was one of the problems I had first presented to Dr. Gautier. I had experienced another failed relationship the previous spring when I was a student in a psychiatric hospital in Boston. In reliving that unhappy chapter with Dr. Gautier, it was becoming clearer to me what a major role my mother was playing in all of this.

I had been introduced to the college classmate of a friend from Long Island, and it was the first time I had been attracted to anyone since the end of my relationship with my Army Captain several years before. We had dated a few times before he graduated and met when we could during the summer and fall, and had made plans to get together when I came down to Long Island for the Christmas holidays. He was living with his widowed mother in an apartment in New York and working in a bank. He had arranged a very special evening of dinner and the theater, and afterwards he invited me back to their apartment. I knew what he had in mind. It was quiet and dark when we came in and without turning on the lights he drew me to a couch and we started making love.

Until I heard the sound of plumbing being used in the back of the apartment I had assumed we were alone.

"Is someone here?" I asked.

"Oh, that's just my mother."

"Your mother's *here*?"

"Don't worry," he said, "She won't bother us. She won't come out."

But I froze. I imagined the sound of her footsteps and her calling out, "Frank? Is that you Frank?" then coming into the room in her robe and slippers saying, "Oh, you have someone with you," and I would have had to confront her in my disheveled state. She *didn't* appear, but that didn't make me any less anxious, and it was hard to explain to Frank why I couldn't stay. He was angry, but took me back to where I was staying —young men did that kind of thing then —and we made plans in the taxi for him to come up to Boston. A college friend had an apartment in Cambridge and Frank could use it when his friend was away. But not long after this I got an I-have-met-someone-else letter and never saw him again. This was hard enough, but what followed was even worse.

Not long after I got a phone call from a stranger asking me if I would like to go out to dinner and a movie. It was Frank's friend, the one who had the apartment in Cambridge. He said Frank had told him that I might be interested in going out. I wondered what else Frank had told him. I was doubtful, but decided to chance it. Maybe I would like him. It took me only a few minutes to decide that I didn't, but it was clear that he was attracted to me. After dinner he said he would rather go dancing than to a movie, would I mind? I did mind, but as I had been conditioned I passively deferred to the wishes of the male. As we danced he pulled me closer and closer and I was aware of his being aroused. Then it all became clear. Since I had been planning to spend the weekend with Frank and since Frank no longer wanted me he had assumed I was up for grabs. I could not wait for the evening to end.

The dating protocol in that era was possibly a kiss on a first date, but nothing more, so I assumed I would be able to close the door after thanking him and be rid of him, but he was furious when I did not invite him in. "That's a nice 'thank you,'" he said, "after giving you such a nice evening!" He grabbed me, forced his tongue into my mouth and lifting my skirt, tried thrusting his penis between my legs. We struggled and then I heard my roommate call out,

"Is someone there?"

"Yes, it's me! Open up! Let me in!"

He was startled long enough for me to stumble into the apartment and slam the door.

After telling all this to Dr. Gautier I began to judge myself less harshly for not yet being married, for these experiences had made plain the roles that *both* my parents had played in making me so anxious about intimacy with men —my fear of Ma's disapproval for being sexual, and my fear of encountering the selfishness and insensitivity of my father as I had in Frank's friend. I was still finding it hard to overcome my fear of talking about sex, but with Dr. Porter almost banished from the room I had no excuse not to tackle the topic more aggressively. Of course Ma was still up there under the ceiling listening to every word I was saying, but she had really messed me up about sex and I decided she might as well hear about it; so I plunged into the topic, devoting hours and hours to it, and getting angrier and angrier.

For as long as I could remember she had denied me the rightful ownership of my sexuality. She had first seized it when she found me comforting myself after Little Brother died, ripping the covers off my bed and enlisting my sisters as spies to report to her if it happened again. Later, as a young adolescent, I came across the word *onanism*. Unaware of the dangerous waters I was entering, I asked her what it meant. She looked painfully embarrassed, then told me it was something a person did with their private parts that they shouldn't be doing. She added, "It's usually something that only dogs and monkeys do." At about this same time she put me in shapeless bras designed to flatten and conceal my developing breasts and told me without explanation "not to do anything with boys" before I was married, and of course I didn't dare ask her what that meant.

I had been struggling all my life to be her good girl and had tried to obey her unspoken rule that *sex is bad,* but this had left me tormented and guilt-ridden about my own desires. She had put me in a paralyzing bind, telling me not to be sexual, but also to bring home an attractive, well-to-do young man from a "good family."

Perhaps she had been harder on me because of Hope. While I would have done just about anything for her approval, Hope seemed to have no need for it at all. When she grew old enough to be interested in boys and became flirtatious and provocative, she and my mother met head on and I knew what would be in store for me if I strayed from the straight and narrow. I was amazed that Hope dared to defy her and more amazed that she usually won the rounds. Mary and I would then get an earful about how bad and willful Hope was, but the puzzling thing about it was that Hope was my mother's favorite of her three girls.

"Do you think it's possible," I asked Dr. Gautier, "for a mother to split sexual conflict within herself between two daughters, saying yes to one and no to the other?"

"It's possible," he said.

I concluded that even though Ma had been *saying* no to both of us, she had been giving Hope a covert message to "go for it," and that Hope's behavior excited her.

All this made me wonder about Mary and how Ma's sexual hang-ups had affected *her.* Unlike me Mary was not afraid of saying or doing the wrong thing. She would talk to strangers and had a way I envied of making people laugh. When she became an adolescent she was friendly and chatty with the boys and became one of the most popular girls, but she never did anything Ma disapproved of. Then she met an attractive young man whom my parents liked and they became engaged. But before they could marry she became seriously ill with anorexia nervosa and was hospitalized. I learned later in my training that such an illness often expresses a young girl's fear of mature womanhood, and this could well have been true for Mary. Fortunately her fiancé waited her out and she went on to marry and have eight children. Hope, who had grown up to be a beautiful, seductive woman, was married by then to another "socially acceptable" young man, so of the three girls I was the only one who had thus far failed in love.

It was painful to be looking like an attractive, promising young woman and, compared with my sisters and friends, to be feeling like such a sexual failure. If I had been ugly I would have had an excuse. I began to worry that I might be sexually abnormal, but how was I to find out? Only more sexual experience could answer that question, but when I looked up at the ceiling, Ma looked down, shaking her head, and my abject fear of her disapproval took me over again. I was also mortally afraid of becoming pregnant, not only because of the stigma, but I had heard about women having harrowing experiences with illegal abortions, and if I were to conceive I could not imagine not having and keeping my baby.

So instead of more experience I asked Dr. Gautier to explain what normal sexuality is. His answer: Except for a small number of biologically abnormal individuals and people who have suffered severe trauma such as incest or rape and cannot experience satisfaction with the opposite sex, men and women are normally attracted to one another. Same sex attraction reflects psychosexually immature development.

Well, I had certainly been attracted to Leo and my Army Captain and to Frank, but I had never told Dr. Gautier about the experience I had had in my dormitory at Smith. I had allowed myself to think that it wasn't important because it was just that one time, but I knew that "honest self-disclosure" was probably the most important rule of psychoanalysis and that I should tell him what happened.

One night a girl in my dorm climbed naked into my bed in the middle of the night and started making love to me. I barely knew the girl and had not been especially drawn to her. When I was thirteen I had had a crush on a senior in boarding school and had made many close women friends over the years, but I had never been sexually attracted to any of them, and to discover that my body was beginning to like this warm physical contact was alarming and confusing.

In boarding school we had giggled about "fairies" and knew vaguely that women sometimes got together romantically, but I really didn't know what that meant. I knew what homosexuality was, but in the abstract, so to speak. Hard to believe, it had not occurred to me before that night that two people of the same sex could kiss and arouse one another sexually. My seducer, I later learned, had a lot of sexual experience with both men and women while I, with my handful of relationships with men, was barely a beginner. When I asked her why she was doing this she told me that my innocence had been tantalizing and that I need 'loosening up." This was true enough, but while we were in bed and my body was saying, "Hey, this ain't all bad," the anxious conformist me was saying, "We shouldn't be doing this." Eventually her ardor subsided, but she *had* loosened me up and jolted me into realizing how abysmally ignorant and unworldly I still was.

Nervously I asked Dr. Gautier if my finding it a "not unpleasurable" experience meant that I was a lesbian. He pondered for a moment.

"Not necessarily," he said.

So if I wasn't abnormal in some way, why wasn't I getting lift off with men?

"We have a surprise for you," Ma called over her shoulder.

Hope, Mary, and I were sitting on the back seat of our car. Robert was sitting on Hope's lap. He was three years old now. Ma was driving and Pa was sitting beside her. She almost always drove. Sometimes Pa did, but his driving was scary.

"Where are we going?" Mary asked.

"Wait and see," Ma said.

We left the village, crossed a small bridge with seagulls standing on it, then climbed a long hill and finally turned into a narrow dirt road. It was like Aunt Carrie's lane, but not so long. We drove until we came into what I came to think of, years later, as the "Small Paradise." On a clearing above the river we had just crossed was a small farm with a house standing beside three tall trees like big Christmas trees. And there were *three* red barns, not just one like Uncle Willie's yellow one. There weren't many trees on his farm, but this farm was surrounded by woods and the only house you could see was across the river. And there weren't any cars, anywhere you looked.

More and more cars had been driving in front of our village house and sometimes driving too fast, and Ma had begun to worry. Then one awful day Jimmy, the little dog that Mr. Carle had given Hope for her birthday, was run over. I was playing nearby. He ran howling into our yard and collapsed on the grass with blood gushing from his mouth. I screamed and people came running. For days I was drawn back to that spot until the rain washed the blood away. Jimmy wasn't mine, but I had loved him and he was gone. All of us had loved him.

Ma and Pa had been wanting to move for some time. They couldn't afford both a place in the country and an apartment or house in the city like their wealthier friends, although they would have liked this. But if Pa continued to commute to his law practice in the city they could afford half of this lifestyle. They were both familiar with English-style country living. Although Ma had grown up in modest circumstances in her father's rectory, she had spent her summer vacations at her grandparent's country place on Long Island, and in his vacations Pa, who was raised in Baltimore, had been welcomed at the beautiful country estate of his aunt who was married to the Governor of Maryland. So when the little farm became available Pa invested everything he had into buying it and living out his dream, transforming it year by year into a country property that would be comparable to those of his friends and business associates.

"We're going to leave our house in the village and move here to live," Ma said, when she pulled up in front of the house.

We three girls burst out of the car like children let out for recess. We raced around, making one thrilling discovery after another. While Pa and Ma and Robert went into the old house, we explored the barns. All the farm equipment had been left behind by the previous owners —old wagons, an old sleigh, old harness that must have been used on a draft horse like Dan, and a mounted stone for sharpening tools that we could sit on and ride like a bicycle. In one of the barns we found a loft with old hay and flung ourselves on it, giving ourselves a fright when pigeons that had been perched on the rafters began flying about. What delighted me most was finding a chicken house like the one at Aunt Carrie's. The little boxes for eggs were empty now, but Ma told us that after we moved we would have chickens and ducks and a cow and a horse like Dan to do the farm work, and maybe another horse or two for riding.

When we went into the house to find Ma and Pa it was dark and gloomy and it had a bad smell. We all said, "Phew!" It was smaller than our village house and I wondered how we would all fit in, but Ma said they were going to make the house bigger so that each of us could have our own room. It would take a while and we would be living in the village for one more year, but this was our place now and we would come over as often as we could while the bigger house was being built.

Before we left that day Pa took us into the woods. I had never been in a woods before and it was dark and I didn't want to go in, but everyone was going, even Robert, and you always did what Pa said. I was scared at first, but then I began to hear birds singing and saw them flying about and it began to seem like a nice place. We followed a little narrow road that wound through the woods, then took us down a hill, and to our surprise we came out on the bank of the river. We stood and watched it as it moved along almost as if it were alive. Further down we could see a pair of ducks swimming and then disappearing behind a bend. Hope picked up a stick and threw it in the river and we watched until it disappeared.

"The river flows out of those ponds where Miss Tyler used to take you on your nature walks," Ma said, "and it flows all the way down into the water where we swim."

"After we move I'm going to get a boat," said Pa.

It was the best thing I had ever heard Pa say! I had loved those walks with Miss Tyler. Ma had arranged for us to go out with her sometimes in the afternoons when our lessons were over and the weather was nice. We would walk around the hunting and fishing club where she lived with her father. As we walked along the paths she told us the names of birds and flowers and trees, and when we came to a boat that was moored in a stream for the fishermen, she let us get in and taught us how to row. It was the first boat I had ever seen. The oars were too big for me, but I was able to learn and I loved knowing how to make the boat go where I wanted it to go. And now Pa had said we were going to have our own boat! I couldn't wait for a year to pass.

And finally we moved.

My days would begin with the sound of swan's wings flying down the river from its headwater ponds and end at night with the whippoorwill calling from the woods. Each day I would go wandering. One day I might make a discovery like the patch of tiny arbutus on a sunny bank by the river or come upon a gathering of pink lady slippers in the woods, and I would always find something to do. There was no pond on the farm for Pa's ducks and I spent days digging a little pond for them, but after I filled it with water and they had a good swim the water disappeared. I couldn't figure out why it didn't stay in the ground like the pond we used to skate on near our old house in the village.

After Pa got his boat I would spend hours rowing on the river. I thought of Miss Tyler as I handled my oars. "I'm feathering them just the way you taught me," I said to her. She would be pleased. I learned how to move with the tide, rowing up when it was coming in from the bay, then drifting down after it turned, watching the scenery go by. I liked the river best where it was narrow and the water was clear and fresh. Sometimes as I drifted down I would see a cardinal flower on its bank. As the river widened and the marshes and the smell of river mud took over I sometimes moored the boat and did a little fishing. I would sit there with my line, dreaming, I guess, and watching the dragonflies darting about. Sometimes I caught a fish or two and brought them back to Delphine who was still our cook.

I missed being on the river in the winters, but there were heavy snows in those years and after they had fallen the sky would become a brilliant blue and the world would be bright and clean. After coming home from school I would take my sled up our highest hill and over and over race down into the frozen marshes. Winter days were short, but when darkness came and I went into the house to do my homework it still seemed sunny, for Ma was kinder to me then and would help me with my projects. One year when I was playing the part of the Happy Prince in a school play she made me a beautiful costume out of gold material. I became more content in these years, no longer lonely the way I had been when we lived in the village, but when we were getting ready to move into our new house I suffered a bitter disappointment.

"I'm going to put Robert and Miss Brackett in your room until he's better," Ma said.

Robert had been sickly during the past year and Ma had become so worried about him that she had hired a trained nurse to take care of him. I couldn't believe what she was saying.

While the new house was being built she had shown Hope and Mary and me the rooms we were to have and let us pick out paper for the walls. I had chosen a paper with pretty little pink flowers. Before we moved I had loved going up to my room and watching while the men were working to get it ready.

"I know it's a disappointment for you," Ma said, but your room is the sunniest and I've put special glass in the windows so the sunlight can come through. When he's well again you can have your room back."

"Where am I going to be?"

"There'll be just enough space in that little room off the sleeping porch for your bed and bureau."

But the "room" had a door to the porch and to the upstairs hall and it was more like a passageway. Pa was supposed to sleep outside for his health, which is why they had built the porch, so after I moved in Pa kept coming through all the time.

After Robert was better and his nurse had gone —and good riddance she was with her red face never smiling and her fat legs in white stockings —I began asking Ma when I could have my room back. She kept saying things like "just a little longer" or "pretty soon" and the months passed. Winter went into spring and spring into summer and he was still there. Ma was breaking her promise and it wasn't fair. One day when she and Robert were out in the car I decided to take matters into my own hands, moving my things back into my room and moving his into the space I had been occupying. When they returned and Robert discovered what I had done, he howled in dismay. Ma came running, sized up the situation, then delivered her verdict:

"What you've done is within your rights," she said, "and you can stay, but it's a cruel thing you've done. Do you see how upset he is?"

What made me even sadder that day was that I liked Robert. He was a nice little boy, and I didn't want to hurt him and now he was going to think I was cruel too. And I was puzzled. When Pa and Ma had four children why had they made only three bedrooms for us? Where was Robert *supposed* to be?

At the end of our first summer in the new house Hope went off to boarding school and Mary and I commuted by train to a small country day school. We lived too far away to spend time with the friends we made there and I liked our being companions again. And, as Ma had promised, the three empty barns began filling with occupants. It was exciting to greet the new arrivals —chickens, ducks, a cow and her calf and my favorite, a draft horse we named Eleanor. She had been pulling wagons in the city, but when trucks started doing her work she needed a place to go. Pa had bought her and she had come out to us on the railroad. On that thrilling day Mary and I and the hired man had walked with her from the station to the farm, with Ma and Robert following in the car. Eleanor was a gentle, friendly animal, and even though she had never been ridden Mary put a saddle on her and taught her to be a riding horse. Mary would have taught me how to ride, but I was afraid.

When Hope came home from boarding school for the summer Pa bought another horse and Hope and Mary went riding all the time. Then Mary went off to school with Hope and I was alone again and as usual, looking for things to do. I often visited Eleanor in the barn, bringing her lumps of sugar. I worried about her being lonely with Mary gone, but there was plenty of work for her to do on the farm. Then that Christmas Ma gave me a bicycle and when the weather warmed up I rode it all over, going out our lane and on to the roads and sometimes all the way to the bridge where I could watch the river flowing underneath and see the seagulls swimming.

Ma had a friend with twin boys Robert's age and they lived on a farm near ours. Every day Robert went over to play with them and to have lessons with a tutor and I used to ride around her farm. She had a donkey and when I rode past him he would run over to the fence and I would stop and pet him. I worried about him being lonely like Eleanor and then I had an idea. As far as I could see he didn't have any work to do. He was just there. If I brought him over to our farm he and Eleanor could be friends and we could find work for him so he would have something to do. So one day I mentioned to Ma's friend that if she didn't need her donkey any more I would like to have him and I asked her if I could buy him. I had saved up my allowance and could pay her $25. She laughed —I didn't know why —and then she said I could. I was thrilled. The next few days I fixed up the stall next to Eleanor taking out the dirty old straw and putting in fresh. He and Eleanor could talk to each other and they could graze in the pasture together.

It had never occurred to me to ask Pa's permission and I don't know how he found out what I was planning. But when he did, he was very angry. I overheard him saying something to Ma that I didn't understand about "making a contract with a minor." Having just turned 11, I didn't know what that meant. I could tell that he was mostly angry with the lady who had sold me the donkey and that it wasn't so much me. A while later Ma told me —he always made her do the telling —that he didn't want a donkey on the place, but later that spring he would give me a lamb.

At that moment nothing could erase my disappointment. I loved my donkey and I believe he loved me. I didn't know what I was going to tell him. Ma knew that I was sad and she tried to cheer me up, taking me to a movie once in a while –Pa never wanted to go –and helping me with my homework projects. And when I played the part of The Happy Prince in our school play, she made me a beautiful costume out of gold material.

Spring came and I had almost forgotten about the lamb, but Pa hadn't. He had a way, I figured out later, of giving things to people that he wanted for himself, and he wanted to start a flock on the farm. So I was sent off with our hired man to pick up a lamb at the farm of one of his friends. It was a lovely little thing, but it was frightened and cried all the way home even though I was holding it in my arms and trying to comfort it. I carried it into the barn, put it in the stall I had fixed for my donkey and the hired man brought it some food and water, but it would not stop crying. The next morning it was still crying and I could not bear to hear it. I asked Ma to ask Pa if I could use my donkey money to buy another lamb and he said that I could. It, too, cried all the way home. When I got out of the car with it in my arms and started towards the barn the first lamb heard it crying and cried back. Then they both kept crying to each other until I set the new lamb down and they raced towards each other and the crying stopped.

Those years growing up on the farm were the best years of my childhood. Although I did not know it was happening to me, just as I had fallen in love with my grandmother's piano years before, I had fallen in love with the natural world. It had become my faithful companion and was always out there for me whenever I needed it. And it was during those years that I began to feel more like a whole person, less like a half, and refused to be called Sister anymore, claiming my given name. I believe it is also possible that in my concern for Eleanor and my donkey and the lambs and in my efforts to help them, the seeds of my vocation as a therapist were being sown.

"Why aren't you talking more about your father?" Dr. Gautier asked one day.

34

"Because I don't want him in here."

It was bad enough having Ma up in the ceiling, but I knew perfectly well that sooner or later I would have to let Pa in, for I was getting pretty sophisticated now in my own counseling work. But I didn't want him in my space because I knew how impatient and rude he would be, and when he was like that I wanted to be as far away from him as possible.

I remembered all too well his response to Dr. Porter when Ma had her breakdown during World War II. I was seeing Dr. Porter then about Leo. Hope, who was living with her two children at the Small Paradise between marriages, was seeing him too, and I had come home to help her with Ma. We called Dr. Porter and he told us to bring her into the city to a private psychiatric hospital where he could treat her. She responded well, no doubt pouring out her grievances about Pa who was also in a hospital being treated for his ruptured trachea. After he was discharged 'Dr. Porter made an appointment with him. He reported to me later that Pa had refused to talk about himself or the marriage, had complained about the expense of his wife's treatment, and had walked abruptly out of the session.

And so, reluctantly, I let him into my analysis and for weeks poured out my own grievances about him to Dr. Gautier.

All through my childhood he had been a distant stranger. I have almost no memory of him in our village house. After we moved to the Small Paradise I rarely saw him in the morning before Ma took him to the train, but when he returned at night, reeking of cigarette smoke, if I happened to be in the path he took from the front door to the liquor closet, he might give me a gruff greeting. His first order of business was downing a shot of whiskey, followed by a baffling grimace, and this ritual added yet another unpleasant odor to his person. Whenever he wanted me to do something or not do something he would speak to me, but never, during all my childhood, did we have a conversation.

I hesitate to say that I hated him because hate is such an unforgiving word. But I never forgave him for killing the cat Ma had given me to help with my disappointment over the donkey. I don't think he meant to harm the animal. He wasn't a cruel man. It was just that what he wanted, or didn't want, always took precedence over the wishes of others. He hated cats and they weren't allowed in the house, but one day mine got in and he opened the door and kicked it so hard that it flew through the air. It raced off. I looked and looked for it all that day and the next and finally found it in the crawl space under one of the barns. It was limp but still breathing. Ma said we could take it to the vet, but it died in my lap in the car before we could get there.

It was hard to talk about Pa without talking about Ma and how unhappy she ultimately became. After coming out of mourning for Little Brother and replacing him with Robert, she recovered much of her old spirit except for her chronic worry about Robert's health. When Pa bought the old farm they were happier for a time, living out their shared dream of creating a beautiful country estate. But when she was about to become the mistress of a lovely home the great depression descended on the country. To deal with his financial crisis and without telling her, Pa fired the architect and instructed the builder to finish the renovations, cutting corners and using the cheapest material and hardware. Ma's dream house had been compromised. After we moved in she made it plain that she was never happy living in it. Pa did not or could not give her enough money to furnish it attractively and I remember her dragging me around the basements of department stores looking for bargains.

On one occasion, after a futile search for a bureau, we rode in a taxi to visit a friend of hers who lived in a large apartment on Park Avenue. Ma's friend was one of the three girls she had taught when she was a governess. She had stayed in touch with them as they grew and Ma and her friend were happy to see each other. They sat down with tea, and cookies for me, and I watched and listened as they talked and laughed and talked and laughed. I was seeing a mother I had never known.

Would I have liked Pa more if Ma hadn't complained about him so much? "Your father hasn't given me enough money this month," she would say to us. "I don't know what I'm going to do." Of course she shouldn't have been talking to her children like this, but she did. Money was always the big thing. I don't think she ever knew how much he made. After we began living at the Small Paradise she complained that he never gave her enough to run the house and was always spending it on outside things like dredging a channel for the boat that I loved but that she never went out in, or on a colt that he raised to run at the track, who never won his races. But in spite of the bad press Ma was giving him I had experienced for myself that Pa seemed incapable of imagining how someone else might feel and of being able to respond to that. I gave Dr. Gautier an illustration:

At breakfast one morning –I was nine or ten –Pa announced that he was taking his boat down the river on the ebb tide to moor it at the dock of a friend. Ma knew that I liked being out on the river and suggested that I go with him. The previous summer Pa had taken Mary and me out on the Sound to troll for snappers. Although it had been a little frightening –you were never sure Pa was in control of a situation –it had been mostly a fun time, a rare experience with him. I didn't want to be alone with him, but with some misgivings I agreed to go. During what came to feel like an interminable and *not*-fun voyage I began to need to pee in the worst way. It is hard to believe that I was in the same predicament that I had been on the train coming home from Aunt Carrie's. The prospect of having to tell him was appalling.

"Pa, I have to go to the bathroom," I finally made myself say.

"Go over the side," he replied brusquely and continued rowing.

"But I can't, Pa."

"Figure it out."

If he had bothered to think he would have realized that for a girl, peeing in this situation would require gymnastic ingenuity, but I did not protest again. Though painfully embarrassed I took my panties down in front of him and accomplished the feat without falling into the river. How easy it would have been for him to row over to the shore and let me hop off, but that would have taken him off course.

"Do you see what I mean about him?" I asked Dr. Gautier.

"I take your point," he said.

Predictably my relationship with Pa made me view men as selfish, inconsiderate and ungenerous, and unfortunately I was to believe this generalization about them for far too long. If there been other benevolent father figures in my life, a grandfather, a teacher, or the father of a friend, I might not have arrived at young womanhood with such misgivings about what intimacy with a man would be like, but most of the men I encountered were like a friend of Pa's who always laughed when he saw me and called me "the egg," making other people laugh. I never knew why. Apparently, with my yellow hair and pale face, I had reminded him of a hard-boiled egg.

So, week after week, fueled by years of unexpressed anger, I vented on the couch about Pa and men in general and began having fantasies of wrecking Dr. Gautier's office. I was entering what psychoanalytic theory calls a negative transference. Within the safety of the analytic rules I lay tranquilly on the couch while mentally throwing chairs around his office and painting offensive graffiti on his walls. I told Dr. Gautier about my fantasies (one of the analytic rules was to share everything I was thinking) and I was rude to him, mocking him for making stupid remarks and for being unimaginative. I seemed to be getting nowhere in the analysis and had begun to have reservations about his competence, so this negative transfer had come easily. Although my reservations remained, this negative phase more or less ended one day.

I had been going on about how much I disliked the father of one of my friends and described an incident that had taken place at our beach club. I had been playing on a raft with some other children when this man swam out and pulled himself up on the ladder. His mere presence threw a damper on our play and we stood around warily. Then suddenly we were all shrieking. He had reached into the water and grabbed a jellyfish and was threatening us with it. Knowing how painful the sting of those tentacles could be we leapt into the water and swam a safe distance, waiting until he threw the jellyfish away and swam back to shore.

"This man was probably just wanting to have fun with you," Dr. Gautier said. "Are you sure he really picked the thing up? Maybe he was just pretending to?"

"I saw it in his hand! And even if he wasn't going to sting us with it, he frightened us. He was being mean."

"I think you need to look at whether you aren't generalizing unfairly about men from your experience with your father," Dr. Gautier said.

Now I was getting really angry. "I was there and you weren't! My father was selfish, but he was never mean like that. Mr. Hall was a sadistic man."

"Mr. who?"

"Mr. Hall. Mr. Bartlett Hall."

"Is this man in the real estate business," he asked?

"I think he is. He commutes to the city with my father."

Dr. Gautier was silent, processing this information.

"I know a Bartlett Hall who lives in your community,' he said finally. "I believe I know what you mean about him, Miss Nicodemus, and I owe you an apology. He is a most unpleasant man. Bartlett Hall is my landlord."

Would our wrangling have continued if Bartlett Hall had not been my analyst's landlord? But he was, and Dr. Gautier's apology freed me to move on and uncover romantic dreams and longings from my early adolescence.

I had been an ardent reader of fairy tales, seeing myself as a princess, of course. I had also devoured books about boy and girl twins, always seeing my twin and me in these stories. I used to wonder if he would have been a handsome boy and if he would have been my protector when I became a young woman. But I had been even more influenced by two books by George Macdonald, *The Princess and Curdie*, and *The Princess and the Goblins*. In these books I had found the ideal parents I had been longing for, and I had fallen in love with Curdie

The Princess in Macdonald's book was an only child. Her mother was too ill to care for her and her father, King-Papa, took her away to a castle in another part of his mountain kingdom to be raised by "country people." Periodically he arrived on a splendid white charger to visit his daughter and to oversee her care. He adored his little girl, When his henchman sounded the bugle to announce his coming she would run out to him and he would reach down and pull her up onto his saddle, holding her "against his heart."

The Princess was a perfect creature —polite, truthful, and so kind and gentle that she did not pick the flowers that grew on the mountainside but would touch them tenderly and say, "Are you all smelling very sweet this morning?" She was "fair and pretty with golden hair like her mother and eyes like two bits of night sky." Curdie was a miner's son. His hair was black and curly and his eyes were "as dark as the mines in which he worked." He was brave and strong. The Princess meets Curdie when she and her nurse lose their way on the mountain and Curdie, who is coming home from the mine, leads them safely back to the castle. She wants to thank him with a kiss, but her nurse tells her it is not proper. Curdie tells her not to worry. She can give him the kiss another time.

One day the Princess gets lost in the castle and discovers her grandmother living in a remote tower. She is seated at her spinning wheel wearing a black velvet dress with a "long mane of silver hair shining against it." She is a magical figure, real and not real, and sometimes when the Princess gets lost in the castle and cannot find her she thinks she is only a dream, *but her grandmother is always there.* Once when the Princess is upset her grandmother bathes her in a silver tub and lets her sleep "close to her bosom in her large oval bed with its coverlet of rose and pale blue curtains all around." But she is not just a nurturing figure. She exacts a high standard of conduct from the Princess —honesty, courage, faithfulness, obedience, and consideration. In return she is always unconditionally loving and protective. To keep the Princess safe she spins a magical ball of invisible, indestructible thread, ties it to a ring and gives the ring to the Princess so that she will *always be connected to her.* The thread will take her wherever she needs to go and will always bring her safely back.

In a dramatic denouement Curdie gets lost in an abandoned mine trying to thwart a plot of the Goblins to kidnap the Princess and marry her to the hideous Goblin Prince, but by running her finger along the magical thread the Princess rescues Curdie. Later Curdie saves the Princess and the King's household from an invasion by the Goblins who have come to steal the Princess, and he returns her to her King Papa. King Papa pulls her on to his white charger and tearfully embraces her. When the Princess tells him that she would like to thank Curdie with a kiss, King-Papa agrees that she should. He holds her down close enough to Curdie for her to throw her arms around his neck and "kiss him on the mouth." Then King-Papa says to Curdie and the Princess, "When you are grown up —if you both will —you shall marry each other and be King and Queen."

Coming out of this magical place as a ripening young girl into the real world of boys and young men was like coming out of a movie on a steamy summer afternoon into glaring daylight, with papers flying about the street and the smell of deep-fry in the air. Curdie never perspired, but the boys who pushed me around the dance floor did, and we always seemed to be stepping on each other's feet. I *wanted* a boyfriend, but the bolder boys scared me and driving with them in fast cars was terrifying. I stayed clear of them, but the shy, fearful ones I did like stayed clear of me. There seemed to be no one in between. My handsome, respectful, and courageous Curdie was proving to be a tough act to follow.

MY JOURNEY BEGINS

It was such a powerful moment that I could be standing there right now in front of my bureau in boarding school, looking at myself in the mirror and combing my hair. I was thirteen. Something remarkable was happening to me. I was metamorphosing into self-consciousness. I was becoming I. I do not know who or what I was before, but I was becoming a separate person with boundaries around myself. Forever after I would be alone in the world inhabiting this body. Would Freud have called this moment the "birth of ego"?

Boarding school was the beginning of separation from my family. Hope had gone there and was home again, studying singing and looking for a husband, and Mary was still at the school. Now it was my turn to go.

I loved being there, although spending four years in a strict, convent-like atmosphere under the watchful eye of a severe, ramrod straight, elderly headmistress would seem like a prison sentence to today's thirteen-year-old. But for me there were invaluable compensations: life-long friendships, being exposed for the first time to classical music, although Pa wouldn't pay extra for lessons, and winning recognition for my writing and athletic ability. But the downside of those years was my abysmal failure as a student. Since the small day school I had been attending did not have enough pupils for an eighth grade, my parents simply sent me off to ninth grade in boarding school, skipping my eighth grade year. I have often wondered how the school rationalized accepting me and giving me a diploma. I was at sea most of the time and humiliated by my inability to catch on to things as rapidly as the other girls. But as I said, there were compensations.

It was during my first months at the school that I formed my first close friendship. In trying to bring Peggy to mind after decades have passed I see someone totally and attractively different from myself. I see reddish hair and a pale, thoughtful face, and I see a grown-up person, someone jelled and self-confident —all the things that I was far from being. She was fully developed physically which I was not, although I was taller, and I still wonder what attracted her to me. I remember her laughing a lot when I said funny things, but I think we were drawn together in some deeper way. Perhaps she sensed my profound emotional hunger and this might have touched some wounded place in her. I see her, even at that young age, being a kind of mother to me, caring about how I felt and who I was. All I knew at the time was that I loved being with her and thought of her as my "best" friend. It was the first time in my life that I had had the luxury of choosing one. In my lean past I had been grateful for any friend who came my way.

Peggy was in the class above me and girls usually didn't have friends in lower classes, but we had come to know each other living in adjoining rooms in a small cottage on the school grounds. She came from New York City and was far more knowing and sophisticated than I, and this intrigued me. Older girls often responded to younger ones as if they did not exist, but Peggy went out of her way to be friendly. We began spending our free time together, although there wasn't much of it. When it was time for us to go home for Christmas vacation I was surprised and thrilled to have her invite me to spend a few days with her in her family's apartment in New York.

Peggy had a stylish mother, totally unlike my own, and a strikingly beautiful older sister, both of whom frightened me. No father seemed to be around, but you never asked why about those things. However, they were kind to me and the visit was the high point of my holidays. But the night before I was to leave something troubling happened. We had been having a wonderful time going about the city by ourselves and I didn't want to leave the next day. I had been sleeping in a room that opened into hers and after our lights were out that last night and we were trying to sleep, but still talking through the open door, I got up and went into her room and crawled into her bed. I didn't want to leave her. I snuggled up to her and in a boldness that was entirely new to me lay my head on one of her already well-developed breasts.

"Can I sleep with you to night?" I asked.

She held me in her arms for a moment, then said, "No. This isn't right. You must go back to your own bed."

Dutifully and respectfully I did, but I was perplexed and deeply troubled by what I had done. She had said it was "not right." Ma was always saying that, and I was afraid Peggy would not like me anymore, but she was friendly the next morning. After our vacation was over and we got back to school, all was as before. That is until the dull, obese, humorless woman who was our house-mother at the cottage and whom we all detested took Peggy and me aside and told us we could no longer be friends.

Apparently this woman had observed us one day sitting together on a sofa looking at funny pictures in a book. We had been giggling and being silly and probably attracting attention. She said we had been sitting "too close" and re-ported this to the headmistress who told Peggy that she should not be having a friendship with a girl in a lower class.

What had the housemother seen? I was bewildered but obedient, hav-ing learned never to question decisions by figures in authority, and we dutifully went our separate ways, but I could not understand what we had done wrong. I was further confused the following year when the headmis-tress, who often placed one or two older girls in a room with less mature ones, put Peggy in a room with me and one of my classmates. Had we by then proved ourselves wholesome? We did not see much of each other, however. We were in different classes and girls spent little time in their rooms, not being allowed in them during the day, and not being allowed to communicate in them after the last bell at night. Checked twice daily at a roll call, we were on our honor to report violations of this and many other rules. But even though Peggy and I spent very little time together that fall, our mutual affection resurfaced easily and I was happy that we could be friends again.

Peggy had some kind of a heart problem, but we had never talked about it. Everyone knew it was why she had been excused from sports and was supposed to be careful and not "overdo." Except for that, she didn't seem any different from the rest of us. When I returned to school after our Christmas vacation I was told that she was ill but would probably be back in a few weeks. I wasn't alarmed, but one evening when we were all at our desks in study hall doing our homework, I was summoned to the office of the headmistress. These summonses usually meant that there was going to be a reprimand for some violation. I went in nervously and was relieved that the headmistress was not looking severe. I sat down. "You know that Peggy has been ill," she began. "Because you will take it the hardest, I want you to know before I make an announcement to the school that Peggy has died."

I did not cry. I disliked the headmistress so much I would never have shown her or told her how I felt, but even if I had wanted to, felt free to, I wouldn't have known what to show her or to tell her because I was feeling nothing.

"You can go back upstairs to your room if you want," she said, "while I tell the other girls." But I didn't want to be there alone. I wanted to be with the others. So I went back to my desk, knowing that they were wondering, as we were always wondering, why I had been summoned and whether it had been good or bad.

There was a gasp in the room when she made her announcement. Then several of the girls began to cry. But I still did not cry. It would not be until many, many years later that I would understand why.

Later that spring our English teacher invited a professor she knew to give the upper classes a series of lectures on English poets. After each lecture we had to write an essay for him. Our teacher would send him our efforts and he would bring them back with his critiques. His final assignment, however, was different. We were to write a poem or a story about a life-changing experience. I decided to write about the death of my pet rabbit when I was about eight.

While we were still living in the village I had begged Ma for a rabbit and she had finally let me have one. It was kept in a small rectangular pen that had no gate but could be lifted and moved around so my rabbit would always have fresh grass to nibble on. I had taken it out to play with one afternoon, but when I tried to shove it under its pen it hopped away from me. I caught it, took it back to its pen and, holding the pen in one hand and the rabbit in the other, pushed it under. Then I found that the pen wasn't level on the ground, leaving a gap it could get through. I pushed down on the pen to level it, but something was in the way so I pushed down harder. Then I realized that the rabbit was half in and half out and that I had been pushing the pen down on its back. I finally pushed the rabbit all the way in and thought all was well. The next day when I went out to play with it I found it lying dead on the grass where I had left it. I remembered the force in my arms pushing down on the pen and knew that I must have killed it. I started screaming and ran back to the house. Hope was upstairs ill with pneumonia and Ma had hired a trained nurse to care for her. The nurse came rushing out when she heard my screams.

"I've killed my rabbit!" I screamed. "I've killed my rabbit!"

"Oh," she said. "I thought something was really wrong. Don't you know that you're not supposed to disturb your sister?" And she turned and went back into the house.

I felt as if I had been struck in my heart. I would never speak about this to anyone ever again.

At the end of my story I had written, "At that moment I made a decision that changed my life. I locked my tears in a little tin box and threw away the key." When my story was returned he had given it an A, and there was also a message for me: "I hope you still have your little tin box. Somewhere someone will have another key."

Two years have passed. I am in the living room of a friend's home in Washington, D.C. and I am experiencing another life-changing moment. This friend has been my most recent roommate in boarding school and we have just graduated. We have made no plans, other than knowing that we both want to marry and raise a family. Most of our classmates are going on to college, but we are not. She is thinking of art school, but I will just be at home waiting for something to happen. I had wanted to go to college too, and I had asked Ma to ask Pa, but the answer was no. I was afraid it would be, but you never asked Pa why. I suppose it was about money. That was what Ma was always complaining about. Hope and Mary had wanted to go too, but he wouldn't send them either.

My friend and I are not alone in her living room. She has an older sister and an older brother and they and some of their friends are there. They are talking about President Roosevelt. Some of them like him and some of them don't and they are arguing. I have no idea what they are talking about. I know nothing about him except that Pa hates him. I remember Ma teasing him when she got the vote, telling him she was going to vote for Roosevelt even though I don't think she was, and how furious he was.

"You'll just cancel out my vote if you do that!" he had shouted at her.

Then the talk in my roommate's living room moves on to world affairs and to people and events I have never heard of. I have no idea what they are talking about. We had only studied ancient and American history in school and if there had been any discussions of "current events" I would not have been interested in them. And of course we had no radios, newspapers or magazines.

For the first time I realize how abysmally ignorant I am, and I am ashamed. I vow privately and passionately that I will somehow get out into the world, out of my tiny corner of it, and find out who is in that world and what is going on there. It is a powerful moment of self-awareness and resolve and I will revisit it many times.

LOVE AND LOSS

I was looking for love, although I didn't know that I was. I was supposed to be finding a suitable husband and securing my place in upper-class society. That was all my parents expected of their three daughters after they graduated from boarding school and Ma had set about to do all that she could to launch us socially. Her view of social classes was a simple one. There were just two, upper, to which breeding —not money —was the ticket of admission, and everyone else. Since "coming out" parties were too expensive we could not be debutantes, so the three of us had just "leaked out." Ma had scored admirably with Hope who had married a "well-connected" Yale graduate and had her first child, and Mary in her turn would be marrying another Yale man and go on to have eight children.

Would Ma be scoring with me?

Time was to become so precious it is painful to look back on my first year after leaving school and seeing myself killing it, moping around the Small Paradise. But what else was I to do? Most of my friends were in college or living in the city with their parents and studying something, but since we lived in the Small Paradise the year round, there was precious little to do.

When Hope had started her singing lessons Ma had found a piano for her to work with and I fooled around on it, not getting anywhere. Ever since I had heard other girls in school playing so beautifully in their recitals I had longed to have lessons and so I approached Ma, and to my surprise, even without consulting Pa she agreed to find a teacher for me. Mary was back home trying to pull her life together after her illness and was planning to enroll in some courses at Columbia University. I decided to join her, and once a week she and I went into the city together, becoming friends again like old times. These were baby steps, but steps, none the less, out into the world.

The following summer I made a new friend. Martha had just graduated from college where she had majored in music and she was going to continue her studies at a school in New York. Her family had rented a house for the season not far from where we lived and she had heard me singing in the bathhouse at our beach club. She told me I had a lovely voice and should have lessons and urged me to enroll in her school. I had never thought of having singing lessons. Hope was the one with the beautiful voice. I told her I was studying piano but had been disappointed in my teacher. She suggested that I find a new one at her school *and* study singing and take other courses, become a serious music student. Why not? Did I have other plans?

It was a thrilling prospect, but would Pa agree? He would have to be consulted about such a big expense and the answer that came back was the no that I had feared. Then I remembered my bonds. Little Brother's god-father had given them to him before he died and they had been transferred to me. If I cashed them in I would have enough to pay for a year's tuition at the school.

I approached Ma again and this time a yes answer came back. To my amazement the following year Pa agreed to pay not only for my tuition, but also for a room in a residence in New York for music and art students. Perhaps my practicing at home had driven him to this. Not infrequently on weekends I had heard him yell from the library where he was reading, "Cut that out!" and of course I had. It was not that he didn't love music. It was because he did. Faithfully, every Saturday afternoon, he listened to the opera on the radio and I knew enough not to practice then. But this was typical Pa. Although he wanted to hear the beautiful sounds that he loved he could not be patient with a daughter who was struggling to learn how to make those beautiful sounds.

But I had not stopped looking for love. It started out with my falling in love with a couple, the Director of our school and his wife, both foreigners with a mysterious allure. Leo and Yvette were both in their early forties, she a tall, beautiful, graceful blond and he, with his irregular teeth and unruly hair, hardly handsome, but a charming man, personable, warm and enthusiastic. All the female students were in love with the two of them, and remarkably they were in love with each other. With perhaps no more than twenty-five students, the school was like a small family and they were our parents. Leo also conducted a community chorus and one evening each week Leo and Yvette and the vocal students —I was one now —would meet at a nearby restaurant before the rehearsal, and there was always laughter and gaiety. Occasionally we would burst into song —singing a section of the choral work we were rehearsing —and I was captivated by this spontaneity. I could not imagine a more wonderful life than making music all the time with people like this.

I spent a great deal of time that winter with Martha in her family's apartment. Her family had become the adopted family so many of us seek growing up when our own family life is failing us. Like the couple in music school Martha's parents loved each other and everyone in her family always seemed in good spirits. The following summer I visited her at her family's camp in the mountains. We hiked and swam, did jigsaw puzzles on rainy days, and played parlor games in the evenings. I learned for the first time what it was like for a family to enjoy life together. It was that same joie de vivre that had attracted me to Leo and Yvette.

Parents, teachers, even therapists have favorites and Leo and Yvette were no exception. Martha, one of the most gifted students, was their number one and I was another. Although a neophyte I was respected because I was "musical," a term used loosely around the school meaning you either "had it" or you didn't, and I was diligent. On occasion we favorites were invited to their apartment for a meal and it was there that I learned to drink wine and to handle food unfamiliar to me like yogurt and calves' brains. Bit by bit I was moving farther and farther out into the world. I could see myself at the tiller of a very small boat with the shoreline of my origins receding in the distance.

It was in the spring of that year that Leo and Yvette invited me to spend a weekend with them in Connecticut. Barely solvent, they had been lent a cottage by a patron of the chorus, and Martha had already been up for a visit. It had just become exciting public knowledge at the school that Yvette was pregnant and would be having her baby in the fall.

After dinner on my first night Leo and Yvette announced that they were going up to their room to read in bed. They invited me to come up and join them when I was ready for bed. I was occupying a small guest room downstairs. I was startled by their suggestion, dumbfounded in fact, and could not imagine being in bed with them. I did not want to be, but they kept insisting. Martha had come up with them, they said, when *she* visited. Learning this about Martha was even more unsettling, but they were not letting me say no. When I appeared they were warm and welcoming and made a place for me between them in their large double bed. For twenty minutes or so we all read silently, or I pretended to, then Leo closed his book, turned out his light and snuggled up to me. A while later Yvette closed her book, turned off her light and slid down in the bed facing away from me. I started to get up, but Leo drew me closer and said cozily, "Oh, don't go yet. Stay a little longer," and it was then that I felt his erection. At least I guessed it was an erection. What else could that thing be?

It may well be that a part of myself I did not yet know was attracted to what was happening, but I was about as virginal a girl then as you could find. I had "necked" and "petted" with a few boys, but that was all. I lay there in the darkness, feeling trapped and panicky. I lingered a few moments, then made a break for it as gracefully as I could. After I was settled in my bed I heard Leo coming down the stairs and go into the bathroom which was next to my room. Then I heard him come to my door, open it without knocking, and come in. I was only dimly aware that I was both afraid of something happening and afraid of it not happening. What was clearer was that I was afraid of not being able to be the woman he was expecting me to be. He knelt down beside my bed and kissed my forehead as if he were putting a child to sleep. "I love you for not staying," he said. He told me that Martha had. Then he left me and went back upstairs. What did that mean? What *had* Martha done with them?

The next morning there was no mention of the night before, not as if it were something that shouldn't be talked about, but because it seemed unimportant. Leo and Yvette were both in a ho-hum-what's-for-breakfast kind of mood. He had come down first and greeted me with a warm hug. When Yvette came down he had kissed her and put his hand on her rounding belly, asking solicitously, "Are you all right?" Naïve though I was, I knew that they had had intercourse after I left and that he was concerned because of her being pregnant. Too much was happening too fast. At the time I had not felt used sexually. I did not even know what that meant, but it seems likely to me now that I served as an aphrodisiac for them without their being aware of what they were doing. Then again, maybe they were.

In sharing our impressions of the Connecticut scene neither Martha nor I said anything about what had happened to us in the upstairs bedroom. Back then, even in a close friendship, sex was a forbidden topic and there was no one else I could talk to about the complicated emotions it had left me with. Then summer came and the school year ended. I went back to Long Island for the summer months and again visited Martha's family in the mountains. She and I were as congenial as before but continued to avoid any mention of what had been, for me at least, the alarming goings on in Leo and Yvette's bed.

Pa was becoming more generous and the following fall he agreed that I could share an apartment with a friend from Long Island. She was eager to live in New York and study music at my school. She was younger than I, and her mother was uneasy about her living in the city but finally gave her approval when an apartment became available in the building where Leo and Yvette lived. It was across the hall from theirs so that they would be nearby to keep a parental eye on us. My parents had met Leo and Yvette during the summer when I invited them to the Small Paradise and Ma had liked them. Pa had been attracted to Yvette and was flirtatious with her but clearly disliked Leo and was barely civil to him.

Meanwhile I was becoming more and more attracted to Leo. After my new roommate and I became settled in our apartment I began having romantic fantasies about him. Supposing he were free, I would speculate as I lay in bed waiting for sleep. Suppose something happened to Yvette. Could I see myself married to him? Although I did not know this was happening, I was being seduced by his attentiveness and responsiveness and his making me feel like an attractive woman, not the clumsy child that I still felt myself to be. I had never known a man like Leo. One day at the school when I was looking for a studio where I could practice he said that I could use the piano in his studio while he was teaching in another classroom. When I sat down to practice and opened the keyboard I found a row of paper-wrapped candies lying between the black keys. I could not believe he had thought about my being there and had wanted to surprise and please me. It was probably at that moment that I fell out of love with a couple and into love with him.

But there were other things about him that made me uneasy. He could fly into rages when he was teaching or rehearsing the chorus. One day in a class he challenged a student to walk three beats to a measure and clap two and when she couldn't he screamed at her, "Why don't you go home and cook!" But I would forget about these ugly outbursts when he was back to being his charming, cozy self. Physically pale, unathletic and with his unruly mane of hair beginning to turn a bit gray, he bore no resemblance to the lean and handsome stranger in my old romantic day dreams, but he had slipped into the part when my back was turned. I could imagine him as my husband even though he was already married, and I could dismiss the fact that he had been married before he came to this country and had a young daughter whom he rarely saw. This piece of news, which Martha had recently shared with me, had been disquieting, briefly tarnishing his image as Yvette's faithful and adoring husband, but not for long. Are not the warnings of the poets dismissed when one is in love?

"Yvette's dead!"

It is early morning and my roommate and I are just getting up. I hear a loud knock on the door and when I open it I find Leo standing there, flinging out the words.

"The baby's dead, too!"

He turns, goes back to his apartment and slams the door.

"What did he say?" my roommate calls out from our bedroom.

"He said that Yvette and the baby are dead."

"*What?*"

As I begin taking in what he has said, my thoughts move from disbelief to replaying the day dreams I have been having of his being free and of being his wife, and I am sickened with shame. My roommate appears.

"They're *dead*? I can't believe it. Do you think we should we be doing something?"

"I don't know."

"Maybe we should call someone." Just then the phone rings. She answers it.

It is the manager of the school wanting to know if we know. Yvette went into premature labor during the night and the doctors do not know why. Everything had been normal. They think there might have been some emotional shock. She tells us that the school will be closed for the rest of the week and that there will be a service on Saturday. Yvette's sister will be coming up from Washington to stay with Leo.

The next day Leo and I meet accidentally in the hall. Before I can say anything about what has happened he pulls me into his apartment.

"Oh, my darling," he says. "I've been waiting for a time for us to be alone." He pulls me to him and embraces me passionately.

"Oh, my darling," he says again. "I need you. I adore you. We must be together. I want you to marry me. Say you will."

I cannot believe what I am hearing.

"No, Leo," I say, pulling away.

"But you *must* say you will. Please say you will. I can wait if you say you will."

"No, Leo. It's too soon. We don't know each other that way."

"But I know you care for me," he insists. "I know you do. I can feel it. And you know how much I adore you. I've loved you ever since I first saw you."

Innocent and unworldly though I am I know this is wrong. How can he be thinking of marrying someone else when he should be mourning Yvette? He should be thinking only of her, grieving for her. More time has to pass. Maybe later, much later, he and I can think about whether we want to be together.

But he is embracing me again, telling me how much he loves me. I cannot believe this is happening. I have dreamed of being with this man, but I cannot say the yes he is wanting to hear.

I draw back. "I don't know, Leo. I just don't know. You've got to give me more time. You've got to let me go now."

I break out of his apartment and run across the hall to mine, fumble for my key, then slam *my* door. I lean against it, my heart pounding, feeling a sickening mix of alarm and elation. Had Leo told Yvette about his feelings for me? Had this been the shock?

Later that day Yvette's sister arrives. On hearing the news, my roommate's mother has called the manager of the school. She tells her that we can no longer occupy our apartment now that Yvette is no longer there and that she is pulling her daughter out of the school. My roommate protests and a solution is reached. Yvette's sister will be our chaperone, sleeping on a cot in our apartment. By day she will be in Leo's apartment and will take her meals with him. But if Eros is looking for cracks in an arrangement of this kind, they will easily be found.

The following day I find a note in my mailbox:

"Forgive me, my darling. Of course we must wait until this whole thing is over. I adore you. Leo."

Just what "this whole thing" encompasses I am not sure. But after a service for Yvette in the Unitarian Church, Yvette's sister moves into our apartment and the school reopens. Leo is resourceful about finding time for us to be together. We are teacher and student by day and sometimes steal out for lunch. We are rarely alone but manage this now and then. He is ardent and I am frightened, driving with my brakes on. Confused though I am, I am clear that I want to remain a virgin until I am married. I tell him this. He is touched, tender, adoring, says he will respect that. Although I am relieved, I cannot understand why a passionate man who has had two wives will accept the limits I will be setting as if I were making out in a car with an adolescent boy.

It never occurs to me to wonder about the propriety of this, or if the faculty and the other students have caught on. But having established with him my limit of virginity I do not feel guilty about our relationship and move into a nice andante tempo of enjoying it. I love being with him. I am a thirsty learner and he is wonderful to talk with about all kinds of things. Our country is at war and I do not understand what it is all about. He educates me, gives me Oswald Spengler's huge volume, *The Decline of the West*. He talks passionately about his interest in the physics of sound and of ideas he has for research into the development of musical modes. He spoils me, gives me jewelry —I have never had any —and makes me a silent metronome for practicing the piano that has a weight on a string I can see moving out of the corner of my eye. I have never felt so loved. But he becomes restless and pushes for marriage. Months have passed since Yvette's death and I know I must give him an answer.

I swing like my metronome:

I love being with this man. *He is old. When I am his age he will be almost seventy. I do not want to be married to an old man.* I love being with this man. *He is not the man I have been groomed to marry, not the suitable young man from a good family whom my sisters have chosen. My parents will be furious.* I love being with this man. He is an accomplished artist and we will make music all the time. *I do not like his body. It is weak. It will never want to climb mountains with me.* I love being with this man. We will have wonderful musical children. Will I ever find anyone I like being with so much?

I finally tell him yes and anxiety seizes me, but if I had told him no, it would also have seized me. He is ecstatic, pushes for soon. I must tell my parents so that we can make plans.

When I was around twelve and bored one day hanging around the Small Paradise, I saw a hornet's nest hanging under the eaves of the chicken house and threw a stone at it, getting a direct hit. Out came an army after me, stinging my legs as I ran screaming. This is the way I remember my parents reacting when I tell them I am going to marry Leo.

Pa and I are in a taxi driving across Manhattan. He says, "If you marry this man you can never come home again. You can never be a part of this family." It is probably the longest sentence he has ever spoken to me. I am devastated. I was prepared for uproar, but not for the threat of abandonment. The price is too high and his strategy works. Perhaps I would have been willing to pay if I had been wildly, unambivalently in love. I break off the brief engagement, quit the school, and go home. I cannot sleep. I cannot eat. I pace. I go on long walks. My parents think they have another anorexic on their hands. They make an appointment for me with the doctor who hospitalized Mary and helped her recover. I am not opposed. I am desperate.

Negative learning is learning how to do something by experiencing how it should not be done. This is my first lesson in how to be a good therapist.

"Musicians are notoriously unreliable" is the first of this man's pronouncements.

"It is selfish to be studying music when your country is at war" is his next.

There is no "How can I help you?" or "This must be a very upsetting time for you" or "What do *you* want?"

He tells me there is nothing wrong with me and that I do not need to be hospitalized like Mary. What he is saying is I agree entirely with your parents. Stop this nonsense and start being a good daughter.

I have no respect for this man. Since he is the agent of my parents, my lack of respect for him extends to them and my fear of their abandonment begins to erode. As I walk out of his office and head in the direction of the school, I realize that if I am to live my own life and make my own choices, good or bad, I must stop being my parents' dependent child. I must find a job and pay my own way. I will have to stop being a student, not because it is selfish to study music, but because supporting myself is the only way that I will ever be free. What I am going to do about this man I am so torn about I have no idea, but my steps take me back to the school and into the office of the administrator, an ample, warm, motherly woman who is fond of me. She jumps up when she sees me and embraces me.

"I've been worried sick about you," she says.

"How is he?"

"He's been frantic. I've had my hands full. He will be overjoyed to see you."

I wonder if a certain incident on Lexington Avenue tipped the balance of my mixed emotions about Leo.

I had left the music school and was working on the clip desk at *Newsweek*, but I was still seeing Leo and still singing in the chorus. His sister-in-law had married, and my roommate and I had found another apartment. Leo was alone in his and I felt free to go there now, but not to stay over. Proper young girls did not do that then.

I was on my way to see him, walking up Lexington Avenue with some guppies in a white carton. His had recently died and I was bringing these for his aquarium. A taxi swerved over to the curb and a soldier in an officer's uniform jumped out. He threw a bill at the driver and caught up with me.

"I saw you walking alone," he said. "You're lovely. I want to spend time with you. Have dinner with me."

He was classically handsome with movie-star white teeth, dark eyes and an irresistible smile. He was every girl's romantic hero.

"I can't," I said. "I'm meeting someone."

"But you must. Can't we just have a drink?" He took my elbow and jostled the container.

"Be careful of my fish," I said.

"You've got fish in there? How marvelous!" He pushed me towards a café. "Let's go in here."

"I can't. Really I can't. I'm already late."

But there we were, sitting down and he was asking me all about myself. I kept looking at my watch. Finally I stood up and said, "I simply have to go. Someone will be very angry. I'd like to stay. I really would."

Leo was more than very. When I told him why I was late he became even angrier. I had expected that he would appreciate how that young soldier must have been feeling, perhaps shipping out somewhere the next day.

I handed him the carton and he busied himself settling in the fish. He would not look at me and did not thank me for bringing them.

Suppose there had been a different ending to that scene. Suppose when I told him about the young soldier he had embraced me and said, "You should have called me. You should have stayed with him longer, had dinner with him. I would have understood."

It might have made all the difference.

When that incident occurred I was back at square one in my relationship with Leo. After a passionate reunion and enjoying several months of the forbidden relationship, he was pushing again for marriage and I was again immobilized by indecision. He was getting more and more impatient. I had finally taken my metronome swings to a psychiatrist that Hope was seeing to sort herself out between marriages. I had told her that I was having doubts about marrying Leo and she thought Dr. Porter might be helpful. A tall, thin, aristocratic-looking man with neatly combed white hair, he had seemed forbidding at first but proved to be attentive and kind and gave generously of his time. Here was yet another man totally different from the men I had grown up with. My parents, no doubt relieved that I was not rushing into marriage, had agreed to pay for the sessions.

Except for those fees, I was supporting myself. In a few months I had been promoted ay *Newsweek,* and in the two years I was there I received a long overdue education. I was not only learning about the topics I was researching, but also about power, intrigues, infidelities and some "-isms" that were new to me —lesbianism and alcoholism. I had already been acquainted in my family life with sexism, favoritism, and chauvinism. I had also had a little story published which nourished a fantasy, going back to my high school years, of having a career as a writer. I loved working there and was proud to identify myself with journalism's credo to uncover truth and to report it honestly.

Before starting my talks with Dr. Porter I had very little understanding of my emotions, but gradually I began to see that my powerful attachment to Leo was a child's need for the attentive, admiring, demonstrative father I had always wanted. But I did not want to marry him as a needy child. I did not want to marry anyone until I was a mature woman like the beautiful wife he had just lost. But how long was it going to take me to grow up and how was I going to do it, and would Leo wait for me? Then one day I saw him flirting with Hope and I was devastated.

Hope was a mature, desirable woman who enjoyed her sexual powers. She had come on to Leo, perhaps only playfully, but his response to her had felt like a betrayal. Dismayed and confused I rushed to Dr. Porter. His response to my distress was to tell me one of Hope's sexual dreams. I did not want to hear it and mentally put my fingers in my ears. I did not want to know anything about Hope's sexuality. Furthermore, how could I be sure that he would not reveal to her or someone else something private that *I* had told him? My trust in him was shaken. However, I was far from ready to end the therapy. My anxiety was mounting daily, for I knew I could not go on procrastinating about Leo.

As I look back on that painful time I had probably decided to end the relationship when I saw those vibrations pass between him and Hope. But I was having a hard time acknowledging this. Once I did I would have to act and Leo would be furious. Even though I was the one who would be ending the relationship I would feel abandoned by him, unwanted and agonizingly alone. But finally, as if I were giving advice to someone else, I said to myself, "You are still a young woman. This is not your only chance to marry. Surely there is still time for you to find the young husband you have dreamed about and have always believed is out there somewhere looking for you."

This is what I told myself then and it was true. But an even deeper reason that I could not say yes to him I can only now put into words: For all its wonderful extravagance I had never, from the day after his wife's death, been able to trust his love.

So I went to his apartment. He embraced me warmly, believing that everything was as before, but I pulled away, afraid that I might lose my nerve. I went into his living room and he followed me. Sitting down on his sofa I picked up an object from his coffee table and nervously turned it around in my hand. It was a beautiful piece of polished ebony that Yvette had given him. Then I spoke the lines I had been rehearsing over and over. He flew into the expected rage and snatched the ebony from my hand. "Don't you ever touch anything of my beloved!" he shrieked. "Get out! Get out! I never want to see you again!"

What I remember most about the weeks that followed was the cold. The only comfort was the safe enclosure of my little apartment and the unspoken understanding of my roommate. I had not been able to tell her what I was going through, but she knew. I walked around the streets aimlessly, but perhaps not always aimlessly, sometimes hurrying down a street past Leo's favorite restaurant, hoping I would not run into him, and hoping that I would. I imagined seeing him eating alone at a table in the window, looking down at his plate, dejected and miserable. Then he would look up and see me and rush out. "Oh, my darling!" he would cry, embracing me. "I cannot live without you!"

But of course he would not be there, and I would continue my aimless wandering.

Winters in the city could be brutal for women in those days. I didn't wear trousers —women didn't then —and the icy wind would blow around the sky-scrapers and up my nyloned legs, and I thought that I would die of the cold. I remember walking with Leo and Yvette one winter night and lowering my head to keep the wind out of my neck. I can hear Yvette saying, "Hold up your head! Pull the air into your lungs! Then you won't feel the cold!" I can see her striding ahead, a magnificent figure, tall and erect in her black coat, and her head with its golden hair wrapped modishly in a black turban, raised defiantly into the punishing wind. And now Yvette was dead and Leo had married again. Just a month after he had snatched the ebony from my hand and ordered me out of his apartment, he married a young college student he met the previous summer when he was teaching a seminar at a New England campus. It hadn't been me after all. It had been anybody. Which isn't to say that I hadn't meant anything to him at all.

He was the brother of a new friend, a war widow who had invited me to dinner with her and her children. There he was, sitting next to me at her table, not the handsome soldier who had jumped out of the taxi but another handsome soldier. I was immediately attracted to his Gary Cooper looks and his somewhat shy but urbane manner. He was an army captain and stationed nearby and often came into the city to stay with her. When you are trying to recover from failed love, you see no future and do not even want one. But the drive for connection is powerful, and before that dinner was over I was falling in love again, hoping that he would want to see more of me. And he did.

I have always been looking for this man, I thought, after he had escorted me home. In my romantic daydreams there had always been a hazy but alluring male figure. When I first looked into this man's face, I felt sure that he was the young man I had hoped would be out there when I finally summoned the courage to end my relationship with Leo.

For a while he and I lived out my dream —dinners, theater, sailing, visiting his family, he visiting mine, everybody liking everybody —and when he wanted me to get fitted for a diaphragm, I was ready to part with my virginity. He had not asked me to marry him, but I felt sure that he would, and we grew closer. Then suddenly the dream was over and I was back in the abyss. Perhaps he had sensed that I was assuming too much about his feelings for me.

"I'm still in love with a girl I was involved with before I met you" were the painful words. "She was the one who broke it off and it's over, but I'm still in love with her."

A sturdier girl, less vulnerable to being the less loved of two, might have waited it out and given him slack. But in the black and white thinking of the child I still was, all I could see was that he wanted someone else more than he wanted me, even though he could not have her. I had no appreciation then of how a couple can reach the edge of a cliff, then stop and negotiate a solution —not just leap off. But when the last petal of my daisy told me "He loves you not," I leapt and did not land on my feet for a long time.

The hectic pace of my new assignment in the War Fronts department at *Newsweek* was distracting, and with Dr. Porter's help I began sorting through the ruins of my romantic life. From the beginning of my therapy I had been trying to understand why I was so fearful and unsure of myself when I had so many assets. Dr. Porter and I had been examining the role my indifferent father played in this, but increasingly I saw my troubled relationship with my mother as more significant, and the focus shifted accordingly. It was during this phase of the therapy that Dr. Porter made two comments that further eroded my trust in him.

When we started examining my relationship with her I had told him about her punishing me for something I had done, wanting recognition from him of how destructive her punishment had been. I was about six. I was alone in her room trying to paint a picture with watercolors and needed something to blot up the moisture. I saw a bolt of material lying across the arm of a chair. Finding some scissors I cut a small square out of the material and went on with my work. Several days later an angry mother asked me if I had done this. She had been planning to make a dress for herself out of the material and it had been ruined. I lied, and of course she knew that I had. "I don't know what I'm going to do about this," she said, "but I'll have to find some way to punish you." Weeks passed. Then one day my sisters and I were being dressed to go to a birthday party and my mother appeared with three dresses that she had made from the bolt of material. She had sewn a patch on the front of mine to replace the square I had cut out and told me that I would have to wear it to the party. "This is not so much to punish you for what you did, but to punish you for lying."

Dr. Porter laughed. "That was certainly a clever punishment she thought up for you," he said.

Here was another instance, like my encounter with Mary's therapist, of learning how to do therapy by experiencing how it should not be done. A more skilled therapist would have tuned into my feelings of mortification and helped me make the connection between being shamed in this way and my low opinion of myself. Therapists are powerful. They have the power to heal but also to harm, and when a therapist says something harmful, that power intensifies the injury. Having that power may gratify some therapists, but it was always a burden to me because of my fear of being a potentially harmful if not malignant person. I do not know what led up to Dr. Porter's second ill-advised comment. All I remember is his making the following pronouncement:

"You are an animus-ridden woman deficient in feeling."

I did not understand what he meant, only that I was in some way fatally flawed. Later I learned that he was referring to Jung's classification of personality types and to his theory that both sexes have characteristics of the other gender called "animus" and "anima." But he had made his "animus" comment with such animosity that I took him to mean "Women are full of feeling. You have none. You are unbecomingly rational like a man. You are a failure as a woman."

His comment hit hard. I had been raised to believe that men were my intellectual superiors, but when I encountered men whom I knew were less intelligent, I had a way of disengaging the gears of my mind, almost unaware that I was doing this. I knew intuitively that I had to protect the egos of men and that if I revealed my good intellect, or used it too well, I could be discarded as unfeminine, as on several occasions I was. And now Dr. Porter was doing the same. But maybe, in a naive belief that I did not have to protect *his* ego, I had failed to disengage the gears of my mind with him, perhaps questioning something that he had said and eliciting this painful rebuke.

As I was growing up, being who I was seemed such a wrong thing to be that I finally retreated inside myself where it felt safe, and became uncommunicative. But my inaccessibility exasperated Ma and she would exclaim angrily, "Don't you care about anything? *Have you no feelings?* In time her view of me became my view of myself, and now Dr. Porter's outburst was echoing her reproaches and confirming my worst fears that I was a cold, selfish unfeeling person. Deep down I knew this was not so, but how to become the person I believed myself to be seemed an insurmountable task.

So I had lost my lover, my trust in my therapist, and soon I was to lose my belief in the integrity of journalists. As a fact-checker I had discovered an inaccuracy in a minor story. I called it to the attention of the writer, but correcting the misstatement would have destroyed his story and he refused to change it. Even though it was a small deception that would probably not be noticed, I was disillusioned by his indifference. Perhaps I was ready to leave *Newsweek* anyway. Even though working for the magazine was classified as an "essential war industry," I found myself wanting to do more for what was called "the war effort." Robert and my sisters' husbands and many other men that I knew were in the service, and a number of my women friends had joined the Red Cross. I decided to join too. I would be able to leave my losses and failed life behind me and plunge into the unknown.

PART II

STUMBLING INTO THE PROFESSION

After spending two years in the midst of the anthill activity of an army camp in the parched, scrub oak terrain of middle Long Island, I had not known how much I was thirsting for the beauty and serenity of the campus at Smith College with its wide green quadrangles and stately trees. I have often wondered how my life would have turned out if I had become a doughnut girl or had gone to Smith as an undergraduate as I had wanted to, instead of being a student in their school for social work.

The Red Cross had declined to send me abroad because of my hay fever and sent me instead to Long Island to work in a psychiatric hospital and discharge center for soldiers returning from overseas. It was not far from the Small Paradise, but gasoline was strictly rationed and I rarely went there. I had been hoping to "see the world" when I had applied to the Red Cross, but this new world was as foreign to me as the South Pacific or war-torn Europe would have been. Although Long Island flora was familiar, I was encountering, as I had in music school and at *Newsweek*, the rich variety of human beings I had been deprived of knowing when I was growing up. I was fulfilling the vow to get out into the world that I had made in my roommate's Washington, D.C. living room after graduating from boarding school.

We "Hospital Workers," all female, were housed in a barracks with Army nurses. Most were there to find husbands and some did. I was still convalescing from the loss of my Army Captain and surprised myself by being attracted to another. He was a doctor in the medical corps and in charge of the clinic for the hospital staff. I found myself flirting with him a bit on my frequent visits to the clinic for allergy shots. While he flirted back he let me know that he was firmly married. Being the kind of committed family man I was hoping to find made him even more desirable, and I was not attracted to anyone else in the two years I was there.

My co-workers and I spent our days interviewing patients who were being discharged. Our assignment was to help them with confusing paper work, but we were encouraged by our supervisor, a graduate of the school at Smith, to be aware of the feelings these men had about what they had been through and their return to civilian life, and to give them as much sensitive listening as time allowed. This woman liked my work and when the war was over she encouraged me to apply to her school at Smith. She believed that with a strong recommendation from her they would consider admitting me even though I would be applying to a graduate program without an undergraduate degree. I knew next to nothing about the profession of social work and had no interest in becoming a professional anything. My life plan, like my boarding school roommate's, was to marry and raise a family, but my supervisor's suggestion had been planted in fertile soil.

After I left boarding school, Ma, in her push to get me connected socially, had arranged for me to become a member of the Junior League of New York. As part of their orientation, a social worker had taken our class to see the living conditions in city tenements. I had been stunned by what I saw. Coming from a house with five bathrooms I could not believe that these apartments had none and that all the occupants on a floor had to use one smelly toilet in the hall. When we visited a family where four children slept in one bed I thought with chagrin about the fuss I had made when Ma had put Robert in "my" room. At least I had had a cot of my own in the room off the porch. But what moved me most about these people was their *entrapment*. I had never known poverty, but I had known how it felt to be trapped in other ways. I was on my way to becoming a professional *liberator*. It is clear to me now that my calling has been to help people free themselves, not only from such tangible misery as poverty or a bad marriage, but also from those interior miseries of guilt, self-hatred, and a host of disabling fears.

My supervisor arranged for me to be interviewed by Annette Garrett, an Associate Director of the social work school at Smith. One of her responsibilities was visiting and evaluating the progress of students on their fieldwork placements, and when she was on one of her trips she scheduled an appointment with me at her hotel in New York. We met in her small, low-budget room and she indicated that I was to sit on the bed while she occupied the only chair. I knew at once that I was in the presence of a powerful, perceptive woman who was comfortably at home in her plainly presented self. She was not unfriendly, but clearly was not going to waste time on pleasantries.

"What do you want to do with your life?" she started out.

"I want to get married and have children," I said.

She laughed. "I mean what do you want to do with your social work training?"

I told her I wanted to work with children.

The way she worded her opening question is an interesting reflection of her times, for it was exceptional then for women to combine marriage and career. Social work education presumably was her life, and she had probably assumed that by applying to the school I had opted for career, but I still expected to marry and have children. Until that came to pass I could think of no better way to occupy my time than to help children in some way.

As the interview progressed I believe that Miss Garrett did not know what to make of me. I was not your usual candidate, if indeed one exists. In that era few women of my class were professional social workers. If they were interested in helping the disadvantaged they would be sitting on the boards of social agencies and doing volunteer work, as Ma had done and I as had done as a member of the Junior League. Miss Garrett was disbelieving about my feeble education, but at the same time I think she was intrigued by me and did not want to pass up an interesting possibility. In the end she compromised.

The school at Smith was unique, using the campus in the summer when the undergraduates were not there for its academic work and placing its students in various social agencies throughout the northeast for nine months of full-time internships. Miss Garrett said she would accept me for the school's first summer semester, and if I could handle the work I could go on with the program. Not having an undergraduate degree, I would not be awarded a Master's. But since graduates of the school were well regarded, I should have no trouble finding a job. This seemed fair enough to me.

I do not recall any reaction from my parents to my decision to enter graduate school, pro or con. I was not looking to them for financial help since I had saved most of my salary while working for the Red Cross and would be able to finance my first year at the school. But after I left the Red Cross and was back at the Small Paradise before heading up to Smith, I overheard my mother having one of those what-are-your-children-up-to conversations with a friend. The isn't-it-an-admirable-thing-Fairlie-is-doing tone in her reply made me feel that she was covering her disappointment and would rather be telling her friend that I had found a wonderful young man and that she was making plans for my wedding. I, too, wished that I had found a wonderful young man, and I was hurt by my parents' seeming lack of interest in the direction my life was taking.

Being ignorant of college life, not knowing the steps, I fell in behind the other students and was braced for a repeat of my high school years when everyone else was way ahead of me. But here our courses seemed far less difficult than Algebra II and Latin Prose Authors, in which latter course I had received the humiliating grade of 36. The history of social work and the minutiae of the public welfare system were pretty dry, but our courses in normal human development, psychopathology and "social casework" were engrossing. I had never heard of "casework" —a counseling method first developed in the 19th century by untrained social workers —and it quickly became my favorite class. Learning how to conduct interviews was fascinating and a revelation. It had never occurred to me that I could be taught to be a kind of Dr. Porter and that in time I would become a more competent therapist. But what I was learning in my courses was not the only education that I would be getting at Smith.

There was one black girl in our class, the first educated black person I had ever met. There had been a building in our town when I was growing up called "The Flats" where the only Negro families lived. When Ma drove us by, warning us not to stare at them, we children were afraid that they might run out and do something bad to us. Although we had never encountered them, I had met the blacks, who worked for Aunt Carrie and her husband on their farm in Maryland, and they were always good to me. But I did have a scary moment with a black man when I was walking along the street in New York City. He brushed against me as we passed each other and muttered "white meat."

I wanted to get to know my black classmate and one day after class I started up a conversation with her. When I asked her to tell me about herself she said that her mother was a lawyer. "She *is?*" I said, being both surprised and impressed. She glared at me and drew away and I realized I had offended her, though at first I did not understand why. I tried to make amends, explaining that *my* mother would never have been able to become a lawyer. At this she became even angrier and stalked away. In spite of my making several attempts to heal the breach she never spoke to me again. It took me a while to realize that my astonishment about her mother betrayed an assumption that my mother, being white, *should* be superior to hers. I had, understandably, brought negative generalizations about blacks into my encounter with her, for I had seen them occupying the lowest niche in society and been exposed to the prejudice of my elders. Naïve as I was, my mind had been trying to be open and was wanting to learn. She too, however, had made negative assumptions about me because of the color of *my* skin. Being very blond I was probably for her the epitome of "Whitey." Sadly, I never did get to know her, but the experience taught me an invaluable lesson about the power of words and the perils of miscommunication. I was on my way to understanding why therapists have to listen so attentively, to hear so accurately, and to respond with such care.

I had not seen much of Miss Garrett, but one day she stopped me when our paths crossed on the campus. She told me that she had heard good things about me at the last faculty meeting. If I still wanted to, I could go on with the program. In due course I learned that I had been assigned to a Family Service

Agency in Connecticut for my first internship and that two of my classmates would be going with me.

By chance Ma's brother and his wife had a house near the agency and this time they were glad to have me stay with them. I had been told that after Little Brother died I kept asking where my twin was and that Ma could not bear to hear it. So she sent me on a ferry across Long Island Sound to stay with them. They had no children. They had been told that I was toilet trained, but apparently I regressed while there and they promptly sent me back. I had not seen much of them during the intervening years and did not know them well, but it proved to be a congenial arrangement, and over the course of my nine months with them they shared some disturbing things about my mother's family that I had never known.

I had known that her younger sister had died in childbirth, that Ma had cared for her baby and wanted to keep her, but that Pa had insisted she be returned to her father's family. I also knew that the eldest of her three brothers died of rheumatic fever in his late twenties. But I did not know that Ma had a little brother who died at about the same age as my twin when she was eleven. But the most startling, the most shocking revelation of all was that Ma's mother had killed herself. She had been hospitalized for depression and this same uncle, who was a bachelor then, brought her to his home to recuperate and she hanged herself in his attic. My grandmother's death had never been spoken of. And no wonder. In that era, along with cancer, sex, and mental illness, suicide was yet another shameful forbidden topic.

What I learned about my mother during those months was the beginning of my seeing her as a person separate from myself with her own painful losses and fears, and with that came a stirring of compassion and forgiveness. While a part of me wanted to weep with her now for what she had suffered, another part of me was still wounded and angry and struggling to be free of her power. Forgiveness would not –could not –come until I had claimed that freedom.

B efore we left for our fieldwork our casework professor warned us not to expect to be able to go out and rescue all the poor and suffering. "You'll be able to make a real difference in some people's lives," she had said, "but be realistic about how much you can do. Don't go out tilting at windmills."

I did not think her advice applied to me for I had no mission, as some of my classmates did, to save the world. I just wanted to help a few troubled people while waiting for my life to begin. But soon after, when I found myself in a bedroom in Connecticut with tiny, miserable, mute Mrs. Dailey and her robust, middle-aged, very vocal, retarded daughter Mary, I was hooked for life in a vocation I had never sought.

Mary and her mother had been evicted from their ramshackle home by the town's health department. Their report in the Family Service Agency's case record described it as an eyesore and a hazard to the neighborhood. "It is heated with kerosene and can go up in flames at any time," the report went on. "These two women are not competent. They do not eat well and the daughter has been seen spending welfare money on Coca Cola and potato chips."

But the Daileys had been happy there. When Mary was a little girl Mrs. Dailey supported them cleaning houses, but now she was ailing and house-bound. Mary had never been able to work, but she enjoyed her life wandering about the town and she had become somewhat of a town character. She loved reading children's books and was a regular visitor to the town's small library. Before their eviction, our agency had found them a place to live on a farm with an impatient, inflexible elderly widow, and Mary and her mother were miserable. When they were moved they could only bring what would fit into the small bedroom they were to occupy in the widow's house and had to leave most of their possessions behind. Mary, who always spoke for the two of them, had been complaining loudly, not liking this, wanting that, and the widow was threatening to throw them out. She was willing to give them a few more weeks, but the complaining would have to stop. My assignment was to go out and make peace.

As I approached the farmhouse in the Agency's car on my first visit I felt like a plumber coming to fix a leak without any tools. I had no idea what I was going to do. But I soon discovered that I did have tools for the obscure trade I was trying to learn —intelligence, sensitivity, friendliness, the ability to listen and observe, and compassion. I would soon discover that I had brought with me my backpack of neuroses and that they were going to make this learning experience extremely difficult.

One of my most disabling hang-ups was my fear of authority figures. We students were closely monitored during our nine months at the agency and, lacking today's tools of tape recorders and videos, spent hours writing verbatim reports of our contacts with our clients. Then our work would be critiqued in weekly conferences with a supervisor. When I began having conferences with mine I quickly grew to dislike her. She was single, possibly menopausal, and may well have been depressed. She also lacked both imagination and a sense of humor and had an intimidating way of looking over her bifocals disapprovingly. She was there to teach me "the right way" to do this work, and my need for correction often seemed a heavy burden to her. In the beginning when I was floundering, her advice had been helpful. As I grew more confident and began questioning her judgment our relationship grew more and more strained. But as I approached the farmhouse I was grateful for her suggestion to "just let them all talk."

I met first with the widow, a short, thin energetic woman with sparse, graying hair pulled into a tight bun. As soon as I walked in the door she began her litany of complaints. She and her husband had run their farm together, but he had died recently and she was finding it hard to do all the work herself. She had taken in the Daileys because she needed the money. She had chickens and ducks and a small herd of goats and had customers coming in and out buying eggs and milk and she didn't want them running into the daughter. If it were just the mother she thought she could manage. The daughter was the problem. "I don't like her. She gets too close to me. And she's always touching herself where she shouldn't. Go on up. You can see for yourself."

The Daileys were expecting me. Mrs. Dailey, a tiny woman, was standing in the middle of their room, her white head bowed, and holding her abdomen. She looked up, but did not return my smile. However, my smile at Mary, a large homely woman with short, badly cut brown hair, brought her leaping from the bed where she had been sitting right into my private space, talking close to my face. I was unprepared for her powerful body odor. I drew back instinctively and went over and sat on the bed where she had been sitting. But she followed me, standing over me, pouring out their grievances:

"My mother hates the milk…She can't drink it…The lady says she has to…She doesn't have any teeth…She hurts down there…(Mary poked at herself to show me where)…It hurts her to go…she has to go all night…she had a potty…We want to get her potty…We want to go home…Please take us home."

I shook my head. "They told me you have to stay here."

I had learned that after the Daileys left their little house it had burned down. Some neighborhood boys who had been harassing them were probably responsible, but since the house was to be demolished, no action was taken.

Mary gave me a sullen look and moved away, then moved right back. "Can't you take us back to get our things? They made us move too fast. I left my *Hans Brinker*. It's my favorite book. I want to get my *Hans Brinker*."

I could see its pages curling in the fire. I shook my head again. "No, Mary. They won't let me do that either."

Again Mary turned abruptly and moved away, but she couldn't stay away long. She came back and again stood close to me. I knew now what was making the widow uneasy. "Can you get us some bananas?" she asked. "My mother loves bananas. You don't have to chew them. Can you bring us some?"

"I'll try to do that, Mary," I said, grateful to be able to say yes to something.

Most of the rest of the visit was listening to the painful story of their eviction and how miserable they were on the farm. Mary was afraid of the country and terrified of the goats. She and her mother stayed in their room most of the time listening to their radio, but "she" was always coming up and turning the volume down. Mrs. Dailey was getting deaf and needed it turned up. I told Mary that I would visit again soon and would see what I could do about the milk and getting a potty for her mother

On my way out I had another talk with the farmer's widow urging her to give it time. I learned that she had an old chamber pot in her attic and would not object to Mrs. Dailey using it if she emptied it herself and did not soil their room, but she was adamant about the milk. She had plenty of good farm food and they had to get used to what she had.

After reading the verbatim report of the visit, my supervisor told me I had handled it well, "but you can't buy them food. You'll be undermining the widow's authority if you do that. They have to get used to what she gives them."

"But I would only be buying some bananas for Mrs. Dailey. She doesn't have any teeth."

"I know, but the public health nurse is going to get her dentures. You'll be setting a bad precedent if you let the Daileys expect that you're going to give them everything they ask for. If you give them one thing, they'll keep asking for more. The widow is taking good care of them. You have to learn, Miss Nicodemus, as you're starting out, that you can't meet all your client's needs. You'll end up an old lady with seventeen cats and not enough money to feed them. Do you understand my point?"

I nodded. I had *understood* it, but I did not agree with it. It seemed like a simple act of human kindness to give Mrs. Dailey something she could enjoy eating, and I believed that giving the Daileys some pleasure would make them less fretful and less homesick for their little house and their old way of life. Furthermore, my supervisor had put me in an awkward position. What was I going to tell Mary when she asked me again for the bananas as I was sure that she would? A less anxious student who was not so intimidated by authority figures, would probably have just gotten them and not mentioned it in her verbatim, or if her supervisor had asked about it would have simply lied about it. But I could not imagine doing that.

It is hard to make believable the depth of fear I had at that time of doing the wrong thing or of being a "bad" person, and of being punished and rejected. "It's not so much because of what you did, but because you lied," my mother had said when she made me wear that dress to the party. Then I had spent four years living under the honor system in a strict boarding school, having to report in a public assembly on any rules that I had broken, and I had become a paragon of virtue. When I made my next visit to the Daileys I had no idea what I was going to do.

The public health nurse had arranged for Mrs. Dailey to be treated for her urinary infection at a hospital clinic, and my supervisor suggested that I provide transportation for these visits. This would get the Daileys out the house and we could talk in the car. Mary was so stimulated on the first of our many trips that she didn't complain once about their grievances. Her mother, glued to the window, was momentarily distracted from her physical discomfort. While she was being treated at the clinic Mary and I walked around the town. She surprised me by taking my hand like a little child and embarrassed me at first by grabbing at her crotch periodically. I realized that this must be the habit that so deeply offended the widow. We were an unlikely pair, Mary and I, and heads turned when we went by.

I had still made no decision about what to do if Mary asked again about the bananas because nothing was right. I couldn't see saying no and disappointing them, and yes would mean deceiving my supervisor since I lacked the courage to defy her openly. And of course on the drive back Mary did ask. I didn't answer right away.

"Well, *are* you?" she asked impatiently.

"Let's see if we go by a place that sells them," I said, evading the hard decision, leaving it to chance.

When we drove through the next little town Mary cried out, "There's a market!"

So chance had made the decision, saying that a little pleasure in their lives was not going to hurt anyone. I went into the market and came out with a banana for each of them.

"Can't we bring some home?" Mary asked.

"No," I said. "She wouldn't like that." I didn't have to explain who *she* was and Mary did not press the issue.

On our next outing Mary said she would prefer ice cream. So I bought Mrs. Dailey a banana and, by now a hardened criminal, bought Mary a double scoop strawberry cone, her favorite flavor. We repeated this ritual on all subsequent trips. My supervisor never knew, and the Daileys never asked for anything else. You might expect that I would have been elated by my "success," but I was still so mired in my fear of her or anyone's disapproval that I could not see this small deception as a step in the direction of my own growth. Even though deceiving my supervisor had been extremely stressful, I had done it. Later, when my fear of her authority led me to deceive Mary the last time I saw her, my guilt about that deception would haunt me and goad me into eventually claiming my autonomy and the right to my own values.

After the last of Mrs. Dailey's treatments at the clinic I visited less often, wanting to wean them from the pleasure these visits gave them, but I continued taking them out for drives and buying them their treats. When we returned to the farm after these outings Mrs. Dailey would return to their room and Mary and I would walk around the farm. I wanted to enlarge her world as much as I could before I had to leave, and I was able to help her overcome her fear of the goats so that she could enjoy petting them through the fence. As my departure approached I began preparing her for my leaving. At first she pretended that she hadn't heard me, but I knew that she had when she asked me to write her after I left. I promised I would. Once again I received a frowning you-can't-do-that response from my supervisor.

"Don't you know that it's unprofessional to continue a relationship with a client after the case is closed? You've done nice work with the Daileys, but Mary has to let you go and think of our agency as the place to turn to if she needs any more help, not you."

This time I protested more passionately, saying that I could not see how exchanging an occasional letter would do any harm.

"How do you know she can even write?" my supervisor asked scornfully. "She didn't get very far in school."

"I know she can *read*! You remember! She kept pestering me to take her back to their little house so she could get those children's books she'd had to leave behind. Don't you remember that?"

"Well, she probably doesn't know how to address a letter and I really doubt that she can write one, but that's not the point. You've become very attached to Mary, but now *you* have to let *her* go and get on with your training and let someone else take over if the Daileys need more help. What's most important is that the Daileys see our agency being there for them. Individuals like you come and go. You'll have to tell Mary that you can't write her. The widow will call us if they need anything."

I left our conference shaken. I would have to break my word to Mary. I knew that she would be hurt and angry and wouldn't be able to understand why, and I didn't want our relationship to end this way. How could occasional letters do any harm? Of course if I wrote her, my supervisor wouldn't have to know, just as she didn't have to know about the treats I had been giving them. But then again how could I be sure? The widow would see my letters, and another social worker who might visit the Daileys after I left would undoubtedly learn about them. With my history of academic failure having made me so unsure of myself and having been on probation when I first came to the school, I did not want my supervisor sending a poor evaluation of me to Miss Garrett, and I was afraid to disobey her. At a remove of half a century it is hard to believe how anxious I was about this, but the child in me was still painfully intimidated by people in authority. For far too long I would continue to be shamed by my inability to muster moral courage in spite of that fear.

On my last visit Mary and I took a long walk down a country road, picking wildflowers along the way. In her enthusiasm Mary sometimes pulled up whole clumps instead of taking time to break off the stems. We brought some flowers back to the widow —at my insistence, she didn't want to —and a bunch for her mother. While Mary took them up to her I had a final talk with the widow. As she often did she spoke about how tired she was caring for the farm alone. I reminded her that Mary could be a useful helper, even learning to milk the goats if she could take the time to train her.

"No, indeedy!" the widow said, "she'll just be in my way!" She always said no, although I did notice from time to time that she had done something I suggested.

"Well, think about it," I said as we parted. Then I went up to the Dailey's room to say goodbye.

"This is our last visit," I said. "I'm going to miss you." I shook Mrs. Dailey's hand, then Mary's. She held on to my arm.

"You write first," she said, "and I'll answer.

I still did not know what I was going to say.

Mary prodded me roughly. "I said you write first, *okay?*

"Okay, Mary," I lied, knowing now that I would not have the courage to. "I'll write first."

I squeezed her arm, waved at her mother who was sitting on her bed, and left them for the last time. After a diplomatic goodbye to the widow I hurried out to the Agency's car. When out of sight of the farm I pulled over to the side of the road and shut off the motor. I leaned forward on the steering wheel, put my head on my arms, and began to cry, anguished that I would not have the courage to do what I had been told not to do, even though my heart told me that my supervisor was wrong.

"I'm sorry, Mary," I said through my sobs. "I'm terribly sorry."

When I returned to the school I bought the most beautiful copy I could find of *Hans Brinker or The Silver Skates* and mailed it to her with a card that said, "Dear Mary, I am thinking of you and hoping you and your mother are well." But I did not include a return address.

M iss Garrett was not only the Co-Director of the school. She also taught the advanced casework class and had the reputation of being a tough teacher. As another authority figure she was even more intimidating than my supervisor in Connecticut, not only because she had more power, but because I respected her. When I was struggling with my supervisor I not only disliked her, but did not respect her, and it is clear to me now that even as a rank beginner I was intuitively a better therapist. But after attending a few sessions of Miss Garrett's class I knew I would have a long way to go before reaching her level of competence, if I ever could. Because of my humiliating failures in boarding school I had carried with me a fear of "not knowing" when called on in a class, so I always sat in the back row and never raised my hand. I thought I was successfully hidden in Miss Garrett's class, but one day she pounced on me and called out:

"In a nutshell, Miss Nicodemus, hiding back there, what is your philosophy of social work?"

And my mind went blank.

I was humiliated to have to say that I did not know and hurried back into hiding, but she was to pounce and catch me again. Her own philosophy was strongly influenced by Freud and we had been studying his theories. We had of course been trying them on to see if they fit and when she pounced the next time I was grateful, for she was making me confront my overdeveloped "superego," as we were being taught to call it. She had posed the following question to the class:

"If you are driving alone in a desert and are coming to a red light and there are no cars in any direction, would you stop or go on?"

A spirited discussion followed about the purpose of rules and law, concluding with the assumption that any normal person would drive through. She started to move on to another topic, but I must have betrayed my perplexity.

"What's the matter with you?" she asked.

"I'm still back in the desert," I said, "trying to make up my mind."

I remember how heartily she laughed. It was only years later when I began acquiring the authority of my own expertise that my fear of external authority began to lessen and I could begin to trust my own good instincts.

A symbol of that growing expertise was what I thought of as my little black bag. The image of that bag first came to me during an interview I was conducting in the psychiatric outpatient clinic of a hospital in Boston where I had been placed for my second nine-month internship. When I said something in that interview that seemed to be helpful I began, for the first time, to think of myself as a therapist who carried useful remedies in a little black bag —a bag like the one our family doctor used to carry when he made visits to our house.

One of the psychiatrists in our clinic had referred a young single mother to the social work unit, and she had been assigned to me. She had come to the clinic because of depression, but he thought it was reactive to her stressful circumstances and that it would lift as those circumstances changed. When I had been working with Mary Dailey I was actively engaged in her day-to-day life in a hands-on way, but with Mrs. Reilly I was sitting in a small room furnished with an old oak desk, two straight chairs and a battleship gray metal wastebasket, talking with her about her problems. What passed between us in our conversation was what would make the difference in her life, if she could act on the conclusions we reached.

Mrs. Reilly was a war widow. She had two people in her family, a 6-year-old daughter who had started to become rebellious —talking back and being generally objectionable —and a complaining, demanding mother. Her only sibling, a brother, had also been killed in World War II, and her father had died shortly after from an early coronary. Mrs. Reilly had been his favorite.

Her work week was spent fending off a predatory employer and coming home to a defiant daughter. Then on her weekends she felt obligated to be available to her demanding widowed mother. She had no life of her own. What she most wanted from me when we started our talks was help with her daughter. Her mother had been very strict with her and her brother, and short on affection. When her brother was bad her mother had made his father spank him when he came home from work and he had hated doing it. Mrs. Reilly wanted to be a different kind of mother. She believed that spanking was wrong and she was trying to be patient with her daughter and to explain why she wanted her to do this or not do that, but to no avail.

With my new supervisor's guidance I was able to help her see that she had overcorrected her mother's mistakes and to accept that getting angry with her daughter, even contemplating a "good smack on the bottom," as opposed to pre-arranged corporal punishment, was *good* mothering. She went home prepared to take action, but never had to. Her daughter had sensed her mother's determination to use her rightful power and had stopped challenging her. Emboldened by success with her daughter she was also able to "set limits" with her mother and to claim some time for herself. One day when Mrs. Reilly was complaining about a particularly objectionable remark her mother had made I said, "Your mother could use a good smack on the bottom too," and Mrs. Reilly laughed and laughed.

I had been apprehensive about my new supervisor, but she was gratifyingly different from my previous one –smart, attractive and, like Miss Garrett, another role model I could respect. She expected me to be an adult and was impatient with my self-doubt. "You've just got to jump in and swim," she said. "You'll make mistakes, but they probably won't be fatal, and you'll learn from them." This woman was good medicine for a chronic worrier, and she clearly thought well of me. One day I stumbled on an evaluation of me that she had written for Miss Garrett. She had described me as "a young woman of superior intelligence." Having teetered on the edge of failure all through high school, those words were thrilling to contemplate. My time with her passed quickly, and under her tutelage I evolved from a self-effacing beginner to a promising young professional.

As this internship grew to a close I had become sufficiently confident in my growing competence to sit back and take a critical look at the work we had all been doing in the clinic. I had been so insecure when I started out that I never questioned our various roles. At that time social workers were seen as experts in a patient's tangible, conscious world and psychiatrists as experts in the terrain of a patient's psyche or unconscious. However, patients like Mrs. Reilly often had weekly sessions with both a psychiatrist and a social worker and I began to wonder in what way these interviews were different. The faculty at Smith had instilled in me such awe of psychiatry I had assumed that what went on between Mrs. Reilly and her psychiatrist was a mysterious process I would be unable to understand and that he was doing "the real treatment." I was just giving Mrs. Reilly some practical help. I had taken this distinction so seriously I even worried sometimes that I might be venturing inadvertently into his terrain. It was all very puzzling.

During our final summer Miss Garrett kept reminding us that we were "caseworkers," not psychiatrists, that we did not have medical degrees, and that she disapproved of caseworkers going into private practice. At the same time she was urging us to become as knowledgeable as possible about our own psyches and even to be psychoanalyzed, if we could, the way analysts in training had to be. In her casework class she was teaching us "the art of counseling" —a topic on which she later wrote a book —but she was also telling us not to step out of our professional niche and cross the line dividing social work from psychiatry. But just what was that niche supposed to be?

Before the 1950's social workers had remained dutifully on their side of the line, working in social agencies and mental health clinics with people who could not afford psychiatric treatment. I remember social workers referring to themselves then as the "poor man's psychiatrist," although poor *woman's* psychiatrist would have been be a more apt description. It was primarily poor women who were seeking help with such problems as poverty, alcoholic and abusive husbands, and disturbed children. As time passed, however, caseworkers who were more confident or perhaps more rebellious than I began making end runs around that line much sooner than I dared to do. Later, when the distinction between the two professions was becoming more and more blurred and I was venturing timidly into private practice, I thought about Mrs. Reilly and concluded that her interviews with her psychiatrist and with me had probably not been all that different, especially then when there were no drugs for a psychiatrist to prescribe.

Therapists sometimes speak of therapy as a "corrective emotional experience" and I think it is likely that what was most responsible for Mrs. Reilly's improvement was her reconnecting with a kind and attentive father in her interviews with her psychiatrist and experiencing a warm, affirming and undemanding mothering from me. By the time my internship at the clinic ended I had added what was to become the number one remedy in my little black bag —the *relationship* I developed with my clients. I had offered this intuitively to Mrs. Reilly. Only later in my career, after I had begun doing supervision myself, did I conceptualize its value.

I did not need Miss Garrett's urgings to know that I needed and wanted to be psychoanalyzed. I had learned a great deal about my emotional handicaps during these years at Smith, how chronically anxious I was and how nearly crippled by self-doubt, and I was tired of carrying this baggage wherever I went.

"You have a good engine," she had once said to me, "but you're only operating on about two cylinders. You need to get the rest of your motor going."

Her comment had lit a fire under me. It was exciting to think that analysis might accomplish this, but perhaps even higher on my psychoanalysis agenda would be taking a hard look at my romantic failures. During the previous year I had added yet another to my list and I was beginning to lose hope that anything in my personal life would ever work out. I decided to ask Miss Garrett how to go about finding an analyst and for suggestions that she might have about a job. During our conversation she wanted to know if I had had any therapy. When I told her about my experience with Dr. Porter she was shocked. "That wasn't therapy!" she had exploded. "You need the real stuff!" Although other schools of analysis were well respected by then she thought that after my bad experience with a disciple of Jung I should go for the "pure Freudian strain." She also had a job suggestion. The Director of Social Services at a children's institution in Westchester County, who was an alumna of the school, had phoned to tell her about an opening on their staff. She was interested in hiring a young graduate. If I took the job, Miss Garrett would refer me to an analyst she knew in New York City, which was an easy commute. He, in turn, would refer me to an analyst in training if he thought I was a suitable candidate for analysis. The fee of a trainee would not be as steep and would be possible for me to manage on a starting salary.

When I went down to New York for my job interview, I decided to make an appointment with Dr. Porter. We had never had a formal termination and I hadn't seen him since I started the program at Smith. Miss Garrett had told me that I had no obligation to tell him that I would not be coming back, but I felt that I should. We had been through a lot together and in spite of his blunders I was grateful to him. I wanted to have a friendly good-bye and to thank him for his help. Not realizing, naively, that he would be deeply offended, I told him that I was going to try a different kind of therapy and had decided to have a Freudian analysis.

"I knew when you went to that school you were going to be contaminated by that Freudian stuff," he said coldly. He stood up, indicating that our session was over and saw me to the door. When I held out my hand he did not shake it and closed the door behind me. This dismissal by a surrogate father I had come to trust was deeply wounding and although I never saw him again, he was to barge into my analysis and remain a disapproving authority figure for some time.

In September 1948, at the age of 28, I boarded a train in Grand Central Station, proceeded north along the Hudson River, and got off at Dobbs Ferry. Then I climbed a short hill to the grounds of St. Christopher's School and reported for work on the first day of my career as a psychotherapist. Obedient to Miss Garrett, I did not call myself a psychotherapist. I was a caseworker, a soon-to-be member of the National Association of Psychiatric Social Workers and a beginner in the social work specialty of child welfare.

I had taken the right job. I loved what I was doing and loved the people I was working with. Since I had to be in Manhattan four times a week for my analytic sessions I had decided to live there and commute to the school. In the early mornings I would walk to Grand Central from the tiny, furnished apartment I had found near the United Nations and board the train, going against the grain of commuters whose cars hurtled by on the railroad's incoming tracks. I could see candid snapshots of them as they flashed by, engrossed in their morning newspapers. I loved the near solitude in my almost empty car. I loved leaning back and feasting on the view, soaring on the thermals with the seagulls and watching the sparse river traffic that seemed frozen in time beside the speeding train.

At the end of the day's work I boarded the train back to the city to meet with my analyst, moving again against the tide of commuters who were returning home, and I would catch glimpses of them standing and lurching in the club car with drinks in their hands. Some of these commuters would be debarking unsteadily into a scene from a John Cheever story, but Cheever could not have woven much of a story about my life. Work and analysis were about all there was time for, or all I was ready for. Although I was living in a vibrant, cutting-edge city that is normally mecca to the young, I had not come there to swing in its fast lane. I was there because of an analysis that I knew I needed if I was going to fashion a full life for myself anywhere.

St. Christopher's School occupied a beautiful old estate overlooking the Hudson. Its purpose was to provide housing and a school for children whose families could not care for them. The children lived in cottages with "cottage parents" and each child was assigned to a social worker. Sometimes after a period of counseling and family repair, the child could be returned home. For children whose stay was going to be lengthy or permanent they were housed at the school or our staff found foster homes, scouring a wide area for families who seemed trustworthy and who would accept supervision.

Our staff was a small, tightly knit group of idealistic professionals. We worked long hours to make the children's time under our care as comfortable and brief as possible. Every few weeks we met with our consulting psychiatrist to present our most challenging "cases" for his assessment. We were like a small close family with our psychiatrist, actually a youngish man, functioning as the wise patriarch.

When I started on this job my status as a professional social worker put me in a position of some authority. I was supposed to know the answers, or at least to know more than my clientele. Perhaps working with children made it easier for me to hide my insecurity, for to them at least I looked like a functioning adult.

One of my first clients was Jenny. She was going on thirteen and had the pseudo-maturity of a "latch-key" kid, but she was still very much a little girl, pretty and fresh looking, and not yet shapely. She was chatty and friendly. Her stay at the school was temporary and was a kind of vacation for her from cleaning and cooking and looking out for her younger sister who was also at the school. They would be going home when their mother, a working divorced woman, was well enough. She was flat on her back, recuperating from a detached retina.

Jenny loved to sit in my office and talk. She missed her grandmother back in Oregon and a cat that her grandmother was keeping. She talked a lot about her parents' divorce and missing her father, and about her mother's new boyfriend. Then she threw me a curve.

"Why do people like sex so much, Miss N?"

Although I was no longer a virgin, I was not married and had no children. The last thing I felt myself to be was an authority on sex, much less a fully arrived adult. Anxious as I was about how to proceed I was grateful to Jenny for assuming I was both and for helping me learn that I had a center of good judgment in myself that I could trust.

After drawing her out I learned that she been aware of her parent's enjoyment of sex before their estrangement, seeing them kiss a lot and hearing them laugh and make funny noises in their bedroom when she was supposed to be asleep. She had come upon them once when her father was on top of her mother and she was worried that he was hurting her. Sometimes when her mother's boyfriend stayed over she again heard laughter, but she also heard her mother cry out. Jenny was confused.

"And Lottie talks a lot about sex," she went on. "I don't know what she means."

Lottie was the oldest in the adolescent girls' cottage. Tough and streetwise, she had become a ward of the state after running away from an alcoholic mother and a stepfather who was abusing her sexually.

"Lottie tells us dirty poems and she smokes. She knows she's not supposed to. What's a cunt, Miss N? When Lottie gets mad she says, 'Lick my cunt, you little runt!' What does *that* mean?"

Apprehensive though I was I decided I had no choice but to give straight answers to her questions and to plunge in and have the talk that her mother might or might not be having if they were together, the kind of talk I wished Ma had had with me, sparing me years of guilt and confusion. In lieu of such a talk she had planted a book for me to find that was supposed to explain the sex act, but all it said was "the man and the woman lie facing each other so that he can put in his seed." I assumed that the two were facing each other on their sides and I read that passage over and over, unable to imagine how that could possibly work. The existence of something called an orgasm —that rather crucial piece of information about making love —was nowhere mentioned in the book. With Jenny watching me intently I proceeded to tell her everything she wanted to know and an hour passed quickly as I covered the basics and such topics as rape (including marital —apparently that had happened to her mother), unmarried sex and out of wedlock pregnancy. I found explaining orgasms the most challenging.

"Will I be having that wonderful feeling when I grow up?" Jenny wanted to know.

"Yes, you will, Jenny."

She was thoughtful for a moment, then said abruptly, "I think we've talked enough, Miss N. Can I go now?"

"Of course, Jenny."

"She went to the door, then turned back. "Thanks a lot, Miss N."

The provocative Lottie was also one of my "cases" and I was not surprised by what Jenny had told me. Her cottage mother complained that she was a troublemaker, upsetting the younger girls, but they adored her and were awed by her façade of worldliness. Lottie was a loud mouth, making her points in tough New Yorkese, and she had no tolerance for injustice. I was especially fond of her, and not long ago I came across a photograph she had given me with that perky upturned nose, her naughty eyes, and irresistible grin. She had written on it with neat circles over the i's: *To My Social Worker and Friend, Love, Lottie.*

I was surprised when she asked me to find her a foster home and was hesitant, since adolescents can be difficult to place. But Lottie kept after me.

"Please, Miss N. I want to live with a family for a while and have them to come back to." There was a vacancy in a foster home in Yonkers, and the staff decided to see what would happen on a weekend visit. The home had been used successfully with several younger children, but Lottie would be the first adolescent to be placed there. There were three daughters in the family, one who was working but still living at home, and two younger girls. The foster mother worked part time in a nearby school cafeteria and was home when the children returned from school. She seemed reliable, saying the right things about home life and family values. Her husband drove a bus for the city and appeared to be a kindly if somewhat detached man who let his wife do all the talking. The trial visit went well and all parties wanted to proceed. Lottie and the older girl had hit it off, and her little foster sisters were thrilled to have her there. The following weekend I took Lottie, her suitcase, and a huge stuffed panda that she had won one summer at a carnival, to settle in with her new family.

A visit several weeks later found everything going smoothly. Lottie had assumed the job of washing dishes with the little girls drying, and the older girl was helping her with her homework. She loved her school and had met a boy she liked. I continued to check in from time to time and there were still no complaints on either side. This was unusual. Normally after a brief honeymoon, a period of painful adjusting sets in, so I was unprepared to receive a telephone call from Lottie when I was on Long Island visiting my family for the New Year's holiday. She asked me to come get her but would not tell me why. Normally loud and voluble, Lottie became almost monosyllabic when she was upset and I realized that she was demanding immediate rescue.

I asked her to put her foster mother on the line.

"We thought it was going good," she said, "I don't know why she wants to leave us."

I told her to tell Lottie that I would come over the next day and try to straighten things out. I could hear her relay the message, and then Lottie came back on the line.

"I'm not staying, Miss N," she said. "I need to leave now," and she hung up.

It was a tough decision. To reach her that day I would have to take a train into the city, board another train out to the school, pick up a car and drive back to Yonkers. But I was afraid Lottie would run and I did not want to take that risk. I called back and asked the foster mother to tell Lottie I would be over that evening. When I arrived I found Lottie, her face grim, sitting by the front door with her bag packed and her giant panda beside her. She did not greet me. Her foster mother had answered my ring.

"I don't know what's turned her against us," she said nervously. "We let her go out last night with her boyfriend and this morning she said she was leaving."

I looked at Lottie. She stared back and said nothing. I knew, reading her dark face, that she was not going to tell me anything until after we left."

"Of course she's been no angel," the foster mother said, "and she doesn't like correction. Right, Lottie? You know you're not supposed to smoke, but you sneak our cigarettes and smoke in the bathroom and when we catch you at it, you talk fresh. Then a while back she let her boyfriend come to the house when we were away and she was supposed to be watching the girls. I really let her have it. My husband thought we should send her back, but I didn't want to give up on her. Poor girl. She's had a hard life."

Another look at Lottie's face made clear that this was not going to be negotiable.

"I think I'd better take Lottie back to the school tonight," I said. "We'll let her cool off for a few days. Then we'll see how things are. I'll call you later in the week."

I loaded her things into the car and on the drive back to the school it all poured out. The urgency in Lottie's cry for rescue had made me wonder if the foster father had approached her sexually. What had happened was not as dramatic as that, although it was almost as serious in its own way. Lottie's new boyfriend had asked her to go out on New Year's Eve and her foster mother had said she could go. When Lottie was preparing to leave with him she asked her when she should come home.

"*I don't care* when you come home," her foster mother had said. "You can do anything you want as long as you don't get me into trouble."

I looked over at Lottie and saw tears rolling down her face. "I *wanted* her to care," she sobbed. "I *wanted* her to care."

After her crying had subsided Lottie said, "You shouldn't send any more kids there, Miss N. She's lazy and she lies. She's only in it for the money."

In the next staff meeting with our psychiatrist he questioned my having gone to such lengths to respond to Lottie's call. "There's no question after what you've told us that she should be back here at the school, but supposing she hadn't been able to reach you that day? Are you supposed to be available on a holiday?"

"But she did reach me."

"But supposing she couldn't. She would have had to wait."

"Or run away. She's done that before, more than once."

"She would have been found eventually. Maybe she would have learned that running away isn't always the best solution. Would you have run away?"

"Never. It would have terrified me."

"So you wanted to protect her from that. How about the rest of you? Would you have fetched Lottie on New Year's Day?"

"I would have had to get a sitter for the boys," our single mother said, and I probably couldn't have on such short notice. I wouldn't have had to face 'would I.'"

"I think she's got Fairlie's number," our young bachelor said. "Lottie's a manipulator. I don't like being manipulated. *I* wouldn't have gone for her."

"But aren't all these children manipulators?" our single mother said. "Haven't they all had to learn that to survive?"

One of the other women said that her husband resents the time she gives to her job and would have given her a hard time about going. She would have felt torn. Worrying about Lottie would have spoiled her day almost as much as going.

"I know you don't run around doing social work," I said to our consultant with uncharacteristic boldness, "but if she was yours and she got *you* on the phone and you were free, would you have gone?"

"Probably."

We all laughed. It was the last thing we expected.

"I would have needed to *know*," he went on. "It could have been something very serious and in a way it was. I thought of the foster father, too, when Fairlie was telling us about it. When I was a little boy I'd find my parents'

91

bedroom door locked sometimes and they wouldn't tell me why. I used to worry that something awful was going on in there. I was desperate to know."

We all laughed again on receiving this rare nugget of personal revelation from the master.

"It's all very subjective, isn't it," he said, "the way we respond to things. It depends on so much —our values, our histories, other pressures we have in our lives, and of course on the particular parents each of us has had. I drew one set, Fairlie drew another, Lottie drew hers. Professional care is a grab bag too, isn't it? Lottie would have had a different experience with every one of us. Would it have been as good, or better, or worse?"

In the professional grab bag Lottie had drawn me and I have often wondered if my work with her and the other children had any influence on the rest of their lives. I like to think that for some of them their time with me may have tipped their balance from despair to hope. It was certainly a plus for them to experience a kind, trustworthy human being, and to be heard and to have their needs recognized, even if they could not always be met.

Lottie would be in her seventies today, if she is still alive. I wish I knew how it had been for her over these many years. Would I recognize her if I ran into her somewhere? Would she recognize me? And would I see the irresistible smile come over her face when she remembered who I was? When I try to imagine her life I am afraid she has been a chain smoker like her mother, that spent, coughing, alcoholic woman I interviewed once and found so shockingly indifferent to her daughter's welfare, and I worry about her health. But I also imagine that overall she has had a good, decent life, been married more than once, had a crowd of rowdy children and been an easy-going mother, but fierce with her kids when they've flirted with drinking or drugs. Her house has been a mess. She has worked steadily all her life —in factories, waitressing, that sort of job —and still works because she likes to —likes being with people, horsing around —and now she's beloved by her grandchildren.

"I've never forgotten you, Miss N," I can imagine her saying if we had met.

"I've never forgotten you, Lottie," I would say.

But what has her life really been like? I will always wonder.

"You're not supposed to be making a major change in your life during the analysis," Dr. Gautier said.

I had explained to him why I was thinking of leaving my job at the school. There were several reasons. Although it was still a congenial place to work I felt that I was just carrying sandbags when what was called for was flood control. Jennys and Lotties would keep coming and going and I could continue to work with them earnestly and tirelessly, but I wanted to do more than that, and I wanted to learn more. I was also becoming restless in my personal life. I had made several close female friends on the social work staff, but my love life was still at a standstill. With my long working hours and the demands of the analysis there was little time or opportunity to meet anyone.

When I came back from a professional conference I made a strong case to Dr. Gautier about the wisdom of a change. I had heard practitioners in the mental health field discussing the latest thinking about the causes and treatment of mental disorders and I had been particularly impressed with the caliber of the presenters from child guidance clinics. When a job became available in a newly opened clinic in a hospital in Philadelphia I was able to persuade Dr. Gautier that it was in my best interests to take it. One of the "perks," perhaps the only one, of being the unmarried daughter of a railroad attorney was having a pass on the Pennsylvania Railroad. With it I had free transportation from my new job to the couch, and much welcome reading time.

It felt right to be leaving my job, but it was hard saying good-bye to the children and my colleagues. I couldn't know it then, but we were the closest, most congenial group of professionals I would ever work with. However, the pain of these losses was balanced by the pleasure of renting an apartment in a beautiful old town house in Philadelphia, acquiring my own modest furnishings, and for the first time creating a space that felt like my own.

My new apartment had a small fireplace and when I got my first good fire going, I thought of the fire blazing in the library of Aunt Carrie's house in Maryland and the welcoming warmth I had always felt when I visited. I walked mentally around her rooms, stopping in the dining room to admire the portrait of my grandmother, then moving on to the front parlor and running my hand along the smooth finish of her beautiful piano. I thought about a house that I would have someday with a husband and children and it, too, would have a fireplace and a piano. The children would learn to play and I would play, if I could remember how. Music had been too painful after Leo and I had distanced myself from it. Yet the old longing to make music began stirring again. As I sat warming myself by my little fireplace the thought crept in that there was room in my new apartment for a piano and no good reason I could think of why I had to wait for my dream house before I could play again. Why couldn't I look for a piano right now? Be extravagant for once? Celebrate the nice raise that had come with my new job? The thought would not leave me.

A week later, standing in the street with a group of onlookers, I watched the Steinway upright I had bought from a retired music teacher swinging from a rope attached to the roof of the house and hovering in front of my third-floor window. When I think now about my move from the Hudson to Philadelphia I see an image of myself airborne as if travelling on the wings of the gulls I had watched so many times from the train. I see myself coming down over the city, making a landing on the piano as it is suspended in the air, then moving in with it through the window to start a new chapter in my life.

When I took my new job I did not know that I was making a right-hand turn out of traditional social work and embarking on a career of counseling individuals and couples that would ultimately give me a new identity as a psychotherapist.

My new clinic was squeaky clean —very structured and organized in contrast to the informal atmosphere at St. Christopher's where our days were often long and emotionally draining. I had come to the clinic to learn more about psychological disorders and the art of interviewing and it was providing me with what I had hoped for. My two years there were like getting a doctorate in much the same way that my years as a neophyte at *Newsweek* had given me the equivalent of a bachelor's degree, and the program at Smith a master's in between.

The director of the clinic was a Freudian psychoanalyst. He ran a tight "Aye, Aye, Sir" kind of ship and had too much ego for my liking, but the standard of excellence that he set *was* to my liking. Committed to the highest level of practice, he fed his staff good educational fare, inviting luminaries in child psychiatry to meet with us, and giving us time off to attend a weekly seminar that another psychoanalyst in the hospital was conducting for psychiatric trainees. I admired this man extravagantly, as I had the consultant in New York, and his concept of "the give-get balance" in healthy relationships became integral to my work with estranged couples. In psychiatric parlance I *introjected* this analyst. Soaking up the person, becoming one with a practitioner I admired, was always my primary way of learning how to be a therapist.

Our clinic was typical of child guidance clinics of that era: a team of professionals —a child psychiatrist, a psychologist and a psychiatric social worker —evaluated the children who were referred to us and their home environment. If treatment was recommended and accepted by the parents, the same team continued with the family. My responsibility, as the social worker on the team, was to meet with the parents and take a detailed history of the child's development and "presenting problem." I also had to take a "psychosocial" history of each parent, evaluate the marital relationship and the emotional health of the family. Then my interviews and diagnostic impressions had to be recorded. The hours I spent doing these evaluations and reviewing them with my social work supervisor —a bright, gifted, congenial young woman —gave me the invaluable experience and expertise I had come to get. My little black bag of psychological remedies was getting stouter and stouter and threatening to overflow, but I needn't have worried. I was about to have my first experience of defying an authority figure and taking something *out* of my bag and throwing it away.

I had been assigned to interview a young couple who had come to the clinic with their first child, a boy, then three, whose behavior was incomprehensible to them. They had read about autism and were fearful that this might be the explanation. As they described his behavior I was sure that he was autistic, but it was not my place to tell the parents. The boy would be observed and tested, and when the parents met later with the team, the Director, would share with them the clinic's diagnosis and recommendations. It was my responsibility in my interviews with the parents to go after the information needed for the evaluation, paying particular attention to what kind of a mother the boy had and how she handled him. The prevailing theory about autism at that time, which the parents had come across in their exhaustive reading, viewed this behavior as a response to deep unconscious rejection by the mother. There was a similar theory then about the cause of schizophrenia with the mothers of those patients being labeled "schizophrenogenic." I could find no evidence that this mother was anything but deeply loving, remarkable in the face of such painful rejection by her child. I wrote in my evaluation:

"The mother of this most certainly autistic boy impressed me as being normal in every way. She was eager for a child and was baffled and deeply hurt when her son would not respond to her affection and pushed her away. She is intelligent, thoughtful, bewildered and apprehensive. I can find no evidence in her of the malignant handling that in the belief of some specialists explains this abnormal behavior."

I can still see this mother's sad face. It was disturbing to observe the pain she was suffering, knowing as she did that she was supposed to be the cause of her son's heartbreaking malady. In the parent conference the diagnosis was confirmed and treatment was recommended for the boy and the parents. When the mother asked if she were responsible for her son's behavior the Director equivocated, saying that she appeared to be providing her son good care, but that the role of parents in this illness was not yet fully understood.

On the assumption that the problem lay in the mother-child relationship, the child was not assigned for treatment to a psychiatrist, all of whom were male, but to my supervisor who was about the same age as the mother. If there were any truth to the theory, the boy's behavior would be expected to change when he was offered a different kind of mothering relationship. I went on seeing his mother and continued to reassure her that I did not believe she was responsible for her son's illness, knowing while I did so that adherents to the theory, which included the Director, would be expecting me to uncover evidence that she was. After several months when the boy did not respond and began to be disruptive, breaking out of his therapy room and barging into other offices, the case was closed. The mother was both relieved and disheartened. She was relieved of her guilt but had to face raising this difficult and ungratifying child with little hope that he would ever change.

Using my own judgment in working with this mother had been a coming-of-age experience for me. When I had come to these same crossroads before in my work with Mary Dailey, I had been afraid to "disobey" my supervisor.

Now I was facing again my fear of displeasing someone in authority and risking reprimand, perhaps even being fired. I was grateful to the mother of this autistic boy for having been so sweet and earnest and bewildered that my compassion for her gave me the courage to overcome my fear and to risk rebuke. In the end I was not rebuked and was not told by my supervisor that I had "lost my objectivity" –a therapist's cardinal sin. In fact my work with this mother probably contributed to the Director reconsidering a dubious hypothesis.

What was happening to me throughout all of this was the emergence of an adult who was taking control *of* and *from* my fearful inner child, and as confirmation of this Miss Garrett visited our clinic and asked me to supervise one of her students during the next school year. But this was only the barest beginning of my becoming a mature therapist. Fear of not doing something exactly right or of harming a client in some way continued to hang over my work and to mar my pleasure in doing it. I was never afraid of violating my profession's Code of Ethics –those admonitions were very clear –but of being censured by other professionals. I felt that an amorphous being was always looking over my shoulder ready to pounce and criticize. For many years I found myself torn between my need to "obey the rules" and be conforming and safe, and to trust another more creative part of myself even if that meant being sometimes daringly unconventional or, God forbid, "unprofessional."

But after I left Philadelphia and was working in a mental health clinic in New Jersey, I dared to break a "no gifts" rule that I had been taught as a student. Exchanging gifts was supposed to blur the boundary between the professional and the personal and to encourage clients to try to turn their therapy into friendship. After awkwardly rejecting several Christmas gifts early in my career I had decided to let clients give them as a way of saying thanks. Except for the book I had sent Mary Dailey I had never given a gift. Now that prohibition, too, was about to fall.

I was counseling a recently married hippie couple about how to manage their new life together. One day the young bride said she had a sexual problem, but she could not bring herself to tell me what it was. I could not imagine what aberration I should be expecting. The sexual mores of this new generation were night-and-day different from my own and I was just becoming used to counseling young women with feelings of inadequacy and failure because they had not yet lost their virginity. Finally the young wife blurted out that she did not feel safe having intercourse unless her teddy bear was with her in the marital bed. Her husband had no problem with the bear. His wife was able to laugh after making her revelation, but even though they enjoyed each other sexually when the bear was in the bed, she was afraid that she was "really nuts" for needing him. I did not see any serious pathology here, and said something to reassure her, but sometimes verbal reassurance is not enough. I asked her to bring in her bear and the following week we were introduced. All this took place just before Christmas and the idea came to me of wrapping a tiny jar of honey and giving this little present to the bear. When she opened his gift the young wife exclaimed with pleasure and we all laughed. I don't know why I thought this would be therapeutic –the word "acceptance" comes to mind –but it worked. We never analyzed the why of it, but she was no longer anxious about being abnormal. Perhaps intuitively, and coming from my experience with Ma, I wanted her to experience permission to be sexual from a woman in authority.

Later in my career, as my more confident therapy style was evolving, I did something even more daring. A closeted, middle-aged homosexual who was chaste and lonely wanted to know what it felt like to take a woman out to dinner and to feel the power of being in the socially acceptable role. He asked me if I would go out with him. This *really* was unprofessional! But I agreed. I put on a glamorous dress, made myself up and he fetched me in his car. He had made a reservation in the best restaurant in town. He escorted me in and experienced the "Oui, *Monsieur*" and the "This way, *Monsieur*" of the head waiter, and we then went on to act out the rituals of dating of the period –his pulling out my chair, ordering the wine, our clicking our glasses, and his lighting a cigarette for me across the table. It was no more than that. He had experienced what he wanted to experience. He had no interest in a personal relationship.

But back at the clinic in Philadelphia I was still only taking baby steps, still afraid of exposing my incompetence and of "being wrong," in spite of the good outcome of the risk I had taken with the young mother. In the privacy of my office I was beginning to function more and more effectively, but in staff meetings I continued to "disappear" into speechlessness the way I had in my classes with Miss Garrett. The Director of the clinic was quite a showman and liked to present cases in the hospital's auditorium to an invited audience of mental health professionals. When one of mine came up I was expected to participate and panic set in. I pleaded with my supervisor to take my place, but she insisted that I go through with the ordeal. I did, and in discussing this crisis later with Dr. Gautier he made one of his more appealing observations.

"You know what was going on here, don't you?" he said. "What you really wanted to do was to leap on that stage, rip off your clothes, and say, 'Look at me!'"

MISGIVINGS ON THE COUCH

I had been in analysis for nearly three years and was beginning to get discouraged. It humiliated me to be single when most of my friends and
colleagues were either married or in serious relationships. This was the early
fifties. Conservative values were still firmly in place and a woman in the small
world in which I grew up was seen as a failure and pitied if she did not marry.
Exceptional women could defy convention and marry or not as they chose,
but for the vast sea of the unexceptional, being a spinster was the worst possible fate. But other young women in the same milieu as mine had been able to
move along on the course we were all reared to follow, hoping for passion as
we all did but being ready to compromise and board the marriage boat before
it stopped coming to port. So why hadn't I? Because I knew without any doubt
that a marriage like that of my parents and marrying a man like Pa would be
worse than becoming an "old maid."

I wondered how Ma had felt when she married him. After she graduated
high school her minister father had told her that she wasn't attractive enough
to catch the kind of husband she would want and should become a nun.
Although painfully anxious all her life Ma had a spunky streak and she had
defied him, becoming instead a governess for the three daughters of a New
York lawyer. This man had recently hired a promising young lawyer from
Baltimore who was soon invited to spend the weekend at his boss's country

estate. When Pa proposed I like to imagine Ma saying to her father, "So, you didn't think I could do it, did you?"

I believe Ma did love the Pa that she married —a tall, thin, sensitive, insecure young man —and was proud of her catch. Hope, who was eight when Little Brother died, remembers some sunny early years —Sunday walks in Central Park with Mary in her carriage and Lindy, Pa's devoted German Shepherd, at his side —and then the twins coming, the move to the village house, and after a few more good years the death changing everything, including Pa.

But why had he changed? Was it one death too many? Aunt Carrie told me that after the death of his beautiful young mother a cheerful, active little boy had become silent and remote. I have often wondered how my life would have turned out if the "slender, sensitive" Pa whom Ma wistfully recalled in later years had not become the heavy-set, insensitive, self-serving and indifferent father who was to make me view spinsterhood as the lesser of sad fates.

As I grew older not having a loving father was not the only obstacle to my marrying. Following the failure of my relationship with Leo I had become financially independent and tasted the freedom to be myself and to make my own decisions. If making a conventional marriage meant losing that freedom, I was unwilling to give it up and to accept an inferior status in relation to a man. At the same time I continued to idealize a future mate who would not require this and who would be those things that have become a cliché in analyzing the failure of marriages —kind, tender, thoughtful and infinitely patient. If this were not enough, I also needed a man who in the courtship phase would persist indefinitely, refusing to take my frightened "no" for a final answer. Abandonment was still high in my priority of fears and I needed to be so sure of a man's love that I would have no fear of losing it. Divorce, still socially taboo as it had been in my parent's generation, would have been emotionally intolerable. It hadn't helped matters either that I was painfully shy. I remember watching other girls doing what had to be done in the mating game and knowing that I was incapable of doing it. Hope had been such a flagrant flirt, making my anxious mother lose night after night of sleep, that when my time came along I had played it safe, retreating into a kind of asexual passivity. It was unfortunate that a young couple couldn't live together then before getting married, for I needed time and a ready escape in order to establish a relationship I could trust.

Doing this painful inventory with Dr. Gautier plunged me deeper and deeper into feelings of hopelessness. One of the hardest things I had to acknowledge was how emotionally immature I still was, for when I looked at myself in the analytic mirror I could see the same needy, dependent little girl who had crawled into Leo's lap. "You're a closet infant," I told myself harshly, "just masquerading as a woman!" Furthermore I was confronting other things about myself that I did not want to see. It was hard to admit that I was committing the sins of envy and pride, often feeling superior to other people, and that I could be inflexible and ungenerous, especially with time, my most precious fast-fleeting possession. The more I thought about all this the more disheartened I became. I felt that I had come to the end of the road.

I was taken by surprise when Dr. Gautier announced one day, "Depression is your primary problem."

It had never occurred to me that I might be suffering from depression. I had learned about depression in my social work training, and knew there were different kinds —one that alternated with mania, one that sometimes followed childbirth or could come with menopause, and one that could follow loss. (Was this mine?) I also knew that it could be inherited and that there had been depressed people in my family: my grandmother had killed herself, my mother had a suicidal breakdown when Robert was in the infantry fighting in France, and the uncle I had stayed with when I was working with Mary Dailey had several hospitalizations for depression. But in spite of knowing this I had never questioned that those metallic gray feelings that often hung over me like heavy weather were not "normal." I had assumed that my recurring moods of despair and hopelessness were appropriate reactions to the far from satisfying personal life that was ticking away from me. Learning that I was "depressed" was almost welcome news, for it gave me a reason other than personal inadequacy for scoring so low in my one crack at life. It also helped explain why, on my weekends off from work, I found it so hard to push myself out into the relationship marketplace instead of staying in my apartment and playing sad music on my piano.

Unfortunately, learning that I was clinically depressed did not cure the ailment. There was no medication for depression then, and although patients could sometimes get relief from "talking therapy," they mostly had to "tough it out." Since I was a good athlete and liked to be physically active perhaps I had been self-medicating without knowing it, releasing endorphins with my tennis, swimming, and wilderness hiking. Perhaps that is why, except for a couple of very dark years during menopause, depression did not interfere more with my functioning. To others I probably appeared as a "normal" if excessively shy and quiet young woman, and although I felt less inadequate with my new diagnosis, my romantic life remained at a standstill. It was then that I began to question the competence of Dr. Gautier and the promise of psychoanalysis.

I was sophisticated enough as a young professional to know that for analysis to "work" patients were supposed to fall in love with their analysts. I had wanted to fall in love with mine, but when that hadn't happened I had assumed it was a luxury I did not need, an icing on the cake. I liked Dr. Gautier. He and I had covered a great deal of productive ground, examining my fears and guilts and conflicts —the usual fodder for analysis —and I had tempered my harsh view of myself as sexually undesirable, selfish, unkind, and so insignificant a person as to be almost invisible. I had been grateful that he was there and up to this point I had trusted the process. I knew that analysts were supposed to be relatively passive and that hadn't bothered me, but when he did make observations they had rarely been "ah ha" moments for me. As I pondered all this it occurred to me that perhaps as a trainee he was hesitant to respond before checking with the analyst who was supervising his work. Although his uncharacteristic pronouncement that I was depressed *had* been an "ah ha" moment, I wondered if it had been his idea or had followed a conference with his analyst. I assumed that this analyst was the consultant Miss Garrett had sent me to and with whom I *had* fallen in love and I began to fantasize what my analysis would have been like if I had been able to continue with him.

This man had come across as warm and nurturing and was the kind of man, I now realized, I had always been looking for unconsciously and thought I had found in Leo. If he had been my analyst I could imagine falling into his arms, not in erotic passion (at least at the outset), but as the dependent little girl I still was. In this fantasized analysis I saw myself on his white charger, leaning back "against the heart" of my own "King-Papa." I would have trusted him to know how long it would have been good for me to be there and when to nudge me gently into dismounting and getting on my own little pony. After a while he would have encouraged me to get on to a larger one and finally on to a beautiful white mare, and I would have been riding along beside him, the confident young woman I aspired to be, and ready for a handsome prince to come galloping up on a black stallion and carry me off.

When I came out of my fantasy this lovely man wasn't my analyst, Dr. Gautier was, and he was far from being an irresistible, androgynous mix of King Papa and the Princess's dream-like grandmother figure. He was a middle-aged New York doctor who had never made my heart leap. Of course the consultant had been a middle-aged New York doctor too, but the difference was that I had transferred all my longings to him in that one hour. But to be fair to Dr. Gautier, before starting my therapy and fueled by Miss Garrett's reverence for psycho-analysis, I had idealized a perfect, almost god-like figure, and surely Dr. Gautier was good enough. All analysts had to be good enough, didn't they?

I n that frame of mind I knuckled down and produced the following dream:

I am a turtle without a shell. I am sitting on the couch in Aunt Carrie's library on the farm in Maryland.

"What are your associations to this dream, Miss Nicodemus?" Dr. Gautier asked.

I went back into the dream, back into the turtle me, sitting upright in my tender flesh on my small turtle tail. I could feel the presence behind me of Aunt Carrie's potted plants in the bay window with the morning sun flooding in. I remembered looking through those windows when I first visited Aunt Carrie as a little child and seeing a beautiful sky —intensely blue with float-ing white clouds —and saying to her, "Little Brother is up there." I remember thinking that I had said something important because she knelt down and hugged me and had on a crying face.

As I shared this with Dr. Gautier a torrent of my own tears came.

"I think the dream is telling me," I was finally able to say, "that because I always felt loved by her it was in her library that I could take off my shell and be vulnerable."

More tears came. I had cried before, but this sobbing was coming from a painfully deep place.

"I think I'm crying from gratitude," I said when I could talk. "I think she saved my life."

I told him then about another memory, possibly my first of her. Sometime after Little Brother's death Ma had brought Hope, Mary and me down to the farm for a visit. We children were tired and irritable after the long journey. Aunt Carrie had supper waiting and I was sitting beside her at the table, fussing and refusing to eat. I must have been grating on everyone's nerves. Suddenly, with a nod from my mother, she snatched me up, carried me upstairs, and put me in the mahogany crib that was waiting for the children she still hoped to have. After she left I felt frightened and alone and punished in the strange, dark room, but in a while she reappeared.

"I thought you might like this before going to sleep," she said, reaching into the crib with a glass of milk and helping me sit up and drink it. Her face was smiling and kind.

Not long after talking with Dr. Gautier about my aunt, I found myself wishing that I were seeing a woman analyst. Of course it was too late now, but I was experienced enough in my own work to know that the gender of the therapist can sometimes make a difference. Ma wasn't reclining overhead quite as comfortably now —I had been saying some pretty harsh things about her —but she was still in the room and her presence and my failure to make my own judgments about men seemed fatally intertwined. I had recently said no to a man I had met in Philadelphia and wondered how much I was still being influenced by my parents' values. Although he was a head shorter than I and far from being the dark and handsome stranger of my adolescent dreams, he was one of the kindest, most generous men I had ever known, but Ma would have written him off as a "homely little Jew."

"Why can't my mother leave me alone and let me get on with my life!" I wailed to Dr. Gautier. "Why can't I get her out of here?"

"Maybe you're too afraid of where your sexuality will take you if she isn't here to keep it under control," Dr. Gautier suggested. It was a plausible hypothesis, and one of his more interesting observations.

After returning from another professional conference where some smart women analysts were presenting papers and talking on panels, I found myself wishing again that I could bring some of my still unanswered questions to a woman. I had been attracted by the flexibility and warmth of these analysts. The idea occurred to me of having a "side trip" with one of them that might take me into some different terrain. Then I would return to Dr. Gautier to finish the analysis. Dr. Gautier knew all too well my hunger for the approval of mother figures and was aware of my pattern, starting in early childhood, of looking for surrogates. I had told him of the time Ma and I were in the post office and ran into a friend of hers. This woman was always very friendly to me. I stood waiting while they talked and then she leaned down to me and said, "How is my favorite little girl?"

"I wish you could be my mother," I said.

Both women laughed, no doubt in embarrassment, but I didn't understand why what I had said was so funny. I had meant it.

When I finally broached the idea to Dr. Gautier of working with a woman for a while, I was surprised to get such a swift, unequivocal no. He said I was "resisting" and should be working out these issues with him. A less obedient and conforming patient might have challenged Dr. Gautier, or even left him and found a woman analyst, but I was afraid to protest his no, assuming that it was based on some esoteric analytic theory I was not yet privy to. Instead I took from his message that I should be trying harder. In hindsight I believe that it was he and analytic theory that was the problem, not my "resistance." It was clear that I needed a relationship with a mother figure who would affirm my worth and give my sexuality her blessing. Although I might well have transferred that need to a more nurturing male analyst, I had not, and knew I would not, be making that mother transfer to Dr. Gautier.

Was it predictable? Was it hostility to Dr. Gautier? Was I rebelling against my mother? Or was it inevitable that not long after this exchange with Dr. Gautier I became romantically involved with a woman? It was the last thing I wanted and it sent me into paroxysms of anxiety It was a brief but intense affair, not with a mother figure but with someone very much like myself and very much my opposite at the same time. Natalie was a social worker I had met at the same conference where I had admired the women analysts. Like the girl at Smith who had tried to seduce me, she was my opposite. Short, dark and experienced sexually with both genders she had been the aggressor. Unlike myself, she appeared unconflicted about where her feelings were taking her. On the surface she conveyed an air of self-sufficiency, but underneath she communicated a deep longing to be loved. I identified powerfully with the emotional waif that betrayed itself under her façade of independence and worldliness.

But this had taken me appallingly off course. Establishing openly what is now called a "partnership" with another woman was unthinkable in those days. It is possible that in a more permissive social climate I might have been less conflicted, but back then homosexuals were viewed as flotsam washed up on the fringes of society. This aberration —seen then as sinful and still illegal in some states —was not openly discussed but would be whispered about in private conversations. Although liaisons of well-known homosexuals might be gossiped about, almost all same-sex relationships were closeted and the topic was one of a number of media taboos. Until the Kinsey reports on male and female sexuality came out in the late forties and early fifties it was hard to find anything to read on the subject.

At first I had been afraid to tell Dr. Gautier about what had happened. We had been cruising along for nearly four years with the shared goal of removing the obstacles to my marrying and now that dream seemed shattered beyond repair. With this development I believed that I had failed as an analysand, and fear of failing and of being exposed as a "bad" person still haunted me. When I finally summoned the courage to tell him I was surprised that he had little to say. Perhaps he was waiting to talk it over with his analyst. His analytic passivity was always a handy tool and more easily utilized behind the couch than in the face to face interviews I was conducting. But I knew his position on the subject, and when he began responding he made that all too plain: Except for a small number of biologically abnormal individuals or people who had suffered severe trauma such as incest or rape and could not achieve satisfaction with the opposite sex, same-sex attraction reflected immature psychosexual development. He added that when such relationships were entered into during analysis the patient's conflicts were being "acted out" rather than being "worked through." This "acting out" often occurred when the end of analysis was in sight and the patient, anticipating impending separation and loss, was saying, "See how sick I am? I'm really not ready to stop." He made clear that this kind of relationship was "sick" and dismissed same-sex lovemaking as "mutual masturbation."

If I had been able to sneak a glance into a folder in Dr. Gautier's file labeled "NICODEMUS, Fairlie," I would probably have found his diagnosis of me something like this: *Clinical Depression in a Psychosexually Immature Personality*. But what more was I supposed to be doing to achieve psychosexual maturity? It was disheartening to have been struggling so long and to be failing so miserably. Early in the analysis when I had examined the question of sexual preference it had been hypothetical. Up to that time I had been drawn to women emotionally and could be stunned by the beauty of some women, but I had never been attracted to them sexually. Now the question was painfully real. Love had been absent from my life for far too long and I could not bear to think of parting from Natalie, but Dr. Gautier was telling me that I must.

Although we lived several hours apart in different cities Natalie and I managed to spend as much time together as we could, either in her apartment or mine, and we had not only been enjoying physical intimacy and our shared passion for music and literature, but also the pleasure of shared domesticity. Having grown up in a home with a cook who didn't want children in her kitchen I was an anxious beginner in mine. Natalie was domestic and a patient teacher and not only taught me how to cook but what cleaning supplies were best and how to do laundry without ruining my favorite clothes. We had been enjoying a lovely, if brief, compatible marriage, and now Dr. Gautier was telling me that it was sick and was assuring me that I could still resolve my hang-ups about men before my biological time ran out.

If my relationship with Natalie had been satisfying in every way it would have been even more difficult to leave her, but she had always held back a large part of herself and this had made me uneasy. She had given me the barest details about her family and her previous relationships, while I, normally reticent, had poured everything out to her. I wondered if there was something she needed to hide. It made me uneasy. Before I left her I had been able to persuade myself that I was just an episode in her much fuller romantic life and that her loss of me would not be that painful. But after I left I knew that I had just been looking for an excuse. The truth was that, right or wrong, I did not want a relationship with a woman. The price of ostracism was too high, the price of no children, the price of no comfortable place in a community, and the price of abandoning my search for Curdie who, I still felt sure, was out there somewhere looking for me.

I had anticipated excruciating pain when I finally closed that door, but not the depression that followed. The darkness and apathy were reminiscent of my ending with Leo. I remembered how I had trudged back then through the motions of existence on those frigid, windy streets in Manhattan. It seemed that wherever my feelings took me was the wrong place to be. Further deepening the depression was another loss, but one that I was not yet fully conscious of –the loss of my childish belief that if I were Dr. Gautier's good girl and did everything I was supposed to do that the analysis would have a fairy-tale happy ending. At that point all I could do, in spite of my increasing misgivings, was to continue down the same road with this man and try to be a better patient.

Single in a Married World

Dr. Gautier and I had been discussing the shopworn question of why I was still single and I had complained about a lack of desirable men. The men I was attracted to were already married or uninterested in me which I had tardily come to realize meant that they were probably homosexuals. We were not yet using the word "gay."

"It's harder when you're older," I said, "There just aren't that many good ones left."

"The woods is full of 'em," he said.

His reply felt like a slap on the wrist and I was hurt. But if "the woods was full of 'em," as he had rather crudely remarked, it behooved me to move to the woods. So I had accepted the invitation of a psychiatrist I had been working with in Philadelphia to join him at a clinic he was directing in Trenton, New Jersey, and rented a garden apartment in Princeton where the woods were within easy walking distance. A small university town with its rich potential for friendship and love, surrounded by beautiful countryside, seemed a perfect place to be.

Moving to a new place can also ease the pain of a conflicted parting. I was still having a hard time getting over Natalie, but my first months in Princeton became a time of distracting firsts. I bought my first car, planted my first garden, and acquired Salomé, a German shepherd, my first dog. Another much treasured first was learning about birds. Searching for the singer of a haunting melody on one of my walks in the woods with Salomé, I developed a life-long passion in both watching and listening. The song of that singer, the white-throated sparrow, is still more beautiful to me than the song of the nightingale that I was to hear later in the hills of Florence.

For a while after the move I felt as if I had fallen in love again. I was not only enraptured with this charming town, but my rediscovery of the natural world was like falling into the arms of an old lover I had not realized how much I was missing until I saw him again. In the high that love brings I found myself longing for music. In Philadelphia I had let it back into my life but had little time for my piano, so I found a teacher and began to study again. But after the honeymoon was over and the routine of my life as a single woman set in, I began seeing families everywhere, taunting me with their togetherness. In the mornings on my drive to work I would see commuting husbands walking to their trains, and when I drove home in the evening, their wives and children and the family dog would be waiting for them at the station in the ubiquitous station wagon. School buses would be swarming like yellow jackets all over the town and I would wait patiently behind their flashing lights as treasured children stepped off into the hugs of waiting mothers. Most painful of all was on my weekends off when I would be seeing this family togetherness played out in back yards —husbands cutting their lawns and tending their barbecues, wives kneeling in flowerbeds, and children throwing Frisbees to the family dog.

Being single had not been that visible in the anonymity of city life, but I could not very well return to that anonymity —find a buyer for my car, a home for my dog, uproot my plants and forget that I had ever heard the song of that sparrow. Like it or not I was single in a married world. I had expected to marry young and that a husband and I would evolve congenially together. When that had not happened I had put myself on hold, afraid that I would become so committed to the kind of life I wanted to live, so set in my ways, that I could no longer accommodate myself gracefully to another person. But now a third of my life, or more, was over. It was time to stop mourning what I did not have and to embrace what I did. Even if I was destined not to have children, I could nurture animals and plants, be a surrogate mother in my professional work and, like my dear Aunt Carrie, be a loving aunt to my nieces and nephews.

For a while in this brave spirit I was more content, but as time passed I found myself evolving into a kind of split personality with two very different selves –a professional self and a personal self. My professional self was maturing and was well regarded in my new clinic. I had entered that middle period in a professional's life when one amasses experience day after day, case after case, and an eager learner becomes a more seasoned, realistic practitioner. My co-workers and I were deeply committed to our troubled clientele and to honing our therapeutic skills. We met regularly to discuss our failures. We attended conferences to learn how professionals in other communities were struggling with the same challenges. It suited my earnest self to be doing scrupulously honest work with idealistic, compassionate people and it was a climate in which I felt entirely at home, although according to my life plan I was not supposed to be there.

My relationships with my colleagues were easy and comfortable and it took me a while to realize what was unique about them. In our work with our clients we were dealing with deeply private experiences and emotions, topics that were off-limits in social conversation, and this made our staff more open and direct in our personal communication with one another. When I had vowed in that Washington, D.C. living room at the age of seventeen to make a different connection with the human race, I had not been thinking about "communication." Who did in those times? But when I compare the rich, uninhibited exchanges I have had with my colleagues over the years with the impoverished communication in my family and many of my personal relationships before the communication explosion blew the lid off everything, I realize how starved I had been for it.

While my professional self was enjoying more open communication with my colleagues, my personal self was becoming increasingly dissatisfied with the more limited, superficial communication I was encountering socially with non-professionals. The old boundaries defining what was appropriate to talk about still prevailed and this made these relationships, with the exception of a few close friends, far less spontaneous and satisfying. To my dismay I realized that I had come to a place of no return. I could never go back to that place of psychological ignorance that was still inhabited by most of the cocktail party crowd I encountered in my social milieu. I could never move back into their "avoidance of discomfort" zone and be content within the boundaries they required after inhabiting the private depths of my clients and some of my colleagues, and of course my own. In a few decades all this was going to change with psychological concepts and jargon turning up in everyday speech and on television sit-coms, but back in the early fifties I was awkwardly, and not very successfully, trying to straddle two vastly different worlds.

This schism was particularly burdensome at parties where my social shyness was already putting me at a disadvantage. At that time most people viewed psychoanalysis with suspicion and distanced themselves from "all that mental health stuff." I tried to avoid talking about my work, but when I was asked by a man —women were different —what "I did" and I said I was "sort of like a psychologist" (the correct label "Psychiatric Social Worker" only muddied the waters) I would get a surprised, "You *are?*" followed by a barely visible withdrawal. But I could always sense it. In today's nothing-is-sacred society it is hard to believe how little people knew then about the kind of work I was doing and how wary they were of mental health professionals. There was a stigma then to needing that kind of help, which has not entirely disappeared.

It was a curious dichotomy. This personal me felt like a failure, while the professional part of my split personality was doing well. Yet I disowned that self. The real me was a young woman edging towards her middle thirties who lived in a garden apartment in Princeton, waiting for her real life of husband and children to begin. She was making enough money to support herself and her psychoanalysis, but she never thought about saving for retirement because before long she would be married and have a husband to support her.

One might think that being a successful professional would have been a big boost to my frail ego, and occasionally I did encounter people -- again, mostly women —who were impressed by the work I was doing and wanted to know more about it. But most men I encountered socially viewed professional women as competent, independent, and sexually undesirable females who had settled for careers because marriage was an unlikely option. Furthermore, social work as a profession, running neck and neck with school teaching, nursing and library science, most of which was woman's work, hovered near the bottom of the professional hierarchy. And of course I got no points from my family for being a successful professional. I had not lived out my script and seemed to have forgotten my lines.

But I hadn't forgotten them. I still believed ardently in my romantic dreams and continued my quest for a husband, setting about to enter as fully as I knew how into the life of my new community. I joined a chorus, became a member of the New Jersey Audubon Society, made new friends and discovered some old ones who welcomed me back into their lives. But in spite of this effort I was finding myself in a social no-woman's land, too old to belong to the unattached, energetic, young-adult set, but out of place with my married contemporaries whose lives revolved around child raising and domesticity and who tended to socialize as couples. I seemed to be in a category of one, having encountered other professional women my age, but none who were still looking for husbands.

Today's young women appear not to worry about finding a mate until they are afraid they won't be able to conceive a child. In my generation, arriving at age thirty was as significant a milestone as graduating from high school or college. When you went through the thirty gate still single, still the same person you were on the other side, you looked down and saw yourself wearing a different nametag. You had passed into that dreaded region of diminished possibility. You were having to face that you had probably "blown it" and lost your chances and others seemed to be looking at you as if you had. About this time I received the gift of a beautiful antique cherry table from my much-loved Aunt Carrie. She had written in explanation: "I would have wanted to give you a special gift like this *if you had ever married*." Even dear Aunt Carrie had written me off, but in her day when marriage was the only option for most women, they married young. But I had not mated then and as I grew older I had become more rational and selective in my search for a mate at the very time that my prospects were thinning out. This was an unfavorable juxtaposition.

When I think of the powerful urge in all animals to mate and reproduce I visualize a scene on a Long Island beach one spring night when I was eighteen. I was "seeing" a young man I had met in music school before Leo and I became involved. He had dropped out of college and, although a gifted musician, worked only half-heartedly at his music. I invited him to spend the weekend at the Small Paradise. The time was ripe and I wanted to fall in love with him, but something was holding me back even though he was the kind of suitor my parents would have approved of, coming from a wealthy, upper-class, sporting family.

There was a full moon that weekend. One evening after dinner he suggested that we take our canoe down the river on the ebbing tide into Long Island Sound. If anything could have ignited my passion it would have been that romantic journey. The river was moving swiftly with the pull of the moon, and the moonlight, reflected in the swirling vortexes of our paddle strokes, created moving shadows that looked alive, almost menacing. Yet I felt entirely safe with him as he guided us expertly down the river and through its mouth into the placid waters of the Sound. We paddled to shore and as we pulled up on the beach we were startled to come upon a large gathering of horseshoe crabs. Programmed by nature's clock they had come ashore and were engaged in their annual mating ritual. We stood in amazement watching this frenzy of reproduction. We, too, had been programmed by nature's clock and my attractive young crab was ready and willing, but I could not say yes. With my values about virginity, saying yes would have meant saying yes to marriage and I did not want to marry a man I did not respect. Attractive though he was, he did not seem to have the promise of accomplishing anything with his life that I could be proud of.

I was barely beginning then and my whole life was before me. Surely a more perfect mate would be out there and I would know him when I found him; but some fifteen years later I was living in Princeton still unmated. Why couldn't I have closed my eyes back then, made a bold leap, and made the best of where I landed? Some of my married women friends wondered why I didn't have affairs. If some husbands were throwing out signals to me, they reasoned, and they were, then their marriages were probably failing. If they were, then maybe the affair would move on into marriage. They knew several women who had gone this route. Hope had, creating a scandal in our Long Island community.

One day one of my friends burst out in exasperation. "Fairl, you're taking all this too damn seriously! Can't you just let yourself have a little fun? Isn't it better to be somebody's mistress than to mope around, waiting for your Mr. Right?"

So I tried a few affairs. Typically they began with a phone call after a party. The husband had been thinking about me and that I might be lonely. He had found me so lovely! Would I consider meeting him in New York where he worked and spending the evening with him? We would have to be discreet, of course, etc. etc. etc. But it became clear that even though their marriages were imperfect, these men were not going to leave their families. Besides, playing the role of "the other woman" went against everything I believed in. Hope could do that, but I couldn't, and Ma was still hovering over me, reminding me that I shouldn't. I believed in family life. I didn't want to harm the wives or the children. Although I wanted the intimacy these men offered I became anxious and inhibited when we met and disappointed them. So I added another failure to my list. I had flunked affairs.

FALLING OFF THE COUCH

I t had been snowing for several hours when I decided to walk into town from my apartment to buy some last minute presents. Christmas was only a few days away. The snow had begun to settle on the houses and to lay a pretty blanket on the frost-browned yards. Its presence in the air muffled the sounds of irritable traffic that was crawling along at the end of a busy shopping day. Maybe this year I would find a gift for Ma that she really liked.

It was that time in the late afternoon when lights start coming on in houses, one here, one there, while in other houses that are waiting for their occupants to return, the darkness is deepening. The interiors of the houses that were lit were brighter now than the fading light outside and looking into them was like seeing a stage set for a play. Through the window in one of the houses I saw two children, a boy and a girl. They were sitting at a table, probably doing their homework. A calico cat was sitting near them on the table grooming itself, no doubt wanting to be close to its humans who had been absent for most of the daylight hours. Through another window in the house I could see a woman at a stove and as I watched her she moved out of sight and appeared where the children were sitting. She bent over one of them, remained briefly, then left and reappeared at the stove. I could imagine the smells of supper, and while there was no soundtrack running with my film, I knew that there would be voices rising and falling, calling out and being answered. Then I saw the woman turn from the stove and come to her window and with a wide embracing gesture pull the curtains closed. In a few seconds she appeared at the children's window and repeated the gesture. The woman had not seen me, but as she closed her family in I felt painfully closed out, and suddenly, ridiculously tearful. I wanted to be in her enclosure, wanted to be both her *and* her little girl, and I wanted the brother to be my brother and the cat to be our cat, but I was out on the street alone, not just a solitary woman standing there, but alone in my life.

I was beginning to get cold, but I did not move. I imagined myself back in my childhood, back in *Sparrow, the Tramp*, a favorite book of mine, and I was playing a part in that book that I had played many times. I was the hungry little match-girl who is taken into a loving home, fed and comforted by the mother and welcomed by the boy and girl who live there. When she is falsely accused of stealing the mother's necklace she is almost sent away, but the family pets are outraged at this injustice. With the help of the sparrow of the title they expose the true culprit. Graywhiskers, an old rat with a broken yellow tooth, is killed by the family cat and the missing necklace is found in his nest. The little match-girl is vindicated and embraced by the family. They had thought she was a bad child, but she had done nothing wrong.

As I stood there on the sidewalk coming out of my reverie, with a dusting of snow on my hat and the shoulders of my coat, the unspeakably sad feeling I had had throughout my childhood of not being welcome in my family rose in my throat. I turned and walked on, trying to head off one of my seizures of grieving. If I let it come I knew it would take me over like a painful uterine contraction and not let me out of its grip until it had had its way with me. I could not let myself fall apart here on the street. I had shopping to do. With a shiver I pulled the collar of my coat around my ears and trudged on into the merry season that was busying itself around the town.

"Christmas with the family was pretty rough," I told Dr. Gautier after the holidays were over. "My mother was in bad shape."

I had become concerned about her mental state several months before when I received a letter from her addressed to "Prinston," New Jersey, but I had not been prepared for her deterioration.

"She gets up in the night now and wanders around the house. One night I found her in our guestroom. She had pulled the blankets off the bed and was cutting them in half with a pair of scissors. Something's going to have to be done about her."

Dr. Gautier was silent.

Although there were maids in the house when Pa was away, that would not be enough now, and as the remaining unmarried daughter I would be expected to take on this responsibility. My siblings were occupied raising their families and I was free and unencumbered and had no life to give up. But as intensely as I knew I should, I knew I could not go back into that house and deal with Ma and live there with Pa. He would just have to deal with the problem by himself. Hope and her doctor husband lived nearby and maybe they could help him find a place for her when Pa could no longer manage her at home. It tore me apart to feel so cold and detached about something so awful. I went on to tell Dr. Gautier about the house I had looked into on that snowy afternoon and about the book I had remembered, and how sad and lonely and orphaned I still felt.

"Will I ever be able to stop being such a needy child?" I asked him. I was crying and angry at the same time. "No wonder I haven't been able to find a husband! I'm still looking for a lap to crawl into. When will I ever feel like a normal grown-up woman?"

Dr. Gautier was still silent.

After I had calmed down and more minutes of silence had ticked away I recognized a growing feeling of anxiety. I knew that I would have to tell him about something else that had happened since I had last seen him, and I did not want to.

I had been changing trains in the Pennsylvania Station on my way back to Princeton from my Christmas visit home and had almost literally run into Natalie. I had not seen or heard from her in over a year. As soon as I saw her I realized that I still had strong feelings for her. We greeted awkwardly.

"I've missed you," I said. "How are you?"

She said nothing, then stepped back.

"May I call you?" I asked. "Is it the same number?"

"It's the same," she said. Then she hesitated. "But I'd rather you didn't. Look. I have a train to catch. I can't talk now," and she started running and disappeared into the crowd.

"Maybe I made a big mistake breaking it off," I said after telling Dr. Gautier about what had happened. "I think she still loves me. Maybe that's the route I should be going after all."

"Why don't you leave her alone and let her get on with her life!" Dr. Gautier burst out angrily, breaking his silence.

I felt as if I had been struck. It was true. I had only been thinking about myself and not what might be best for her. But wasn't Dr. Gautier supposed to be my therapist, helping me, not more concerned about her? And now he was chastising me for not being considerate of her and for possibly doing her harm, for being again the hurting twin. It was a fatal error on his part.

During the endless analytic hours I had been struggling to shake off my feeling of being a bad person who could be cruel and hurtful and I had come a long way with this. I had begun to understand where Ma had been emotionally after Little Brother died and could not bear having me around. I had been edging towards forgiveness of her, but even though I knew that the primary task of the analysis was learning to accept and forgive myself, I could not do this in an emotional vacuum. I needed Dr. Gautier's support and belief that I was a good person and would be able to make peace with the past.

Dr. Gautier was a powerful authority figure. Although I had never found him personally appealing I had respected his expertise as a purveyor of psychoanalytic wisdom. But with his outburst I had lost that respect. He had not only hurt me where I was most vulnerable —my fear of hurting others and of not being sexually normal —but he was also oversimplifying a complex, sensitive issue, reaffirming his belief that only the heterosexual route was mature and psychologically healthy. His outburst would not have been so painful if it had conveyed the message, "I don't want you to rush into this because I'm not sure it's what you really want." Instead the message I had heard was —"I need to stop you from hurting someone with your deviant impulses." His anger had betrayed his feeling of repugnance and in expressing it he had lost control of his role as the analyst. Had he listened more closely to what I was telling him he might have seen my renewed interest in Natalie in the context of my loneliness, my mother's worsening dementia, and my growing discourage-ment about ever being able to have a family of my own. I doubt that I had any serious intention of trying to reestablish a relationship with Natalie, much as I still loved her. Seeing her again and recalling the pleasure of intimacy and companionship had reminded me of the huge void in my life.

When I next saw Dr. Gautier he apologized for his lapse, but it did not "make it all better" the way a parent's comforting hug can reassure an over-rebuked child. Today, as a therapist, I can understand his frustration when a patient he thought was coming along well seemed to be regressing and head-ing into a wrong turn. But his outburst had been unfortunate, leaving me feeling abandoned and very much alone.

I continued my visits to Dr. Gautier for almost a year, probably because it was too painful to accept what I subliminally knew —that his outburst about Natalie had terminated a flawed and unfinished analysis. When that exchange took place, the invisible, supposedly indestructible thread that had been spun by the Princess's grandmother and that had become a metaphor for me for the connection between therapist and patient had suddenly snapped. I no longer trusted him. I was unable to shake the feeling that with his uncon-cealed distaste for my relationship with Natalie he had entered into an alliance with my mother and they had become conspirators. I never let him know how injured I had been. My early pattern of dealing with rejection had been to shut down emotionally and to withdraw, and at that point in the analysis I unconsciously regressed into that behavior although I continued to bring up issues to work on as if nothing had changed. I do not recall Dr. Gautier trying to probe my reaction to what had happened. Perhaps he thought his apology *had* "made it all better" and that we could just go on as usual.

It had been a little over five years since the long journey with him had begun. It had started when I was commuting along the Hudson River between my job at St. Christopher's School and his couch. Just having him there, hour after hour, listening without passing judgment (at least in the beginning) had provided much needed cathartic relief. I could be freer in his presence than in my face-to-face conversations with Dr. Porter. I had finally been able to talk about sex although this topic had ultimately led to our fatal falling out. And there had been other good things that happened in those first years, or that had started to happen. Exploring my troubled relationships with my parents and theirs with each other had occupied many painful but fruitful hours. Talking about my twin's death had freed me to open that forbidden topic with Mary and our learning that we were not alone in carrying our burdens of guilt. Over time, though, I had grown less confident in Dr. Gautier, and my high hopes for the analysis had begun to fade. So had it failed in the end?

I had wanted an A+ experience, leaving on the arm of a husband, or at least being in a committed relationship, but with pass/fail grading, this analysis lay somewhere in between. I had come into the process with a trunkful of emotional baggage and gone out with only a suitcase. During the analysis I had learned that I had clinical depression and should not be blaming myself for all my failures. Although I was still part woman/ part needy child, the proportions had improved. But I had carried out with me most of the fears that I had brought in. For the most part they were less disabling and at times I felt almost free of them, but after running normal for a while they would flare up again like a fever in a viral infection. I was still fearful of *being* or *doing* wrong and of being criticized and unwanted, and although my fear of failing was less, it could still paralyze me. Finally I was still afraid to trust the love of men, fearing their lust and power, and I was still confused about my own sexuality.

I have often wondered how Dr. Gautier scored the analysis. My guess is that he thought it was successful and that he had rescued me from deviancy — setting me on a healthy heterosexual path.

The final moment of parting was harder than I had anticipated. This close, yet not close, relationship with a man I barely knew, but with whom I had spent nearly a thousand hours, was about to end. It was unlikely that I would ever see him again. While I had entered into the analysis wanting passion with my analyst, my relationship with Dr. Gautier had been more like an arranged marriage. We had done together what we were there to do, had our marital spats, and had become used to, perhaps even fond of, one another over time. When I parted from this "husband" I had not chosen I felt grateful for his essential decency in spite of the ways in which he had failed me. I knew that for a time I would miss him. At the actual moment of parting he shook my hand. Other than our initial handshake on greeting, it was remarkably the only physical contact I had with this person I had known for so long and with whom I had shared this strange, one-sided intimacy. He said, "Good bye, Miss Nicodemus. It has been a pleasure working with you." I had no reason not to believe him and was able to accept this small parting gift. I was tearful, of course, as I had been off and on in anticipation of the finality of this ending. But when I stepped out of his office onto the street I had a sense of exhausted relief. Adjusting my eyes to the sudden brightness of a sunny spring afternoon, I headed across town in the direction of the Central Park Zoo.

I had often cooled out there after sessions, responding to some gravitational pull towards these caged creatures. I had been especially drawn to a ceaselessly pacing red fox and to a lethargic, defeated-looking yak that stood motionless, munching its cud. Visiting them had become part of the analytic ritual, a brief interlude before walking to the subway and catching the train back to my life, such as it was. On this particular morning I lingered, knowing that I might not be seeing these animal friends for a long time, probably never again. Strangely, this parting felt even more painful than the one that had just taken place in Dr. Gautier's office, with my hand in his for the second and last time. Even though I knew that my visits had no meaning at all for these animals, I had identified powerfully with their entrapment, and leaving them felt like an abandonment.

When I reached the park I found a bench where I could sit and rest and try to put the pieces of my life together. My mind went back into the analytic space, seeing myself in my late twenties crossing that threshold and lying down for the first time on Dr. Gautier's couch. I was absolutely confident, absolutely certain that I could accomplish the task at hand and be free of all those things about myself that I disliked so much. And I remembered looking up and seeing Ma hovering above me and knowing with a heavy heart that it was not going to be a quick and easy fix.

During those months in the analysis when I had been struggling to resolve my conflict about Natalie I had almost forgotten Ma's presence in the room. My relationship with Natalie, perhaps my first conscious act of disobedience to her, had been threatening her power, and although she was still there she had become more ghostlike. Where was she now, I wondered? I had wanted so much to celebrate her departure as I was struggling in that space to reclaim myself, but she had won that round. I had failed to evict her, and since I had failed I realized that she had of course come down from the ceiling when I was having my parting moment with Dr. Gautier and followed me out of his office and down the street. I looked beside me, half expecting to see her sitting there, even though I had known all along that it was my interior space she had been inhabiting. I realized that if I were ever to exist as a free spirit, I would have to find another way to get her out. That prospect made me so deeply sad and weary I did not even *want* to cry. I stood up and started walking to the subway, then stopped and looked back.

"Good-bye, Yak," I called out. "Good-bye, Fox." My voice choked.

Then I turned and hurried on to catch my train.

Adieu Ma and Pa

Before Ma's final departure into nursing home care, Pa invented an inspired way to deal with her dementia. She was very overweight by then and sedentary on her doses of the early tranquilizer, Reserpine. In this condition she was not likely to run away from her keepers. My father had free transportation including a drawing room on all the railroads in the country, and with work obligations frequently taking him across the country he simply took Ma with him on his trips. She sat contently in their drawing room, watching the scenery go by. He was able to navigate her several times a day through the lurching train to the dining car for the tasty meals that were available in those vanished days. The nervous smile with which she had negotiated her relationships as a younger woman served her as before. To other travelers she probably appeared a pleasant if not very interesting and perhaps not entirely well companion for this solicitous man. When Pa conducted his business in the cities they visited he would park her briefly in their hotel.

When she became less manageable Pa was advised to have her evaluated in a mental hospital and asked me to drive them there. I had not seen Ma for some time and was shocked by her deterioration. Her sparse, now graying hair had not been styled, probably for months, and she had become enormously heavy. No doubt her height –5'11" when she was a young woman –had made her seem even larger. She had also developed a problem of urinary frequency.

On our drive along the Long Island Parkway Ma sat contentedly in the back seat commenting like a small child on things she saw —"red" when we passed a red car, "dog" when she saw one looking at us through its back window. Then she announced, "I have to go to the bathroom." The parkway system still had rest stops and I pulled into the first one we came to. It was difficult enough getting her out of the car but almost impossible for me to wedge her into the rest room's narrow cubicle. I could barely get myself in with her to pull down her voluminous panties and steady her on the seat. This was the last time I would touch my mother.

After she was led away from us in the hospital and Pa and I had met with the admitting psychiatrist, we went out to our car to start the drive home. I looked up at the building we were leaving and was shocked to see Ma in an upper window, looking down on us. I was sure it was not coincidence that she was there and that she knew we were going off and leaving her. I waved to her, and she waved back.

"Ma's up there at a window waving at us," I said to Pa, but he did not look up.

In a few weeks she was transferred to a nursing home on Long Island. Pa could have turned his back on her then and left her there, making nominal visits, but he did not.

I have often wondered why Pa was so attentive to her during these last years of her life. It seemed out of character for him to be visiting her every day, sitting beside the bed of a vanished human being who lay there incontinent, not recognizing him or her children. I came with him once and could not bear to go again. I found it unspeakably sad that she could not know he was there in the way she had wanted to him to be when their relationship was falling apart. Or did she know? How do *we* know? How do we know that she did not recognize his voice when he greeted her, or that some primitive part of her may have identified his smell? Perhaps it is our not knowing that makes us keep returning to these bedsides. Did Pa think about it in this way? What *was* he thinking as he sat there? Is it possible that with her approaching death he was also reliving the loss of his beautiful young mother? In the psyches of many if not most men, mother and wife lie very close.

Only now, in recalling the two events that had caused Pa's medical cri-
ses —Little Brother's death and Ma's "nervous breakdown" during World War
II —did I realize that this man whom I had always perceived as heartless and
who normally was a master at repressing unwanted emotions, had feelings
that went so deep they had burst through a weakness in his trachea.

Ma joined Little Brother and the infant son of my nephew in the cemetery
of our Episcopal Church on Long Island. She was seventy-four, and I did not
think then that it was an especially early death as we would today. It is a beautiful old cemetery with an avenue of cypresses and plantings of hedges and
shrubs that separate one family's domain from another. At one end, nearest
the church, marble markers lie in the shadow of old trees with their worn,
hand-carved letters becoming harder and harder to read, while at the other
end, machine-carved granite monuments in shades of gray and pink make
bolder statements in bright sun of more recent deaths.

My parents had planted boxwood to mark the boundary of the plot they
had bought for Little Brother, but had never placed a marker on his grave (nor
had my nephew on his son's) so I did not know where in that piece of ground
my twin lay or the little crib-death boy who had joined him. I wondered how
the men who came to dig the huge cavity for my mother had known where
to dig without disturbing them, but maybe they *had* been disturbed. Maybe
they had been wakened from their sleep and had had to make room for the
huge casket.

I stood there on the emerald, faux-grass carpeting that covered the riled-
up, muddy December ground, with Pa on one side of me making his small
moaning sound, and Ma's old cook on the other. The same stiff hair that I
had hated as a child was still growing out of a mole on her chin. I was not
listening to the prayers. I was crying, being moved in some primitive way by
the finality of Ma's death, but feeling unclean. My tears would be seen in this
gathering of family and friends as the grief of a child for its mother and I was
not grieving for her. In the last awful stretch of her life I had felt compassion
for her, but I had still been unable to forgive her. I was crying because of the
overwhelming sadness of this drama —for my lost twin, for myself and for
this tragic lady with her unfulfilled life who was lying now beside the beloved

son whose death had almost destroyed us both. Would there be room for me, too, in that ground, I wondered, sometime in a future? Might I perhaps lie on his other side? And where would Pa fit in when his time came? Would he bring discord? Would my siblings, Hope, Mary and Robert who were standing nearby with their heads bowed, want to be buried there, or somewhere else with their spouses, or would they choose, as I might choose in the end, to be thrown to the wind? Standing there I wondered what it would have been like to have a mother I did love and for whom I *would* be grieving. I would never know.

Very slowly after Ma's death an embryonic new self began to emerge and with it came a reawakened urge to write. I had had no time for it as I pursued my professional career, but that was not the only reason. Even though Ma had never seen anything I had written, her mere existence had been censorious. As long as she was alive, even in her advanced dementia, she had not lost her power over me and I had not lost my fear of her disapproval. I knew of course that all this was irrational. I had done my psychoanalytic homework. I knew that my real enemy lay within myself —the self-doubting, self-hating being that had been her legacy to me. But after she died, after my flesh and blood mother was gone, her power over me began to subside, although the battle within myself was not yet won. For far too long I would bring my internalized, disapproving mother with me wherever I went like a too-heavy child who still demands to be carried.

Out there somewhere in the real world I still had a father, but I expected little from him and had little to give him. I did not see him often, usually only when I visited Robert and his family who were now living with him in the Small Paradise. I was not sorry. We seemed to have agreed, tacitly, to maintain a formal distance and to meet only the minimum of father-daughter obligations. I was therefore unprepared when he called me one day and invited himself to Princeton for an overnight visit. He asked for the name of a restaurant where we could meet for dinner. He would walk there from the railroad station and I could join him when I came home from work. This was the last thing I wanted, but how could I tell him not to come?

He was pleased with the restaurant I had chosen and delighted that they could produce his favorite whiskey, pure Maryland rye. He was always loyal to his home state. He wanted me to try it —Ma never drank —and I did not want to displease him. While I could not drink it straight the way he did I was able join him with a cocktail and we got off to a good start. He enjoyed his meal, became flushed with his whiskey and became garrulous, launching inevitably into his ethnic jokes, but I had still not worked up enough courage to tell him how much they offended me. Our relationship was too fragile.

After dinner I drove us back to my apartment, apprehensive about sharing such close quarters. After airing Salomé I made up my hide-a-bed for him in the living room while he sat watching my preparations. Over the bed hung a large abstract impressionist piece that had been painted for me by my Jewish suitor in Philadelphia and Pa wanted to know where it had come from. I told him. He studied it for a while, then pronounced his critique: "That's atrocious." I did not reply. Silence had always been my best defense. It was the only comment he made about my place.

Morning came. I drove him to the train and went on to work and came home that night to the disheveled hide-a-bed I had not had time to make. Pages of *The New York Times* that he had fetched from my stoop before I woke had been devoured and scattered on the floor. When I went into the bathroom I found a soaking wet towel in the tub and tiny dark hairs in the sink from his morning shave. They had repelled me when I was a child and still did. Invasions like this were to take place fairly often and followed much the same pattern. Gradually our conversations became more relaxed and it was gratifying to me when on one of his visits he pointed to the painting over his bed and said, "You know, that thing starts growing on you."

I had been puzzled at first about Pa wanting to make these visits, but it began dawning on me that he was lonely. He probably liked being in the company of an attractive young woman and he might even have been taking pride in the fact that she was his daughter. I had felt so distant from him all my life I had never thought of him as a human person with his own needs and emotions the way I thought about my clients, and I began to be a little warmer. But when he invited me to go to Europe with him I was again unprepared. My feelings about the trip were profoundly mixed. I dreaded the prospect of spending so much time with him, but I had longed to travel abroad, and so I decided to go.

In 1958, crossing the Atlantic was a luxury affair and we traveled first-class, bringing large suitcases and dressing each night in formal clothes. There was no limit to the delicious food and wine available on *La Liberté* and Pa indulged himself shamelessly. In the weeks that followed, the distant man I had grown up with metamorphosed into a complicated father, sometimes exasperating and humiliating, sometimes humorous, and surprisingly often a compatible companion.

Although sociable, he was, to my surprise, socially insecure. When we entered a socially challenging gathering, he would go behind me, take me firmly by both upper arms and push me ahead of him as a sort of protective shield. Had he done this with Ma? But in encounters with people he believed to be beneath him socially, he was often insensitive and rude. He could also be socially clumsy and inappropriate which at times made me ashamed to be his daughter. Robert had gone to Cambridge after leaving the service and when we were in London Pa called some of Robert's classmates and asked if we could stay with them. Fortunately, being mannerly young men with mannerly young wives, they received us for the most part with remarkable courtesy. Robert was mortified when he heard about it. Perhaps I could not have endured his social ineptness had he not been willing to do a number of things that I liked and to go to places that I wanted to see. In Northern Ireland after he had "invited" us to visit the estate of another of Robert's classmates, we spent a day walking on a beautiful remote beach, and in Scotland we abandoned our itinerary to follow signs to a sheep-herding trial, and lingered all day with the locals with Pa enjoying his fill of scotch whiskey.

From there we went on to France to visit the country home of a cousin of his from Maryland. One of the governor's daughters had married and settled there. I listened with fascination to their conversations as Pa's cousin repeatedly called him on the fatuous remarks he was prone to make. She had no hesitation putting him in his place. Pa received her rebukes sheepishly and clearly enjoyed the attention she was giving him. I wondered if he might have had a young man's crush on her as they were growing up. Aunt Carrie had once hinted at that. His cousin was the kind of self-assured woman he should have married –a woman who would step on him nimbly whenever he went too far. Weak, bullied Ma had been so painfully miscast for the part.

As we continued across France on our way to visit the family of Robert's Austrian wife, Pa continued to indulge himself with delicious French food and wine and by the time we reached Salzburg, Robert's brother-in-law, a heart specialist, had him hospitalized for severe dehydration and skyrocketing blood pressure. Although chastened and trying to follow doctor's orders, Pa never fully recovered from that final episode of self-indulgence. However, we continued our trip through Italy, following the itinerary Pa had planned, with him resting in our hotels while I saw the sights. When we reached Naples he insisted on joining me to explore the ruins of Pompeii and Herculaneum. He had been reading about those cities in preparation for our trip.

I had no idea that Pa had this interest. I had never thought that he and I were alike in any way, but in fact we were. We were a pair of autodidacts. Neither of us had been educated outside our professional specialties, but we were both intelligent and curious and voracious readers. For years he had been buying books from an antiquarian bookstore in London, building up a non-fiction library, and this had not just been for show. I remember him working his way through all the volumes of Gibbon's *The Decline and Fall of the Roman Empire*. Probably the reason our trip had gone as well as it had was because we *were* both intellectually curious. Ma, I realized, had not been. If Pa had been able to enjoy more intellectual companionship with her, perhaps their relationship might not have eroded to almost non-existence before her dementia set in. On our return journey, crossing through the flotsam and seaweed-laden Sargasso Sea with flying fish leaping off the bow of the *Guilio Cesare*, Pa invited me to join him on the deck at dawn to see the sun rising out of the ocean.

Several months after we returned, Robert called to tell me that Pa had died. After the failure of his colt to become a racetrack winner he had become an avid duck hunter and he had gone out early that day onto the marshes of the Small Paradise with his shotgun and his Chesapeake Bay retriever. When he failed to come in for breakfast at his usual time, Robert found him lying in the marshes. He had been sitting in a blind on the riverbank and fallen when a fatal aneurysm struck. He could not have arranged a more perfect death.

Pa was a large man, too heavy to be carried across the muddy marshes, so he was brought home by boat on the river that he and I both loved. He was laid out in the living room under the portrait of Little Brother. On the opposite wall was a beautiful portrait of Ma that he had commissioned her friend, Alice, to paint from a formal photograph of her that had been taken just before their marriage. Aunt Carrie came up for the funeral and I remember her standing for a long time looking down at her brother, perhaps remembering a solemn little boy at the time of their beautiful young mother's death.

So once again on a cold December day, with Aunt Carrie by my side, I was standing on the faux-grass carpeting in the Episcopal cemetery beside another huge cavity that was waiting for its occupant. I wondered what the non-believing Pa would be making of the prayers that were being offered for his soul. When we were burying Ma, I feared that he might bring discord when he joined her and the little boys, but in their last years he had become kinder to her and I now believed that he would not disrupt them. But I also believed that he would claim all the space he needed to make himself comfortable, even if that meant discomforting the others. Pa would always be Pa.

As I stood there holding Aunt Carrie's hand I was grieving again, but as with Ma, not so much for the loss of Pa, but for the marriage of these two that had started out with such promise, then come apart after my twin's death and deteriorated during those miserable middle years when Ma had almost taken her own life. And I was grieving, too, for the sadness of those final years before her death when he had become attentive again, but she had probably been too far gone to know.

In the years following Ma's death, Pa, that brusque, frightening, unaffectionate stranger I had grown up with had been fleshed out into human being with whom I had more in common that I had realized. Instead of wanting to disown him I could be grateful for the gifts he had passed on to me. He had the reputation of writing outstanding briefs. Was that where my writing ability had come from? Perhaps, too, he had passed on to me his passion for music.

But probably the most cherished gift he gave me, indirectly, was the beautiful natural world he had made available to his family when he moved us to the Small Paradise and with which I had fallen in love. He had loved it, too, and like his books had not just created it for show. It did not matter that he had acquired it primarily for himself in his selfish way. Pa was who he was for reasons I could only guess.

A Fork in the Road

This was the time in my professional career when I should have been moving into a leadership role. I should have been writing papers and presenting them at conferences, becoming active in professional organizations, and perhaps teaching or doing some research, but I had no wish to do any of these things. Feeling as I did that my professional self wasn't my real self, and that I was just marking time until I married and started a family, this next step seemed dry and uninviting although I admired and valued the scholarly contributions of other professionals. When I was a student I had been in awe of the expertise of accomplished professionals and I remember asking Miss Garrett, "Will I ever be good enough to be a you?" and she had replied presciently, "You won't want to be." How did she know?

What held me in the work beyond the necessity of earning a living was the human connection. I loved the work, but not the role. With each new client I became aware of the rich range of human beings who were out there beyond the confining walls of my upbringing. I had loved learning the craft and becoming skilled at helping these people untangle themselves and be more content, and to continue to do this well do this well I would need to keep up with developments in my profession, but I would pay just enough attention to changing theory to be able to add useful remedies to my little black bag.

This decision had far-reaching consequences. With it I took myself out of the mainstream of the profession, positioning myself on its periphery, and forever after I would trade money for time –time for everything else that I wanted to do with my life. I would remain committed to maintaining a high level of practice, keeping abreast of important innovations in therapy via workshops, conferences and the professional grapevine, but I would earn just enough from my professional work to keep me afloat.

Did I say *time for everything else that I wanted to do with my life?* Where was that time going to come from?

I had decided that I did not want to be a Miss Garrett, but I still worked long hours at the clinic five days a week. I had become the clinic's Chief Social Worker and was dividing my time between administration, therapy with clients, and supervision. There was only one solution: With uncharacteristic self-confidence I resigned as Chief Social Worker, reduced my hours from five days to four, and fixed up a small office in the basement of a friend's house where I could start a private practice. I was now confident enough in myself to "disobey" the disapproving Miss Garrett and to make a delayed end run around the line she had drawn dividing social work from psychiatry. Any lingering doubt had vanished when I realized that the psychiatric social workers on our staff knew as much or more as the psychiatrists, while earning less in the basement of the professional hierarchy.

On my first long weekend I had an intoxicating feeling of liberation. I had been so committed to my work I had not let myself know how much other parts of me had been starving for time. I had already let music back in, but now I would have time for serious practicing. I would have more time for my garden and woodland walks with Salomé, and there would be enough time on a long weekend to see more of my family and friends. Martha, whose marriage had failed, had recently resurfaced and wanted me to go backpacking with her. Finally, and perhaps most important of all, I wanted to get back to my writing.

Throughout my school years writing had always been my best skill. After graduating, I had taken some English courses at Columbia University and the professor in my short story course had given me high praise and strongly encouraged me to go on writing. This was thrilling, of course, and I could see a career as a writer coexisting nicely with my responsibilities as the wife and mother I expected to be. I believe that if I had not found myself in Mary Dailey's bedroom in the widow's house a decade later after all the Leo uproar in my life had subsided, and had not heard her urgent cry for rescue, I might have become an Ann Beattie-kind of novelist. But I *had* heard it and gone on rescuing one more Mary after another. So why had my desire to write surfaced again? Because I believe that writing *was* my true vocation.

During these past fallow years I had been accumulating more and more that I wanted to say. For some time I had wanted to write about my work, and when the wife of one of my colleagues told me that she had been selling stories to the confession market, I decided to write some in my new time, and I would weave into them some simple psychological truths. I had not expected to be so successful, but after selling six of them I realized that writing them took as much time as writing what I thought of as "quality" fiction which was the kind of writing I most loved. So I decided to go back into that place in myself that produced the kind of stories my professor at Columbia had thought of so highly. But I could produce nothing. Every weekend I would return to my blank page and still nothing came.

I had heard a number of creative artists talking in interviews about psychoanalysis in much the same vein as the movie director, Werner Herzog, who said that he would rather jump off the Golden Gate Bridge than be analyzed. The writing I had done as a young woman had predated my psychoanalysis and I began to worry that I had talked away all my good material. In this unhappy state I saw a notice in the public library that the novelist, Caroline Gordon, was offering a writing course. The timing was perfect. Taking the course would either free me from this painful block, or Caroline Gordon would tell me to "go home and cook!" I would never forget Leo yelling those cruel, sexist words at an ungifted girl in my class in music school.

PART III

ENTER BETH

"I love your psychiatrist!" a woman in the writing class said after my story had been read. "Do you have her phone number? I think I'd like to make an appointment."

The other women laughed. "I think she's a poet," the woman went on. "The psychiatrist my husband and I are seeing is very good, but he's a prose person, quick and smart, but all prose. It never occurred to me that a psychiatrist could be sitting there, listening and being helpful and not wanting to be a psychiatrist at all. Here's yours with her mind wandering all over the place. I love that business about the conditioned rat and how she sees herself pushing the lever marked 'therapy hour' to get her pellet of food and knows it's too late to have a different life."

The class had been open to anyone but had only attracted women. We had been an earnest group of ten, producing our assignments faithfully, reacting to each other's work, and being critiqued by our teacher. This was our last class. Carolyn Gordon gave approval sparingly. She had said nothing to me about my writing until this last meeting and then she had read an entire story of mine to the class instead of a few pages as she usually did. "I'm afraid she has a gift for metaphor," she said wearily. I was elated, of course, but also sobered, realizing from her demeanor that the world didn't need any more aspiring writers, only writers who were so good they didn't have to aspire. She was probably only teaching us because she needed the money.

Her reluctant encouragement had left me stranded where I was before, not knowing if I should keep on struggling to find time to write or accept that my life had taken a different course. Caroline Gordon had confirmed that I had talent, but she had also made clear that becoming a published writer would demand as much of me as my professional work, and of course I wanted to be published. What writer doesn't? But the therapy hour in my story wasn't fiction. It was my pellet of food, and my better judgment told me that it was time for me to let the writing dream go.

When I shared these thoughts with the woman in the class who had responded to my story —we were all milling around after the course was over, reluctant to disperse —she cried out, "No! You're much too good! You need somebody to take you in hand!"

"Don't tempt me," I said, "I'm trying to be realistic."

But she persisted. She had a friend who worked for an agent and she wanted to send her my story. She was sure the agent would want to send it out. She had to rush now to pick up her little boy at nursery school but suggested that we meet again to talk more about it. We agreed on lunch the following week.

I also had admired this woman's work —several short pieces that were cleanly and economically written and submitted with apologies. If she could write anything well, she had said, it would be poetry. Later on, in that period in early friendship when each is learning about the other, she showed me a collection of accomplished, understated poems about loss that she had written in college. Occupied with the rearing of three young children, she had written little since, but now that the youngest was in nursery school she was hoping to get back to it.

During our lunch she pressed me again to let her send my story to her friend. I told her I was still unsure that I would have the time or energy to continue writing, but if I could produce another story she liked she could pass them on to her friend. In this first meeting we talked mostly about writing and parted with an ambitious plan: we would pursue our interest in literature and writing and meet one evening a week as if continuing the course by ourselves; we would agree on a reading project and bring in our writing when we were ready for the other's critique. We would meet at her house on the night her husband saw their psychiatrist in the city and stayed over at his club.

When I rang the bell the following week at her modest suburban house with its needing-to-be-mowed lawn and a barbecue grill on the back patio, I thought, "I'm going through this portal into one of those houses I drive by where happy couples are nesting. I don't belong here. I'm not a member of their club." But I trusted the relationship with Beth, my newfound friend, and felt sure I would be welcomed. She was giving her son a bath when I arrived. "Come on in and chat while I finish him," she said, "and here are my two girls." They eyed me curiously, shook my hand politely, then went back to their rooms. The house had a casual feel to it. The necessary furnishings were there and Beth's décor struck me as neither attractive nor unattractive. She led me to the bathroom.

"Darling," she said to her little boy, "We really have to get you out of your bath now. We'll put the ducks on the ledge and they'll go to sleep and be waiting for you tomorrow."

She was calling him "darling." I had never heard a mother do that. And later, when he was on her lap and she was reading to him she held him close as if she wanted him to be there. I loved what I was seeing. A few weeks later she would be calling me "darling" and in time I learned that she used endearments words with everyone she cared about, but I still liked it. After her son was settled and her girls' lights were out she offered me a drink. I didn't want one, but she fixed one for herself, then sank wearily into her sofa. "Let's hope he doesn't call out for a glass of water," she whispered, "or say he can't find his cuddly, or needs to pee." She held up her glass as a welcoming toast.

The first assignment we gave ourselves was to read and discuss the books of Virginia Woolf. I loved Virginia. She had become a role model for me, a brilliant, accomplished woman (not an unstylish, frustrated housewife like poor Ma) who had been able to transform suffering into beautiful literature. Beth and I started out on our journey in high spirits as if attacking a plate of delicious food and were unprepared for where our enterprise was going to take us. But the darker, more provocative the terrain Mrs. Woolf led us into, the more subjective, more self-revealing our responses to her writing became.

Being a college graduate and an English major, Beth was far more knowledge-able and better read than I and she became my mentor, continuing in that role as our relationship deepened and moved in other directions. I had known nothing about the Bloomsbury crowd and their carryings-on and I had been amazed to learn that Virginia's "Orlando" was based on Vita Sackville-West and that Virginia had had an affair with her.

"I thought she was happily married to Leonard," I said.

Beth had burst out laughing. "But that doesn't mean they got along sexually."

"But how did they get away with it, Vita and Virginia?"

"When you're Virginia Woolf you can get away with almost anything. She was loved by everyone she cared about, so she could let Vita seduce her and not worry about what people would think."

"But what about Leonard? He must have minded."

Beth laughed again. "My goodness, you're conventional. If he knew about it, and he probably did, he would have been more afraid that she'd be upset by it. He adored her. He loved living with her. He was more of a parent really, not a conventional husband. It just amazes me how you can do the work you do, and you obviously do it well, being so unworldly. Where have you been? Reading fairy tales?"

How did she know? It was true that I was able to counsel unhappy couples, although I was winging it a bit. Even though I was not inexperienced sexually, I knew nothing about the day in, day out challenges of living with another person. Here was this new friend, laughing at me affectionately and telling me to grow up and learn what went on in other people's beds. It was a fluke that I had stumbled unwittingly into the inner sanctum of the married and had found someone who was prepared to educate me in its mysteries. I loved the direct way she said things without worrying about what other people might think and it amazed me that she had caught on to me so quickly.

During our first evening together the seeds of a deep friendship were be-ing sown. The more we talked about ourselves the more I sensed that she had been struggling in deep water and was reaching out for a steadying hand. I, in turn, without being aware of it, had been letting let her slip into my uncon-scious as the embodiment of the earth mother figure I was always searching for. She had a soft, heavy, unathletic body and her breasts were full although she was no longer nursing her son. And, while her appearance was hardly evocative of a little boy, somehow my twin had gotten in there too, again without my being aware of it. Perhaps it was because of the somewhat boyish cut of her hair and a slight resemblance to the face and head that had been looking out at me all my life from the portrait that was still hanging in the living room of our house on Long Island.

After that first evening we became less and less structured about the reading and eventually abandoned it altogether. Getting to know one another and sharing our complex and painful histories became the more pressing and inviting agenda.

Although I had often felt like an "orphan" and sometimes believed that I was adopted —impossible, of course, being the twin of a wanted brother whose lavender dress, little shoes and lock of brown hair I had once come upon in my mother's bureau drawer —Beth *was* an orphan and *had* been adopted. Her American mother and English father had died within a year of each other when she was eight and her brother was ten. They had been living in London, which explained a slight, attractive accent I had been unable to place. Both their parents came from literary, artistic, politically liberal, but not solvent families. It had seemed a wonderful idea to the surviving childless relatives — an uncle in America and three aunts in England —to accept an offer of adoption from a wealthy American couple who could provide all the material advantages that their relatives could not. While these domestically disinclined relatives had not had to alter their independent lives, the children had been left feeling unwanted and abandoned as they clung together on an ocean liner, without escort, to be claimed by strangers.

Beth's brother Toby, while always correct, had remained aloof from their new parents, which left Beth feeling guilty and disloyal for trying to ingratiate herself with them. But it had not taken them long to learn that it was only their new mother who had wanted them. Their adoptive father resented his wife's new preoccupation and made the children feel unwelcome. Beth had grown fond of her new mother though, in deference to Toby, did not call her "mother." She asked if she might call her Tillie, never revealing that this was the name of a cat they had had to leave behind. Tillie could not have been more different from Beth's own mother, who was beautiful and exciting but easily distracted and forgetful. Tillie was a plain, well-organized woman who remembered everything. The two children did not call their remote new father anything, having instantly disliked him, but when Beth's girls began calling him "*Big* Daddy" that was who he became —a huge, soft, overweight man with only the faintest echo of having once been a good-looking Harvard football player.

Later, in trying to understand why it had happened, Beth guessed that after early efforts to conceive had failed, Tillie left the marital bed. When Beth started to mature her adoptive father began hovering inside her bedroom door after Tillie was asleep and exposing himself. There had been no overt sexual act —perhaps he had just wanted to arouse himself for later gratification —but his palpable desire, persisting throughout her young girlhood and reappearing on her vacations from college, had driven Beth into an early marriage. It had been an unfortunate mismatch, decent and agreeable as Eddie had been.

Beth had forgiven Eddie, the only son of a widowed mother, for giving her a hateful, disapproving, manipulative mother-in-law, being aware of the tentacles in which his mother had entwined him. She had forgiven him his lack of ambition and for not being a stimulating intellectual companion. But she would not forgive him his drinking. Although she understood his desperate need to be liked by the men he worked with and that competitive drinking was a test of manliness in that fast Manhattan crowd, she would not forgive his coming home night after night, too far gone to be either a father to the children or available to her. She had found Dr. Carter, a psychiatrist she liked, and she and Eddie had been thrashing all this out with him.

"I'm afraid you're going to think I just want free therapy from you," Beth said after she had told me her story, but if either of us was going to be getting free therapy from the other, it was I, for I had cast her in the role of the woman analyst Dr. Gautier had refused to let me see and was being drawn like a magnet into her earth mother lap.

When I told her *my* story she listened attentively, not interrupting to pursue some association of her own as listeners so often do. And she did not get up once to fill her glass, which she often did in our evenings together.

"Bless that aunt of yours," was all she said. "I hope I meet her someday."
"You will," I said.

As each of us learned more about what the other had experienced growing up our compassion for one another kept drawing us closer. I wanted to make her losses up to her in some way and to make things right for her now and I sensed that she was feeling the same. Intuitively she had been doing this with her enthusiasm about my writing. I remember thinking, this person I respect really likes me, she really thinks I'm a nice, all right person. I'm sure she would do anything she could for me and expect nothing in return and I knew I would do the same for her. Was this love?

One evening Beth suggested that I come earlier the following week and that we eat together after the children were in bed. She was tired of fixing meals for Eddie and then eating alone. He had come home late one night the previous week, taken the plate of food that was warming for him in the oven and thrown it in the garbage. She usually tried to wait for him when he missed his train, which he often did, and she would have a drink by herself, but then one drink would lead to too many and she couldn't let that happen when she was trying to help him stop. At least one of them had to be sober for the sake of the children. It was a shame, she said, that their best time together had been when they were drinking partners in the early years of their marriage. They had been living in New York, eating out a lot with other young couples, and everyone was drinking too much. It had been hard for them to settle down into suburban domesticity, but it was better for the children. Tillie had helped them get this house, but after Eddie had gone through the rite of passage of becoming a homeowner, he tired of caring for a house and yard and returned emotionally to the city, shirking his duties as husband and father.

So Beth and I were both lonely. I had thought mine was the only impoverished life. I imagined hers as full and satisfying and had idealized it in my envy. I, too, hated eating alone, hated living alone. It was a life I had never wanted and now this new friend was asking me to sit at her table where her husband was meant to be. The following week, after airing and feeding Salomé, driving over to her house and sitting down at her table for the first time, I started inexplicably to cry. Beth jumped up and put a comforting hand on my shoulder. Had something happened? Why was I upset? I told her I had no idea. I had not felt sad when I came in. I was happy. I had been looking forward to being with her. I collected myself and we went on with our meal.

After dinner Beth settled herself on her sofa with her usual scotch and soda. She often teased me about living in a fantasy world and I had brought my old worn copies of the Curdie books to read to her. I wanted her to know how real those characters had been —how Curdie had become a brother/lover figure for me, and King-Papa and the Princess's grandmother had become my parents.

"You break my heart," she said when I finished reading.

"Why do you say that? Are you laughing at me?"

"No! That's the last thing I'm doing. How close did you ever come to getting married? Were you ever engaged?"

"I got as close as having a Wassermann test. Do you remember when we had to have them?"

"To marry whom?" She got up and filled her glass.

It was the first time I had told her the whole Leo saga and she was mesmerized.

"Oh, sweetheart!" she said when I finished. "That was such a hard one for a beginner!

You were so young! I can't decide whether it had a sad or a happy ending. Did it make you bitter?"

"Devastated, but not bitter. I tried again and I think I was even closer to marrying that one, but in the end he loved someone else more than me. I still want to marry, but I hate the humiliation of looking for a man. I want it to happen when I'm not looking, but it doesn't. I'm beginning to think I'm resisting it for some reason I don't understand. I should have been able to figure all this out in the analysis and I thought I had."

"You need to get out more. I'll give lots of parties and introduce you to every man I know, but it isn't a disaster, you know, if you never marry. You don't know how many women there are who envy you your freedom.

I wasn't at all sure when I was young that I wanted to be married and I never saw myself having children the way you do. Sometimes when I'm homesick for England I think about my aunts over there and wish I could be like them, doing something in the arts. We were a kind of Bohemian family. It's in my blood, I guess. I'm afraid it comes naturally to me to be unfaithful. I suppose you're shocked, but you might as well know that I've had a few affairs. I don't think it's wrong to find pleasure when you're trapped in a relationship you don't want to be in. It was exciting at first, but it's too risky when you live in a fish bowl like this. But I shouldn't be telling you all this, should I? I don't want to discourage you. There can be wonderful marriages. When it works it's the best of all arrangements. Like democracy. She raised her glass. 'Here's to marriage! Here's to all those blessed unions!"

She'd gotten a little drunk. I'd been worrying about her drinking ever since we met, but I had assumed she was working on that with her psychiatrist.

"I worry sometimes about your drinking," I said.

"You shouldn't," she said. "I have it under control. But I shouldn't be talking to you about all this. I shouldn't be disillusioning you with my sordid marital revelations."

"Have you ever thought about divorce? You must have."

"Of course I have, but Eddie will have to leave me. I would never do that to the children. I would never deprive them of a father. They love him in spite of his lapses, and he loves them. And he needs me. He likes my looking out for him and not making demands on him. Except of course about his drinking. Marriage is a wonderful cover for him. He can go on flirting with the men he works with and not have to worry about himself. Marriage is a good cover for a lot of people."

She had tossed out yet another disturbing revelation, this suggestion that her husband might have homosexual leanings. Before I could think of a way to respond we both heard the fretful crying of her little boy. It was time, anyway, for me to be leaving.

We couldn't believe it when it happened again the following week —my bursting into tears when we sat down to eat the meal she had prepared for us. We couldn't just dismiss it as a one-time fluke. The tears kept flowing as if a well digger had just hit a deep vein.

"I can't believe this," Beth said. "I'm totally baffled."

"I think I know now why this is happening," I said when the tears finally stopped. "I think maybe you've opened the box. I think maybe you have the other key."

"What key?"

While we ate the meal that had been getting cold I told her about the death of my pet rabbit and the little tin box and the professor writing on my story that someone somewhere might have another key. I began sobbing again and went over to her sofa and threw myself down, burying my face in the pillows. She came over and sat beside me, rubbing her hand on my back.

"But why me?" she asked when I had quieted down. "Why do I have the key?"

"I think it has something to do with feeling so safe with you, feeling I can say anything to you, tell you any awful thing about myself and that you won't be repelled. I think you really care for me. Maybe I'm crying because you seem to like me so much. I don't know why you do."

"But why wouldn't I? You're a wonderful person. Are you telling me that you've never cried in all these years? You can't be."

"I cry sometimes when I'm alone, and I cried a lot during the analysis, but never like this. I guess I never got to the bottom of the well. Maybe it was because I never felt a hundred per cent safe with my analyst the way I feel with you."

"For once I'm at a loss for words," Beth said. "You're expecting so much of me and I don't want to disappoint you. I'm touched by what you're telling me, deeply touched. I feel honored in some way, but I don't want to let you down. I would so hate to hurt you."

She got up and walked over to her bookshelves. "Tillie had me baptized when I got here," she said, looking for a book, "and she had me confirmed in the Episcopal Church. I adore Jesus, of course, but I don't believe all that any more. I took a course on religion in college. All religions are the same. They say the same things. They just have a different cast of characters." She took out the book she was looking for, a concordance to the King James Bible. "There's something in my ear that I want to place. I did a paper once on the language of the King James. I love the poetry of that language. Here it is. It's from Isaiah. 'Thou trustest in the staff of this broken reed.'" She put the book back on the shelf, then came over and stood looking down at me. "I don't know exactly what it is that you're going to need from me, but I'll do everything I possibly can to be the person you need me to be."

But I was so needy I thought she had just been expressing feelings of modesty. I couldn't see that the last thing she needed was another child. So, without shame, I put on my bib and stuffed myself at her table. I had sensed, of course, that as much as she disliked the preparation of food and the obligations of domesticity she was as hooked as I into feeding emotional hunger and caring for the orphans of the world. She had once told me a story about herself that had changed her life. Tillie had sent her to camp her first summer in America. She was still homesick for England, and the other girls mocked the way she spoke. They were all well to do and she had taken to raiding their generous supplies of chewing gum. Tillie hadn't sent any with her because it wasn't "ladylike" to chew. She hadn't known why the director of the camp wanted to see her. When she walked into her office this woman had taken her on her lap and filled her own with packages of gum.

"Why didn't you tell me that you needed these?" was all she said.

So Beth filled my lap with chewing gum and, although I didn't understand then what I was giving her, as our relationship played out I fed her hunger and she fed mine like the people in hell —in a parable she was fond of telling —who had no elbows. They were continually being presented with tables of delicious food that they could not bring to their own mouths, but they could take the food in their hands and feed it to one another.

When I left Beth that night and drove home I found myself thinking about the Princess's grandmother and the invisible thread she had woven for the Princess. I had once thought that I had this thread connecting me to Dr. Gautier, but it had suddenly snapped. I knew now that Beth was holding the thread and would hold it as long as I needed her to. But unlike the Princess I was only partly a little girl. I was also partly *her* grandmother and Beth was also connected to me.

Beth's comment weeks before about Eddie's sexuality had made me think more about my own. I wanted to bring up the topic of sex with her, but I was hesitant. Sex was still an off-limits topic in polite society and in the media. I had never talked about it with anyone other than Leo and Dr. Gautier, not even my closest friends. But I was beginning to realize from my conversations with Beth and my novel reading how ignorant and apprehensive I still was on the subject. I was still anxious about my experience with Natalie, and just as I could almost believe that I had never squandered the virginity I had wanted to keep as a gift of love to a husband, I could almost believe that I had never been involved with a woman. Ten years had passed since I had that relationship and while I had not felt attracted to a woman since, I was never free of uneasiness about my sexuality. Maybe I only believed that I wasn't a lesbian because the idea of being one was so intolerable.

Before long the topic of homosexuality came up in one of Beth's I-can't-believe-how-naive-you-are tutorials. I had told her how disappointed I was that an attractive professor I met at a party and had talked with most of the evening had failed to follow up with an invitation. She sighed. "Don't you know that he likes little boys? I thought everybody knew. Why do you think he has a suite on the campus?"

It had never occurred to me. He was a good-looking muscular man, in no way the stereotype of "fairy" we had whispered about in boarding school. I realized then that I had also bought into the stereotype of lesbian. Lesbians were rough, tough masculine women, and all women athletes were lesbians. I had thought of lesbians as "dykes," but Natalie had been small and slender and totally unathletic. Even though I was an active "outdoor" girl I could hardly describe myself as rough and tough and carrying myself like a man. So where did this leave me? Despite its vicissitudes I had come out of analysis feeling ready to find a mate. Perhaps in my desire to please Dr. Gautier I had colluded with his wanting to effect a "cure" and to discharge me as fully heterosexual. Getting a woman's point of view about all this was one of the reasons I had wanted to see a woman analyst. One night, after relaxing with her usual evening highball, Beth, my surrogate analyst, opened the topic herself.

"Do you think one of the reasons people are fascinated watching a magician like Houdini get himself out of impossible situations is because it's a metaphor for marriage?" she began. "I woke up at four this morning and I lay there thinking about all the people who are in beds they don't want to be in, but they just can't put their legs over the side and get out. There are all these invisible barriers. I wasn't just thinking about myself. I lay there listening to him breathing and I thought, 'This poor man doesn't want to be in my bed. He probably wants to be in his boss's bed. He talks about him all the time. I don't think he likes making love to me at all, or maybe any woman. How could he with that mother of his? But here he is trapped in this marriage even though I know he loves the children. No wonder he comes home drunk every night. Then we don't have to do it. I truly don't think I'd mind if he had an affair. How can I, when I have? He probably wouldn't want one with another woman, but of course he couldn't let himself have one with a man." She was silent for a few minutes. "But I don't think marriage is all that easy even for couples who get along pretty well. How many couples are there, do you think —I'm talking now about nice, good, heterosexual couples who care about each other and their children and who took their marriage vows seriously the way you would —how many do you think would still prefer making love to the same partner year after year if they had other options? It used to be scandalous to get divorced. Now more and more people are doing it. Of course men have always had their affairs, but most women of our mothers' generation didn't. Or I don't think they did."

"You're so cynical, Beth! If I had to give up believing in marriage I think it would destroy me. I know good marriages exist. I've seen them. I know those fathers, the ones I see carrying their children on their shoulders. Those are the men I'm attracted to, but they're already taken. I should probably give up hoping."

"Of course you shouldn't. I know I sound cynical sometimes, but lots of people are happily married. My parents had a wonderful marriage, but then they were cut off short. They were only ten years older than I am now when they died. It's hard to believe. Maybe it wouldn't have held up forever, but I think it would. I've always thought my mother had an affair. I'm sure you think that means it wasn't a good marriage, but I think it may have made it better. I think my father knew about it, but just let it run its course. I don't know. There was an attractive man who used to come to our house a lot. I don't see why people can't give this to each other more often. I'm not talking about being promiscuous. But why does there have to be such a huge thing about fidelity? Why can't you give the experience of falling in love to one another now and then if one of you stumbles into it and wants it? If your marriage is good, the person you're married to will come back, especially if there are children. But I suppose if people were so loving and easy about this there wouldn't be any more novels. That's a dismal prospect."

"Maybe I shouldn't be trying so hard to help couples be happy. If I ever get around to spending more time writing there won't be anything left to write about."

"You can always write about loneliness. I was thinking about you, too, this morning and your not being in anyone's bed and what a waste that is, and I wondered whether it's worse to be trapped or to be lonely. It's such a waste, your living all these lovely young years of yours alone. Do you think the reason you're not in anybody's bed is because of Dorothy?" Beth had taken to referring to our mothers by their first names and I liked that. It helped me see my mother as a woman, not just a mother, and I started doing that too in our conversations.

"I know it's *one* of the reasons. We spent hours on that in the analysis. Sometimes I say to myself, 'Go ahead. Take your chances. If the marriage doesn't work out you can just leave, but now you're telling me it isn't that easy to leave. And then there's this other side of me that wants things to be forever. I don't think I could ever say the marriage vows and not mean them. I know people do. I keep waiting to feel absolutely sure, but I never do. I know one never can, but knowing doesn't seem to help."

"I don't know what to tell you. My own philosophy is to say yes when I'm in doubt and that hasn't always worked out, but when you say no all the time, as you do, you're protecting yourself from being hurt, but you aren't giving yourself a crack at pleasure. I guess I *am* telling you what I want to tell you, but I'm not sure you're going to listen. You're very set in your ways, you know."

"I know I am, but please don't give up on me. Please don't."

A few weeks later when we were in her living room after dinner we met the topic of same-sex relationships head on. Beth was sitting on the sofa with her drink and I was lying on the floor to ease the pain in my back from overdoing in my garden. She had seemed preoccupied that evening and I'd noticed that she'd had a drink before I came. She usually waited to have a pre-dinner drink with me when I did like one.

"You've told me all about your boyfriends," she said abruptly. "Have you ever slept with a woman? You don't have to answer. She just sent my poems back, a woman I've been involved with, *was* involved with, I should say. She'd forgotten that she had them. She hoped I was still writing. There wasn't anything personal in her letter. I could just as well have been one of her students. I never thought I'd want that kind of relationship and it kind of floored me that I liked it. Are you shocked? I'm always afraid I'm going to shock you. You're so incredibly chaste. You'll think I'm a bad influence."

"I'm not all that chaste. I'm just a coward. Go on."

"I think I was awed by her being so interested in me, or at least I thought she was. She's published some books of poetry and she teaches. I met her at a party in New York. There were lots of literary people there. My uncle told her about my poems and she said she'd like to see them. It was the classic seduction thing and of course I fell for it. She invited me to her apartment the next time I was in New York and to bring my poems. She barely read them. We met for a few months. It was pretty intense. Then she dropped me. She just ground me out like a cigarette she was finished with and that was the end of it. She smoked a lot. That's one thing I didn't like."

"Are you still in love with her?"

"No. I'm not sure I ever really was. In the beginning it was exciting. It was all so new. Now I feel hurt, and I'm angry. I feel used. I *was* used. I tease *you* about being naïve. The whole thing makes me feel so clumsy."

She got up and filled her glass.

"Dr. Carter told me it was mostly a psychological affair," she said when she came back, "not just a physical one. He said it was all about my English aunts and wanting to be like them and wanting their attention. He said I wanted to be her, not who I am, not the kind of a person she is but an accomplished poet, a poet-in-residence somewhere, leading a different life."

I was silent. I *was* shocked, but not morally. I was shocked because what she had told me was so totally unexpected and startling. Since she was married

I had assumed that she would only be interested in the opposite sex, in spite of her saying that she believed Eddie might want relationships with men. I was further shocked and dismayed by being aroused sexually by what she had told me. Was this simply a kind of voyeuristic response or was it telling me that I had sexual feelings for her myself that I did not want to acknowledge? I hated this woman she had been with, this lady poet of hers. I was jealous of her having been involved with Beth and felt betrayed by Beth for having had the affair even though she and I were not lovers. While I had always loved hugging her ample, motherly body when we greeted and parted, and could sometimes see myself in her arms when she held her children, I had never imagined us being together sexually. But now my thought of her doing it with this other woman was turning me on and making me angry at the same time, angry at them for letting themselves have pleasure, and angry at myself for being so hopelessly hung up.

For Beth this was probably just another episode in her life about which she would feel very little guilt. For me, being involved again with a woman would be close to catastrophic. It would mean the end of everything I had hoped for. At the same time I longed for intimacy. I wanted to be physically close to another person, wanted to touch and be touched, and Beth's revelations had stirred up these longings. Would she want to make love if I wanted her to? *Did* I want her to? Maybe she had brought all this up because she *was* wanting us to be lovers. I began to think I didn't know who she was anymore. Did I know who I was? Had she and I been falling in love all this time without my being aware of it?

"Of course we have, Silly," I could imagine her saying. "Are you just catching on?"

As I lay there on the floor my anxiety was mounting, wondering what was going to happen next. She had asked me if I had ever slept with a woman and if I was going to be honest with her I would have to let her know that I had. I would have to exhume that chapter in my life and I had thought only Dr. Gautier would ever have to know.

"Would you please get up from the floor and talk to me?" Beth said. "I want to see your face. You're so far away down there. I want to know what you're thinking."

I got up and sat beside her.

"You're so beautiful," she said, studying me. "I keep forgetting that until I see you again. *She* wasn't at all. She really wasn't that attractive physically. I wish I were a sculptor. I'd like to sculpt your face. She reached over and ran her fingers over my nose and cheekbones. "That was the first thing that attracted me to you," she said. "Your beauty. I'd love to sculpt all of you, make a beautiful Rodin figure with your head bowed –'The Sorrowing Woman.' I'm so plain, and now I'm fat. I'm surprised she wanted to have anything to do with me. I wonder why she does that? Having one relationship after another. Never letting herself get involved. She has to be afraid of something. You pros know more about these things than I do."

I didn't respond.

"You're so silent. Have I upset you talking about this?"

I shook my head. "Not in the way you think."

"What do you mean?"

"It's hard to talk about."

"So talk about it."

I felt a rush of fear. Supposing she liked me so much because she thought I *was* a straight arrow. Maybe it was all right for her to do these things, but not for me."

I plunged in. "It turned me on hearing you talk about being with that woman. She sounds horrible. I didn't know I'd have those feelings anymore. Feelings for a woman."

"I didn't know you had, sweetheart. All you talk about is wanting to find a husband."

"You asked me if I'd ever slept with a woman."

"That was kind of rhetorical. I just needed to talk. I didn't expect you to tell me that you had. Have you?"

I nodded.

"You never cease to amaze me."

"Have you ever had those feelings for me? Wanting us to make love?"

Beth paused, searching her mind. "I don't think so," she said. "I adore you, of course. Admire you. I'm moved by you. I want you to be happy, but I've never had fantasies of our being in bed together, if that's what you're asking. I'd love it, of course. You know me. But you've never given me any signal that you wanted that. Do you?"

"I don't know. I don't think so. But when you touched me just now, touched my face, I loved your doing that. I'm starved for touching. I wanted to grab your hand and say 'don't stop.' I don't think you were trying to start anything and I don't even know if I want you to. But I have a yearning to be physically close to you and have you hold me and that scares me. Maybe it means I'd rather be with women and I don't want that. I don't see why you can't touch people, even hold them without it always having to mean something."

Beth took my hand.

"Adults aren't supposed to touch each other unless they're making love," I said bitterly, "but why can't you just touch someone because you love them, the way you can touch a child? Why do you always have to be with someone sexually to be physically close?"

"Come," Beth said. "Come where we can lie down."

I hesitated.

"Come," Beth said again. "Come. Trust me."

I had never been in her bedroom. It was the domain of her marriage. Sacrosanct. The queen-sized bed with its pale blue satiny cover was the place of their union. It was no longer a happy place, but it had been for a while when it was in other rooms and before it had been carried into this space by sweaty movers and pushed up against the blue and white vertical stripes of the papered wall. Beth disliked that paper but had never bothered to change it. This room was their private place with photographs in frames on his and her bureaus —pictures of mothers, fathers, children, a brother, and the two of them when they were young and slender. I could imagine Beth's children clambering onto the big bed on Sunday mornings when "Daddy" was home, and I could see Beth rising while the children were crawling all over him, and walking sleepily down the hall into their kitchen to start cooking the Sunday ritual of pancakes and bacon.

"Come," Beth said. "Lie down with me." She had stretched out on the bed and her arms were open.

I took off my shoes and slid across the bed into her arms. Why do arms say it so much better than words? Is it because there is no mistaking the message of arms? No miscommunication?

We lay there together at this crossroads in our friendship, motionless. It could go either way. If I moved towards her she would respond willingly. If she moved towards me I would also respond and then be sick with regret. I had never imagined our being together sexually, but I could imagine passion taking us over at this moment and sweeping us away.

"Don't be afraid, sweetheart," Beth said. "I'm not going to seduce you."

"I'm not sure I don't want you to."

"I'm not sure that you do. Just let me hold you for a while. There's no rush about anything. You're right about the touching. There should be more of it. I just do it whether I should or not. My mother was a big toucher. My real mother. She was very physical with us and she was playful. She'd suddenly chase us around the house for no reason and we loved it. She'd forget things, too, but we didn't mind because she was such fun when she was around. We always knew that she loved us. Tillie was different. She wasn't much of a toucher. She was probably more like your Dorothy, more formal, teaching us manners, that kind of thing. I do love holding you. I think I understand now why you had that psychiatrist in your story wanting to hold that ugly woman in her lap and then worrying about her impulses. Are you all right?"

"If I love being here with you so much does that mean I'm a lesbian?"

"I think of lesbians as just being turned on by women, not wanting to do it with men. That doesn't seem true for you. I don't think I'm one just because I had that affair. If you want to put a label on us I suppose you could say we're bisexual, but I don't see why people have to be labeled."

"You sound so sure about everything, Beth. I wish I could be. But it's different for you. You're already married and you've had your babies. Maybe being with a woman was just a side dish for you. I haven't had my main course yet."

Beth laughed. "You haven't told me yet what happened with that woman you were with. What was she like?"

"Well, first of all she wasn't a woman."

"I assumed she wasn't a man. What *was* she? A chimpanzee?" We both laughed.

"What I mean is she was just a girl. We were both young. I didn't think of us as women then. We met at a conference. I noticed her because her face looked so sad. From the moment we met she seemed to be crying out to me to love her, almost pleading. I wanted to hold her the way you're holding me. There was something about me that attracted her. Maybe she sensed my weakness for being a rescuer. She didn't *say* anything. She just kept throwing out these signals. When I got back she looked me up and it took off. It was very passionate. She was dark. She had dark hair and dark, searching eyes. I always seem to be attracted to dark coloring. Do you know anything about Jung?"

"I've read a bit."

"Do you know about his shadow, the shadow part of ourselves, the dark underside? I think she was my shadow. I didn't understand that then. I was terribly drawn to her and I didn't want to be. I didn't want that kind of relationship, but she did. She was experienced with both men and women and she said she preferred women. She didn't want children, so she wasn't in conflict about that. What she wanted was to live with someone and wake up with them and have the morning orange juice together, and I ran. I was a coward as usual. I just disappeared without telling her. I still feel awful about that."

"What did your analyst think?"

"He said it was sick. Abnormal was his word. He said I was 'acting out.'"

"What's acting out?"

"It's taking a conflict out of the analysis and living it out with someone in the real world –avoiding the analytic work. He didn't analyze the relationship the way your psychiatrist did, seeing something positive in it. We talked about my fear of men and my dislike of my father. He didn't connect Natalie with my mother and I didn't either then. He said it was immature behavior. Mutual masturbation was what he called it. He said a fully mature woman would prefer intercourse and that was the way she should be having her climax. He made me feel even more strongly that lesbians are freaks –kind of untouchables."

"Whatever you are, darling girl," Beth said fiercely, "you aren't a freak or an untouchable! Excuse me! I have to use the bathroom." She got up. "That makes me very angry," she called out.

"Maybe I'm not being fair to him," I said when she came back. "That was the way *I* felt when I started the analysis, but he didn't make me not feel that way. He made me feel I had some kind of disease or abnormality, but that he could cure it if I was a good patient. Now that I look back on it I think he hated homosexuals. I think they got to him in some way."

"Why in the world did you stay with him? Why didn't you go to someone else?"

"I did want to talk with a woman analyst, but he wouldn't let me. I assumed he had a good reason. He was the analyst. He was supposed to know everything, and I wanted him to. You wouldn't have been so docile about it, would you?"

"I certainly would not! I'm still fuming! What did *you* think was going on with this girl? Why did you let yourself do it when you thought that kind of relationship was so wrong?"

"It just took us over. It was as simple as that. And there was probably some rebellion in it. Natalie didn't seem to have any conflict about sex and that was freeing for me. I think she was starved for love the way I was. She never talked much about her family, but her mother must have been worse than Dorothy. She sounded very cold. I loved making Natalie feel loved. And I do think what I was telling you about the shadow thing was in there. I think in loving her I was accepting the dark side of myself, giving myself permission to be sexual. Does that make any sense?"

"I think so. It's a little complicated."

"The freedom I felt with her was extraordinary and wonderful for a while, and then because I was with a woman doing this forbidden sick thing, the guilt came back. It took away all the good feelings and left me with a crime I've been trying to hide ever since."

"That's a terrible way to feel about it! You needed that relationship!"

"I ran into Natalie about a year later. I told my analyst I was still attracted to her and was thinking maybe I should go back to her and he was furious. I kept on seeing him for a while, but that really ended the analysis. I couldn't trust him after that. Why do you think people get so upset about homosexuals?"

"Why did you *stay* with that man? This makes me so angry!"

"But why *do* people get so upset about it? Is there some primitive fear the race will die out?"

"I suppose that could be part of it. All the religions preach against it. I overheard a woman talking about it on the train the other day and she said, 'God doesn't want it,' and I thought, "How does that woman know what God wants?" But I don't think it's going to make us an endangered species if that's what you're asking. I think most people would rather have intercourse. The way I look at it nature gave us orgasms so we'd want to do it a lot. I don't think our *bodies* care one whit which sex turns them on. They just want their orgasms any way they can get them. I remember being blown away when I was turned on nursing my first baby. Then I thought, 'my breasts don't care whose sucking them. They just like it.'"

"You're something else," I said, laughing. "Did you like the sex as well with that poet of yours?"

"It's hard to compare. The seduction made it exciting, but I think she was more like a man, taking over, moving it along. But once you're aroused I think orgasms are pretty much the same with anyone. I like having the man inside. How was it for you?"

"If men were women, I think I'd like it better with men."

Beth laughed. "But how *was* it for you with this woman?"

"Very passionate, like I told you, and I never felt used by Natalie the way you did by your poet. Do you think there's such a thing as an *emotional* lesbian? I feel the way you do about the physical part of it, but it's powerful for me to feel loved by a woman. Maybe I'd outgrow that if I had enough of it, but I guess having sex with anybody has always been spoiled for me by worry. When I was with a man it was wrong because I wasn't married and it was a huge sin to be with a woman. I'm afraid I'm more comfortable not having sex with anyone."

"Oh, sweetheart! Dorothy really did a number on you, didn't she?"

"But my father was in this, too. He didn't make relationships with men look very desirable."

"I was lucky. My father was sweet and affectionate. He was a low-key kind of person. Very dear and kind. He adored my mother. I've always thought of him as being a moon to her sun. I've always been more attracted to men, in spite of Big Daddy. It's so sad the way you've always run away from the people you've loved. If you didn't have to worry about pleasing your parents or that awful analyst of yours which of them do you think you'd most like to be with now?"

"That's a hard one. I guess the first person you're in love with you sort of never get over. I really loved Leo, but I was so worried about him being so old, and he was only forty-five! Just a few years older than we are now. I think I might have chanced it if Pa hadn't threatened to disown me. I never thought seriously of staying with Natalie. It wasn't just because I'd be ostracized. I really did want marriage and children and family life and I still do. I think one reason I was able to let myself go with her was because I didn't have to worry about getting pregnant. I never could have had an abortion. It wouldn't have been just giving up the baby, but the whole awful business of having to go to some stranger somewhere in some sordid place and having that horrible secret."

"I suppose you won't want anything more to do with me if I tell you I've had one."   "Oh, Beth! I don't judge other people for doing it just because I couldn't. I'm a coward, I keep telling you. It must have been awful for you."

"It was. I'll tell you about it someday. But go on. You were telling me which one of your loves you'd have most wanted to stay with."

"My army captain, I guess. I was very attracted to him and my parents liked him. I can't pretend that wasn't in there. He wanted a family and I think we would have liked living together. He asked me to get a diaphragm and I never would have done that if I hadn't thought we were going to be married. It never occurred to me that I was a rebound relationship for him. I think it might have worked out if I hadn't been so immature. I was still looking for a father, and a mother, and he wanted a woman. He was the only one I didn't run from, but maybe I would have if he hadn't left me first."

"Did you like sleeping with him?"

"I did, except that I was always scared. I know I disappointed him. I didn't measure up to that other girl, or woman. She was married, which is why he couldn't have her. I think I was always afraid Dorothy would burst in."

"Supposing she burst in here. What do you think she'd make of us lying here together?"

"She'd be appalled. She'd have that look on her face. That terrible disapproving look."

"I think she might be envious," Beth said. "She would probably have loved being in a woman's arms. She needed to be adored just as much as you do and your father wasn't giving her that. I don't know how daring women were back then about having affairs with each other, but she would have been too frightened. Women are bolder today. They can meet in each other's homes for coffee after their husbands have gone to work and their children are in school. Believe me. You and I aren't the only two lonely women lying together in someone's marital bed. It's a lot safer than having affairs with men."

"Beth! You make it all sound so matter of fact as if it has nothing to do with love. All these unhappy, frustrated housewives having affairs with each other! 'Would you like more coffee? Do you want another muffin? How about another orgasm?'"

Beth laughed.

"You make sex sound so unromantic. Like it's just another body function. I know it is, but didn't you ever have romantic dreams like me? You're always teasing me about mine."

"Maybe I envy you for still having them. Of course I had them, darling girl, but they were taken away from me before I could let them fly. Why do you think I write poetry?"

"I'm sorry." I buried my face in her arm "That was a stupid thing to say."

We lay there quietly for while.

"I'm afraid it's getting late," Beth said. "We ought to be getting some sleep."

"I don't want to leave you."

"You could stay here tonight. Why don't you?"

"I have to get back to Salomé."

"You could go over and bring her back. The children would love finding her here in the morning. And it would be lovely to have you sleep with me. I won't seduce you, if you're still worried about that."

"I'm still not sure I don't want you to."

Beth was silent for a moment. Then she leaned over and kissed me on the lips, lingering a bit. Then she drew back.

"Do that again," I said and she did.

"Again."

But this time she pulled away and stood up. "I would so love to give you pleasure," she said "but then you'd fly away like you did with the others." She reached down and touched my cheek. "I don't want to lose you," she said "I need you in my life. You've saved me from despair. Get up now. Get back to Salomé. We'll talk tomorrow."

SECOND CHILDHOOD

eth was a yes-sayer, I a no. "I know it's because you're afraid," she said, "but you've got to start saying yes more often." But she also knew and respected my increasing desperation about finding a mate and having some children before my reproductive time ran out. It hadn't taken her long to find inside the persona of a sophisticated and competent therapist an emotionally hungry little girl. So instead of the all-consuming passion of an affair, she let me put on a bib and pull up a highchair to her already overcrowded table.

In becoming an appendage to her family, I helped it balance its emotional books, being nourished in return by belonging. I was able to keep Beth sane, cheerful and more sober, which was a bonus for Eddie, and her wish to spend time with me also gave him more freedom. These years were the last when I might be able to conceive a child and it made me anxious to be using them up in my "therapy" with Beth. But my child self was not about to give up what it had been hungering for and thought it had found in Leo —a kind person who loved me and who took pleasure in nurturing, affirming, and often indulging me. Thus instead of having a child, I was allowing myself to be a child within the cover of an entirely acceptable friendship.

Shamelessly I took everything Beth was willing to give and the only downside of my attachment to her was losing fertile time. Dr. Gautier knew about Beth but not that she had become the woman therapist that he had refused to let me see. I often wondered what he would think, but she and I were a fait accompli. Conception had taken place and we were creating a deep, mutually loving, mutually admiring friendship, borrowing from each other what each of us needed —for her, more restraint and for me, more abandon.

True to her word, Beth gave parties for me and included me in outings to New York where she and Eddie often met for dinner with Toby and his wife and old friends from those early, unencumbered years of their young marriage. There would be much heated political talk around tables in Italian restaurants. Toby and Beth had the same dark, sad eyes, but he was as reserved as she was outgoing and outspoken. He and I, although mutually attracted, were both too shy to make much connection. I was awed by Beth's confidence and passion as she held forth about civil rights and the horror of our having dropped the bombs on Japan. I was mute —hiding my ignorance and feeling ashamed of my political passivity. I realized that in being so preoccupied with the inner lives of my clients I had not been paying enough attention to what was going on out in the world. So while Beth continued to indulge me with one hand, she kept after me with the other, pushing me to grow up and wise up both politically and socially. I badly needed this prodding.

She, however, would have been the first to say that our contract was not all one-sided. Salomé became another and much loved appendage to her family and I became Beth's guide in exploring the natural world. When I introduced her to bird watching and she looked through binoculars for the first time, she was disbelieving. We had a lucky view of a black-crowned night heron sitting on a branch in a swamp in the late afternoon sun. Its colors were vivid in this light —its white, black and gray feathers, its yellow legs and piercing red eye. Eddie was out tending the barbecue when we came back. "Darling!" she shouted from the car. "I've seen God!"

When people we care deeply about enter our lives we want our families and friends to know them and to love them and to show them places that have special meaning for us. When I presented Beth to the important people in my life I felt like saying, "Look what I've found!" as if she were an exquisite stone I had just picked up on the beach. During the first summer of our friendship she and I took a number of trips to introduce one another to our families. I had already met Toby and his wife and Beth took me up to the Adirondacks to meet Tillie and the infamous Big Daddy in their summer house. I liked Tillie, who was cordial to her daughter's guest but loathed Big Daddy on sight, and it was not just because of what he had done to Beth.

"He's a big baby!" I said to Beth when we were driving home. "I can see him in his high-chair, banging his spoon and demanding service."

Beth laughed, but she surprised me by defending him a bit.

"I've thought a lot about what happened back then," she said. "I think Tillie married him just to have children. You had to have a husband then. When that didn't happen there was probably no more sex. I'm sure he was a terrible lover and she'd just endured it, but people didn't divorce in those days. I think instead of giving him sex she spoiled him and gave him everything else he wanted. It's sad to see what he's become.

When I took Beth to the Small Paradise to stay with Robert and his family and to meet Hope who lived nearby with hers, she was stunned by the beauty of it all. She had never experienced this English-style country life –large comfortable houses on beautiful properties overflowing with children and animals. I showed Beth every corner of my childhood world, leading her through the dusty old barns, picking wildflowers in the woods and marshes, and sharing with her one of my favorite places in the world –the beach on Long Island Sound.

Robert was trying to carry on Pa's life-style as squire of the Small Paradise, but without a resident caretaker. He had inherited the farm without enough income to support it and was struggling to hang on to it from his earnings as an investment counselor. He and his hard –working Austrian wife did most of the farm work themselves. When we visited, Beth plunged in, helping with the weeding and harvesting of their large organic garden. Later she stood in disbelief in the barn watching Robert milk the family cow with a crowd of milk-hungry cats mewing around her legs. Conversation at mealtime was lively, with Beth challenging Robert on his politically conservative views. But they enjoyed each other's wit, and there was much genial laughter.

One night Hope invited us to dinner with her doctor husband and some other couples.

"Does Hope always flirt like that?" Beth asked me later.

I nodded.

"I guess she can have anyone she wants," Beth said. "She's stunning. No wonder you became shy and retiring."

But before we left Beth had connected with another side of Hope. I had told Hope that Beth wrote poetry and Hope had just started writing poems herself. When we left that night Hope gave Beth a sheaf of papers and Beth promised to critique and return these first efforts. Thus Beth became Hope's writing mentor as well as mine and they corresponded for some time.

Next on our itinerary was a visit to Aunt Carrie in Maryland and a stopover at Mary's on our way home. Aunt Carrie was in her middle seventies then and had been a widow for some time. I remember her standing in her front parlor by the rosewood piano when we came in, smiling, with her welcoming hand stretched out to Beth. It moved me profoundly to bring these two kind, gentle women together and to know that I was loved by both. Beth, the free thinker, a lapsed Episcopalian and student of the King James Bible, and Aunt Carrie, a devout Methodist, a daily reader of the Bible, and the main support of her small, rural church, bonded as if they had been born spiritual twins. Beth was enthralled by Aunt Carrie's account of her pilgrimage to the Holy Land. When I could claim Beth I took her on walks around the farm and showed her the stalls of the draft horses, long gone, and told her about sitting on Dan's back and feeling so safe and comforted astride his warm flanks. Whenever I visited Aunt Carrie wanted me to play something on the beautiful rosewood and even though I was badly out of practice I did my best with one of my easier pieces while she and Beth sat out on the veranda enjoying the evening breeze. "That was lovely, dear," Aunt Carrie called out. She always said that what I played was lovely, even when I knew it wasn't.

On our way to visit Mary I briefed Beth about Mary's anorexia and how her doctor —the man I had disliked so much —had told her to stay away from the Small Paradise because her family was the cause of her illness. She had been painfully homesick but visited there only once, bringing her little boy with her. While there he had burned his finger on the toaster and screamed as if he had been mortally wounded, and she had fled and never visited again.

Like Hope and Robert, Mary was living on yet another beautiful country estate. It was a Sunday afternoon when we arrived and Mary's family and friends were coming in from "beagling," a weekly event and passion of her husband. Half scholar, half sportsman he was a university professor and the owner of a pack of beagles. With permission from neighboring property owners the little hounds were let out to run over the countryside after rabbits, and people ran after the beagles. It was good aerobic exercise.

"I can't believe what I'm seeing," Beth said when I introduced her to Mary's husband. As Master of Hounds, he was wearing a smart green hunting coat, a black velvet cap, and white trousers. Beth's eyes went from him to the "whip," a man in similar attire, who was herding the panting beagles back to their kennel.

"Is what I'm seeing really happening?" she asked. Mary's husband beamed, taking this as a compliment. Then Mary joined us and I introduced her to Beth. Mary was immediately attracted to Beth and began talking with her as if she were continuing a conversation that had just been interrupted. She went on talking almost non-stop as the three of us wandered around the beautiful grounds. Wanting to give them privacy I lagged behind. Had Mary intuitively picked up on Beth's capacity for understanding and unconditional love? One of Mary's children had been killed in a tragic riding accident earlier in the year and from the bits of their conversation that I overheard, Mary was telling Beth about that terrible day.

Mary's response to Beth was strikingly different from her response to me. She had given me her customary "Hi, Sis" greeting when we arrived, showing neither pleasure nor displeasure at my being there. I had stayed in touch with her over the years, visiting her in her various homes as her family grew. I would be greeted pleasantly but never fondly, and felt sometimes that I might as well have been the family dog. Mary had been my friend when we were growing up, but after she married and left home with the warning about her toxic family, the Mary I knew and loved had disappeared. When we were driving away Beth commented on the casual way Mary had greeted me.

"And her children didn't greet you at all! They're so different from Robert's. His three seemed so happy you'd come."

Mary *had* been telling Beth about the death of her daughter. She had also told her about the death of my twin and how she had always been afraid that one of her children would die.

"She's adorable, of course," Beth went on. "One of a kind. I find her absolutely fascinating, but she seems frozen in time somehow. She's like a little girl in a woman's body —having all those babies, but afraid of being a woman. I'm sure she still loves you, but maybe you're just too painful a reminder of the past. And of course her children have picked up on how she feels. I know why you like to visit. Families are so powerful. But I don't think it's good for you, being tolerated but not a welcome member of her tribe. I don't think you should go so much."

The more I thought about it, I realized she was right.

As the months passed Beth kept after me on all fronts in her role as my mentor and personal trainer. Although my interest in finding a marriageable man was on hold as I enjoyed our closeness, she persisted with her introductions. "You never know," she said. "You have to keep your antennae out. You have to keep in practice." She also kept after me to produce the second story I had promised. When I finally finished it Beth mailed the stories to her friend. Two weeks later we were sitting at a restaurant in New York having lunch with Beth's friend and the agent.

It was thrilling to be told by the agent that she felt sure she could sell one of the stories and that she wanted to see more. Beth was elated and I was too, being in the heaven where I had longed to be years before, a published or almost published writer. After Carolyn Gordon's writing course ended I had been high for a while on the gratification that experience had given me, but had come to accept, not without some sadness, what she had made clear —that I was a talented writer, but a writer manqué. Now with the encouragement from this agent, I was soaring again on a new high. In my early years, praise for my writing had been food for the hungry and was still seductive, if not addictive. Hearing the agent's praise was like inhaling a cigarette after trying to break the habit and getting hooked again. But I had also been "hooked for life" in Mary Dailey's bedroom in a vocation I did not want but had come to love. Could I squeeze both into one life?

169

In this confused state of mind, I was unexpectedly offered a job by a friend of Beth's at a finishing school for American girls in Italy. Her friend owned the school and did some of the hiring, but the day to day operations were the responsibility of a full-time director. She was looking for a woman to be in charge of one of the residences and to be responsible for the physical and emotional health of the girls under her care. It would be a nine-month assignment starting the following fall, so there would be time before leaving to wind things down with my clients.

My professional work was going well and I was not especially attracted to the job she offered, but the fringe benefits were hard to resist: I would be living in a beautiful villa in Florence and could start learning Italian; I would have an all-expenses-paid trip to Europe with opportunity for travel at the end of the school year. And while the girls were in their classes I would have my mornings free for writing. Free of professional responsibilities I could once and for all put up or shut up about my writing. I wondered how Beth would feel about my going, but I might have known that the yea-sayer would be all for it.

"You've been moping around a lot lately and I think you need to shake yourself up. Think of all the writing you can do in those nine months. If I were free I'd fly like a bird!"

Her children had been asking for their own dog and they would be over-joyed to keep Salomé while I was away. But was I ready to leave Beth?

Just then I was seeing a little girl in play therapy who was being pushed by her mother to higher achievement in school. She was responding by get-ting bad report cards even though she was very smart. Sensing her need to regress for a while I held her in my lap in a series of sessions and let her drink chocolate milk out of a bottle. Over time her need for this diminished. Then one day she pushed the bottle aside and said, "Let's play pick-up-sticks!" Uncertain as I was about what lay ahead, I knew it was time for me to play my own game of pick-up-sticks. It was time to snip the invisible thread that had connected me to Beth ever since I cried at her table and we discovered that it was she who had the other key. But I knew how difficult it would be to snip that thread while Beth and I were still spending so much time together. I also knew that if I were ever to grow up and take charge of my life we would have to be apart, at least for a while.

Much as I adored Beth there was an exhilarating sense of freedom as I walked the decks of the Stockholm, breathing the fresh ocean air. Like an adolescent I was making the break from "home." Unlike an adolescent I was in most respects a mature and confident adult, so at this point in the adventure I was thoroughly enjoying the fringe benefits that were coming with my new job. I had a friend in Denmark I wanted to visit so I was sailing there, then going by train to Wolfsburg in Germany where I would pick up a Volkswagen Beetle I had bought before leaving home. I would drive down to Italy and the following June when the job ended, I would spend a month in Europe as a tourist, then sail home with my new Beetle in the hold. What lay between then and now in those nine months in Florence was the price I would be paying for the opportunity to travel and to have time to write.

I arrived at the school elated at having made the trip from Germany without mishap, but on reporting to the Director I was told that I would not have the job I had been hired for. I had expected to be in charge of one of the residences, but instead I would be living in the residence where the Director was in charge and serve as her secretary in the school's office. There had been a miscommunication with Beth's friend in the U.S. who had hired me. The Director had already hired someone else for the job I expected to have. In that job I had anticipated establishing a surrogate mother relationship with the girls under my care and of being able to make some use of my professional expertise. The prospect of spending nine months in an office doing clerical work was devastating. If Beth's friend had offered me the job I was about to start, I would never have taken it. As I feared, the most challenging assignment I was to have was calculating the girl's weekly laundry bills (one panty = 5 lire, etc.) and then becoming an unwelcome bill collector.

The Director was a good woman, cultured and intelligent and passionate about the course in iconography that she would be teaching the girls, and if she had been a warmer, more outgoing kind of person it might have made all the difference. But she was not these things. She was a widow of my parents' generation, formal and reserved, sharing nothing personal about herself and showing no interest in who or how I was. I was her employee and as such was treated courteously and correctly. Once again I found myself in a relationship with a mother figure who had control over my life but gave no evidence of pleasure in my existence.

My disappointment was to cast such a dark shadow over my first weeks at the school that it took me far too long to appreciate the beauty of the old Villa and of having a comfortable, spacious room with my own bath. There was a wobbly desk for me to write on —I wondered uneasily if it was a metaphor for failure —but I had barely settled into a work routine when the Director told me that I would be going to Venice with the girls and their art history professor to view the art treasures there. I would also be their chaperone on trips to other cities during the fall semester and would be taking some of the girls who were not going home for Christmas to Austria for two weeks of skiing. Although momentarily dismayed by this interruption to the challenge I had given myself to produce some good writing, I reasoned that there would be enough time to meet that challenge after the holidays and threw myself into enjoying what seemed more like another unexpected fringe benefit than work. But after these trips were over I was back at my wobbly desk in the mornings and on duty in the office in the afternoons and evening.

Ever since I arrived I had been pouring out my disappointments in letters to Beth, although she had recently received some cheerful postcards from my trips with the girls. But a few weeks after those trips ended I wrote her the following letter.

Dear Beth,

"Confine a forty-three-year old woman who is sensitive about her aging and romantic failures with twenty nubile females and picture a horde of freshly shaven young Italian males in pointed shoes baying at the Villa gates, and what do you expect to happen?"

Would you go on reading that story? I can't go on writing it because I am living it and the answer is that the woman goes into a depression. I'm afraid another has got me by the throat. I told you I had started a story I liked and that it had been moving pretty well, but now I can barely produce a page a day. I wish I hadn't given it the title, "Winter Landscape," for I fear it is descriptive of the cold, dark days that have moved into my life, both outside and in. As is usually the case, I didn't identify at first what was happening.

You couldn't have known when you wrote that this is a hard time for me to hear that the agent wasn't able to sell my story. You say she thinks it was too long for periodicals and that she's looking forward to my sending her some shorter ones, but all I can do now is drag myself from one day to the next. I'm sorry to be so gloomy. One good thing though. I have started taking Italian lessons with a Signorina de Rossi. She's slim, erect, very correct, but anxious and fluttery and gives off the impression of repressed passion. We work well together and it's a relief to be focusing on something so unambiguous instead of being in the no-man's-land of my floundering story.

In spite of my dark mood I try every morning to get something on the page, but usually end up doing everything else but work, like finally steadying the wobbly table, or doing a load of laundry in my bathroom sink and hanging it in my window to dry. I pace around my room like my red fox in the Central Park Zoo, trying to get my endorphins going, and when that fails I slump lethargically into my chair like the yak, without even the energy to chew my cud. I feel as trapped as those animals, not only by the job I dislike so much, but also by being caged in this building day after day when I long, as they longed, to be out roaming in the fields and forests. If this weren't enough, I'm also feeling hopelessly trapped by the writing assignment I have given myself. It won't move along, but I won't let myself abandon it.

After mornings like this I have lunch in the Villa's dining room with the students and staff, and I am often silent and remote and probably disliked as much by the students as I disliked my depressed supervisor when I was working with Mary Dailey. I spend my afternoon in the office, then am on call until bedtime when the Director takes her time off and usually goes out. The part of my job I dislike the most is on weekends when the girls are allowed to go out in the evening. When they are due in, I have to be at the entrance to the Villa, unlocking its heavy iron gates and checking them in, one by one, as they say their goodnights to their dates. I feel like a jailer, rattling my keys. Much, much love, dear Beth

In this way one dreary winter day followed another. I believe what finally rescued me from despair was beauty —the beauty of spring —for a shift in my mood seemed almost miraculous. It started one night in April when I was awakened by a song so beautiful that I knew it had to be a nightingale. The next morning my senses felt re-aroused as if from as long sleep. When I walked through the Villa's inner courtyard on my way to the dining room

I noticed its graceful proportions for the first time, and when I sat down beside the housekeeper and looked into her beautiful old face, it was as if I were seeing her for the first time. She had heard the nightingale too. In that one breakfast she and I became friends and my goodbye to her when I left was the most painful, for neither her English nor my Italian were fluent enough to nourish our connection in letters and I knew that I would never see her again.

When I got back to my room that morning I looked out the window at a scene I had looked at, unseeing, all these months and I wanted to grab a paintbrush. Stands of slender green cypresses, marking the gardens of prosperous villas, were descending the hill to the old city with its mosaic of terra cotta rooftops and the dome of its great cathedral. Instead I sat down at my no –longer-wobbly desk that had, as it turned out, foreshadowed failure, wanting to share with Beth the good news of what was happening to me. I wrote her about the nightingale and of my new friendship with the housekeeper:

You would love her, Beth. She is a retired portrait painter, probably in her eighties, a liberated old Florentine aristocrat with an engaging sense of humor. I was able to keep her laughing all through breakfast. She doesn't drive and rarely gets out, so on my next day off I'm going to drive us to some of her favorite old towns in Tuscany. When I came back to my room after breakfast and looked out my window at the gorgeous view I have been blind to all these months I saw a small farm tucked way down in the valley with a pair of white oxen plowing the land. I felt like crying it made me so homesick, bringing back images of Aunt Carrie's farm and of Eleanor plowing our fields at the Small Paradise. In case you are wondering if I am going to be bringing this new energy to my desk and try to make up for lost time, the answer is no. We can talk more about that when I get home. Instead I will go down every morning to the treasures in the old city and soak up all that beauty while there is still time. All my love.

Early one misty morning, the day after the school closed, I drove out of Florence, looking down from my car on that beautiful city in a last farewell. Then I climbed to the Apennines. After elbowing my way into the stream of cars that were speeding north on the Autostrada, I felt a mixture of relief and profound sadness. It wasn't just the pain of any parting —always hard for me —but a huge regret that I had been unable to deal more creatively with the situation I found myself in. But I hadn't just been trapped by a job I disliked. I had also been trapped by my own malady. .

It was the first time it had defeated me so totally. When I was depressed at home, except for seeing clients I could keep to myself, but from my job at the Villa there was no escape. It was painful to acknowledge that during those dark months I had been an extremely unlikable person to have around. After my mood changed and I became more outgoing and friendly even the Director had warmed up and consulted me about several of the girls she was worried about. So I was learning the painful lesson that a depressed person is not only feeling miserable but is also driving other people away, or worse, making them exasperated. "This has gone on long enough. Just pull yourself together." If only one could! I wanted to get as far away from this failed experience as I could and set my compass to the north of Scotland.

Dear Beth,

On my first morning here I rode out on a rented bicycle into this funny little treeless island and when I took my first breath of the intoxicatingly clean air and heard the cries of sea birds I vowed that as long as I have control of my life I will never again let myself be so painfully separated from the natural world. Unlike Italy with its chaos of polluting automobiles there is only one car on this island, so no incessant honking of horns. There is only the sound of the birds and the ever-present wind. The car belongs to a shy young agricultural agent from Glasgow. He is also staying in this croft and I think he's finally gotten over being afraid that this "older" American woman will try to "take advantage" of him. He's trying to help the impoverished crofters make better use of the island's resources —such as harvesting an overabundance of rabbits. He has taken me on his rounds and after supper we have been going out and walking in the long light-filled evenings.

Last night we walked across the island to the western cliffs and looked out across the Atlantic and I thought of America lying on the other side of that great expanse. Do you remember a sampler I showed you at the Small Paradise that was made by my great,

great, great grandmother? She had cross-stitched a poem on it and you and I were much taken by the line, "Long Island is my Nation." As I stood there I imagined the fish's tail of Long Island, my nation, reaching out to me and calling me home. The shy young man, seeing me tearful, took my hand and it was sweet strolling back together as the late light began to fade.

Will we know each other, you and I?

ƒ

REPRISE

Before I returned from Italy I had received a letter from a friend of Beth's and mine expressing concern about Beth. I knew that Beth had been taking a sculpture class and that she had found a congenial friend there. What I didn't know until the letter came was that they had often been seen lunching together and were, as my friend wrote, "three sheets to the wind." Beth wasn't looking well and she had put on a lot of weight.

There had been no hint of this in Beth's letters. I was afraid that she had finally lost control of her drinking and almost dreaded our reunion, but when we met it was a joyous moment with Beth and me in tears, Salomé leaping and crying with pleasure, and Beth's children standing by, watching in amusement. Beth had invited me to stay on for supper and after the excitement of the reunion was behind us we found some privacy on her back patio to talk.

Beth did *not* look well. Her face had the red flush of someone who drinks too much and she *had* gained a lot of weight, but I was relieved that she minced no words about herself. "I've gotten terribly fat," she said, "and I've gotten into bad habits drinking at lunch with a friend I met in the sculpture class. I never did that before. My doctor says I have to lose weight and I know I have to cut back on the drinking, but you were so depressed over there I didn't want you to have to hear about my woes. Eddie's lost his job and it's been horrible having him home. I decided to take a part time job to help tide us over and at least that gets me out. That's why I couldn't meet you at the boat. Eddie's still drinking, of course, and on top of all this Big Daddy's got Alzheimer's. Tillie's been amazing. I feel so weak, such a disappointment to her. But you're back and you're safe and you look wonderful. We've all loved having Salomé. I've promised the children we'll get a dog of our own now."

It had all poured out as if she hadn't had a real heart to heart with anyone since I left. They couldn't afford Dr. Carter after Eddie lost his job and they hadn't gone back, but she knew they needed to. I felt so selfish listening to her. Here I was just back from vacationing all over Europe. What troubles did I have compared to hers?

"I loved your letters," she said, "especially that one from the little island. Your whole experience over there was such a mixture of wonderful and awful. I was so envious of your being in England. You wrote that you were going to talk with me about your writing when you got home. Is this a good time?"

"As good as any. I thought a lot about it on the boat coming back. I don't think I'll ever know if not being able to write makes me depressed or if it's the other way around, but in a way I'm relieved that I'm going to be able to let it go. I think maybe when I went over there I was in a kind of mid-life crisis, allowing my old dreams of glory to take me over again. I can't escape the fact that I'm not young anymore. It was painful to imagine how those ripe young girls must have been looking at me."

"Oh, sweetheart! I'm sure they thought you were lovely."

"No, I *wasn't*. Believe me. I've been wondering why I got so carried away with the writing fantasy and I think it had a lot to do with wanting a different life, being free to circulate more and meet different, exciting people. I truly love my work, but I hate spending so much time cooped up inside doing the same thing over and over. Of course every client you have is different and I should be grateful that I'm good at the work and that it supports me, but I guess a part of me will always be restless."

"Are you sure about this?" Beth asked. "Are you absolutely sure about letting it go?"

"Very sure," I said. "And by the way I've been wanting to ask you if you think part of your giving me so much encouragement was because *you* wanted to go over there and have time for *your* writing. Your psychiatrist told you that you were attracted to that poet of yours because you wanted to be living her kind of life. You said you envied me being in England."

Beth took a long time to answer. "It's very likely," she said finally. "I hadn't thought of that. I hope my encouraging you wasn't bad for you."

"No. Don't worry about that. I had to go. I was pursuing my own dream, and I had some growing up to do."

After settling back into my old routine I didn't see as much of Beth for I was no longer as needy. Although Eddie had finally found a job, Beth was afraid to give up hers and had little free time. She was also more occupied with her children's needs now that they were getting older. I was busy trying to build up a private practice in addition to my part-time work at the clinic. When I set off for Italy I had been nourishing a dream of becoming a published writer. Having failed with the writing I might have resented getting back into my old therapy harness, but it was comforting to feel welcomed and valued by my old colleagues and to reconnect with my old competence. I was grateful to my clients for being there and for needing me. Sitting in a private space with someone who is looking to you for relief will pull you out of yourself from even the darkest of places. Once again I found myself reaching into my little black bag for remedies that I hoped might be helpful, and it was good to be able to lose myself in this way.

While returning to my work had been healing for me, returning to my apartment had made me painfully aware that I was still living the solitary life. I went away as often as I could, and on one of my weekend visits to Long Island, Hope introduced me to a man she thought I would like. I did like him and we formed an immediate bond in our distress about what was happening to Long Island. Ever since World War II acres and acres of fertile farmland had been disappearing under suburban sprawl and high-rise commercial buildings. This man had grown up on the island and was managing the estate of a wealthy businessman. He was thinking of getting property of his own while it was still available and had been looking further out on the island where there was still some good open land. Maybe I would like to go out there with him some time.

When I had looked out across the Atlantic from the Outer Hebrides and imagined Long Island lying over there beckoning to me, I knew that sometime I would have to live there again. Now I had met a man who was as deeply connected to this place as I was. Soon I was driving over every weekend and having the kind of dates I most enjoyed —exploring unfamiliar regions of the island, having long walks along its shores and looking for interesting wildlife. One moonlit night he introduced me to the remarkable mating ritual of the woodcock, and I remembered a night long past when a young man and woman traveled by moonlight down a river to the sea and encountered the mating frenzy of horseshoe crabs. I had persuaded myself then that I had all the time in the world to be particular about which young crab I would chose, but how much longer could I go on wasting what Beth had called my "lovely young years"?

"What do you two talk about?" Beth wanted to know. She had met him the night before when I had come by to pick up Salomé.

In that ritual of serious dating he and I had driven down to Maryland to meet his parents and then over to Aunt Carrie's. He had already met Robert and his family and I had walked with him all over the Small Paradise.

"We talk about what we're doing," I said to Beth. "What we're seeing. What we want to do next. Things like that."

"But when you're driving in the car on a long trip like this? Do you talk about ideas? What else is he interested in besides the out of doors? Do you go to movies? Does he read?"

"Of course he reads! Do you think he's a moron just because he didn't go to college? I didn't go either, remember? It's very obvious that you don't like him."

"He doesn't happen to be my type," Beth said, "but I'm not the one going out with him. I don't have all that outdoor Long Island connection you have. Do you know why he's never married?"

"No. He doesn't talk much about himself. We've obviously both been hung up about making a commitment."

Beth shook her head. "Is he a good lover?"

"Beth! Lay off, damn it!" I rarely got annoyed with her.

"Well, is he?"

"That part's okay! It's fine!"

But Beth wouldn't lay off. "Are you in love with him?" she asked. I was silent. "Well, are you?"

"Do I have to be? Passion doesn't last, remember? I've learned that from you."

"It doesn't, but it's handy to start out with. I guess what I really want to know is whether you love this man and whether you like him. That's what you need for the long haul. Does he love you?"

"Not wildly. Maybe I'm missing that."

"For God's sake, sweetheart! Be careful! Don't marry him just because you're running out of time and want a baby!"

Then suddenly it was all over. I had met someone else, re-met someone else and fallen in love, re-fallen in love. It was an amazing twist of the plot.

It happened in the supermarket. I was on my way home from my last appointment, pushing my cart around when I heard, "Fair*lie!*" Only one person I knew put the accent that way on the last syllable. Then I saw Leo, pushing *his* cart. It had to be Leo. Was he wearing the same black beret after all these years? The same black raincoat? We greeted ecstatically. I knew he had divorced the girl he had married after we broke up, leaving her with a son to raise, and that he had married one of his students at the college where he had gone to teach and had three more children with her. What I did not know was that he had moved his family to Princeton after his retirement for a two-year teaching appointment just as I was taking off for Italy. He would be leaving in a few months. Leo told me that his wife was a busy doctoral student at the University and that he was shopping for supper. He had to get back to the children, but he was longing to see me and we made a date for lunch later in the week.

When we met at the restaurant he looked shaken. He had been leaving a store on his way over and a young man who was coming in had pushed him aside and said, "Get out of my way, old man!"

'Oh, Leo'" I said, "that was horrible." I put my hand on his to convey my concern and when he clasped mine in return I was surprised at the feelings our touching aroused in me. He was still an extremely attractive man. Although he was seventy-one now, he did not seem that much older than the forty-five-year-old man whose age had been such an obstacle for me in those distant years. I remembered counting on my fingers how old he would be when I was thirty…forty…fifty …wondering if I would still want to be with him when he was old. His laugh, his sparkle, his intensity were all still there. He was still alert and curious, still the wonderful company he had always been when things were going well between us. His hair had more gray and he was a bit stooped, but otherwise he seemed unchanged.

Time flew as we shared what had been happening in our lives in the intervening years. Then, as lunch was ending, he mentioned almost casually that his wife was leaving him. She had fallen in love with another student and they planned to marry at the end of the academic year. She was distracted and absent a great deal and he was doing his best to keep things stable for the children. His son Émile, who had just turned twelve, was having emotional problems and not doing well in school. The divorce was messy but proceeding, and his finances would be tight since his wife would need a good part of his retirement for child support. She and her new husband would be going abroad and taking the girls with them, and Leo and Émile were returning to the community in New England where they had been living. Émile could go back to his old school where he had been happy and he would be company for Leo.

"Darling," Leo said. "You're still so beautiful. You haven't changed at all. I can't believe you've never married. I want you to come up and visit us as soon as we get settled."

But he needed me to know that Émile was not an easy child. He had been seeing a therapist up there to whom he was very attached and he would be seeing her again when they got back. Leo was sure his son would settle down when all this divorce business was over. Émile and his mother had never gotten along.

That night I called my old friend Martha to tell her about my encounter with Leo. When I was last with her hiking in the mountains we had talked about Leo, reminiscing about the old days and how appealing he was. She was riveted by my news and we speculated about Leo's divorces and why he was always attracted to young women. What would he go for next, we wondered, a nymphet?

Leo kept calling, wanting to see me again. It was hard to find time, but we were able to manage lunch now and then and quickly fell back into our old, easy intimacy. I had forgotten how much I enjoyed his lovely sense of humor and his delight in the ridiculous. Beth was fascinated by these developments and eager to meet him. She asked me to bring him over some night to have supper with her and Eddie. As I had anticipated, she and Leo made an instant connection. Later that night she called me.

"Darling!" she said. "This one *is* my type! He's absolutely charming. I can see the whole thing now. Of course you were smitten back then, but he is a kind of rascal, isn't he? Eddie didn't like him at all, but I wouldn't have expected him to. Has he proposed to you again?"

"No, but he's asked me to come up and visit him after he leaves."

"He will, of course. He'd be a fool not to. Do you want it?"

"I don't know."

"I don't know either. I don't know what to think about it. You looked so lovely tonight. So happy."

Actually, my mind had been racing with the possibility of this thing. Even if I only had ten good years with him they could be wonderful years. I had finally begun to be more realistic about not being able to conceive at my age, but if we got right to it, maybe I'd be able to have a child after all. In any case I could be a mother to Émile and make his girls welcome when they visited. I decided to have a small cocktail party before he left to run him past some of my other friends.

"He was a great hit with the ladies," Beth reported the next morning. "Of course the idea of your connecting with him again is so romantic. But none of the husbands liked him. I guess he's just too different —all that hair and those tacky clothes. They think he just wants you up there to take care of the little boy."

So had Leo's grade been a pass or a fail? In the end it didn't matter, for I was tuning out what I didn't want to hear.

In a last meeting over dinner Leo put his hand over mine and made a formal proposal of marriage.

"It's going to turn my life upside down," I said, "but I think I want to do it."

"Oh, my darling," Leo said. He leaned across the table and kissed me. "You'll never regret it. I want so much to make you happy."

It sounded like dialogue from an old movie, but I'm sure that he meant it. It occurred to me as we sat there that I had been in this same restaurant with my father many times, often sitting at this very table. This juxtaposition felt like the ending of a short story. I recalled the strain of my first dinners with Pa, trying to find some connection with this totally self-absorbed man who had no idea who I was or gave any indication of caring, and I wondered what he would think if he were in some realm where he could be observing Leo and me. Would he still be outraged by what I was preparing to do? But he had no power now. He and my mother were dead and no longer had a home I could be banished from. I was sure that my siblings would welcome Leo and would be glad that their restless sister had finally found some happiness.

The next day I phoned Beth at work and asked her to meet me for lunch.

"What's up?" she asked when we sat down.

"Leo proposed last night and I told him I would."

"Oh, my God!" Beth said. She went silent.

"What are you thinking?" I asked.

"I've often imagined a scene when you tell me you've found a wonderful man you want to marry and I throw my arms around you and hug you, and now I don't know what to say. Maybe it's the mother in me, but I just can't not worry about how it will work out for you. You're taking on so much. But he's an enormously appealing person. I can understand why you want it."

"I was such a child when I was with him before. He makes me feel like a woman now, the woman I've always wanted to be."

"And now Leo's the child," Beth said. "You've always wanted one."

"Beth, please!"

"Can he still do it?"

"Do what?"

"Good God! Don't you want some good sex after all these years? Haven't you two been sleeping together?"

"No, we haven't."

"I can't believe this. Are you going to wait for your wedding night like a young virgin? Dorothy would love that! What one will this be for Leo? His fifth?"

"It's not as if we don't already know each other that way."

Beth sighed. "There are so many questions. You said he won't have much money so you'll have to get a job up there."

"But it's so close to what I've dreamed of. Maybe we can find a farm. It would be wonderful for the children. I could have a huge garden. Raise our own food. Bake bread."

"While you're working somewhere? And how are you two going to be able to buy a farm?"

"Why are you trying to spoil it?"

"Because I love you. Shouldn't you have waited to see what it's like up there? And what about the boy? Do you like him?"

"I've just met him once. He looked right through me as if I didn't exist. It's going to take time. He'll be seeing a therapist up there when he goes back."

Beth shook her head. "This just amazes me. I've been trying all this time to get you to live more dangerously and to say yes once in a while and now you're way out ahead of me and I'm trying to rein you in. Couldn't you have just said, 'maybe' or 'I don't know?'"

He was renting a small gray house in the village near his old campus. A garden at the back, now a jungle of perennials and weeds, had clearly at one time been lovingly tended. Perhaps an old woman had recently died. He was welcoming, overjoyed, bear-hugging. Then he took me through the house. The woodwork was dark and the rooms were papered in old-fashioned florals, faded now and in some places beginning to peel. Leo's old Steinway was already in place in his living room, bearing the huge, familiar bust of Beethoven's head. Looking into that frowning face took me back to the apartment in New York where I had first encountered it and had been so happy and so anxious and so anguished. I had fled from music then, but had come back to it and was thinking of finding a singing teacher at the college. It was too late for piano, but Leo and I could do Lieder together.

We carried my things up to the spare room, going past Émile's closed door. Leo knocked on our way down, but Émile did not open it and did not come out the whole time I was there. Just before supper Leo went up again and I heard entreaties, exchanges of anger and the sound of objects being thrown. Presently, a defeated, dejected old man walked down and joined me at a table that had been set for three.

But Leo and I had enjoyed preparing our meal together. He loved food and good wine, and perhaps his favorite time of day was happy hour, a coming together after the day's work and relaxing with a cocktail –nibbling, talking, laughing. He was a cozy, domestic man, almost always cheerful except for those fortunately rare times when something made him enraged, and those other times when things were not going his way and he put on a long face. He apologized for Émile's behavior, but I told him it was understandable that Émile could be wary of someone he did not yet know and resentful of my intrusion into their lives. I urged Leo to let it work itself out. Émile would make a move when he was ready. But privately I was disappointed. I wondered how I would feel if I were getting different signals from Émile, shy glances and questioning looks that might be saying, "Have you got anything for me or is it all just for him?"

After we had eaten Leo took a plate of food up to Émile and I started cleaning up the kitchen. When he came down he gave me another bear hug. "It's so lovely having you here, my dearest. As soon as the divorce comes through we can get married and you can stay."

When he spoke of our getting married I thought of my sisters' weddings and how I had once dreamed of having a beautiful one of my own in that little country church where Ma and Pa and the little boys were buried, but I did not want that kind of wedding now. Getting married seemed almost redundant. In a way we were already like a married couple who have been weaving in and out of each other for decades. Soon we would be weaving our way upstairs to a familiar and expected intimacy. There would be no Mendelssohn and bridesmaids and Robert (in Pa's absence) giving me away, and there would be no wedding night for me. That dream of giving my virginal self to a man I would vow to love till death did us part had long since drawn its last breath.

A while later Leo went upstairs to get Émile ready for the night, leaving me with an album of old photographs of his years with Yvette and of the old music school days. There were even some pictures of a shy me that he had taken one day when we visited the Cloisters. I was aware of busyness upstairs, of doors opening and closing, but when an hour had gone by and he still had not come down I decided to go up to my room and get ready for bed and wait for him to join me. It must have been several hours later after I had fallen asleep that he finally climbed in beside me in the narrow single bed.

"What have you two been doing?" I asked sleepily. "I gave up waiting for you."

"I'm so sorry, my darling. I lay down with him and I guess I fell asleep. We always go to bed early. But I shouldn't stay here too long. I don't want him to wake up and be upset when he finds I'm not there."

"Do you two usually sleep together?" I asked, wide awake now.

"Yes, we do. Ever since his mother moved out of our bed he's been sleeping with me. He crawled in one night and said he didn't want me to be lonely. He's very affectionate. I like having him with me."

It had never occurred to me that Leo and I would not be sleeping together.

"How is this all going to work out when we get married?" I asked.

"Oh, don't worry about that. He'll get used to having you here."

He started to fondle me. When he had first joined me in bed my feelings for him had been aroused and then they had gone into a holding pattern while I was taking in this new information. I did not know what to do with it. But when he began kissing me I let myself respond. I can worry about all this tomorrow, I thought, and then I heard Leo say, "This little thing of mine isn't good for much anymore, but I can still make *you* feel good. Let me go down there."

"No, Leo. I don't want that. How long has this been?"

"Oh, let's not talk about that now. I want to make *you* happy. I'm still good for that."

"No, Leo."

He started to protest and then we heard Émile call out, "Dad?"

Leo jumped up like a guilty child. "Damn it!" he said. "I was afraid this would happen."

He didn't even say goodnight as he hurried across the hall to Émile's room.

It was a long time before I could fall back to sleep. I ran the scene over and over in my mind. Why was Beth always right? I both loved her and hated her for it, but she was never one to say I told you so. I knew she would be loving and compassionate about my devastating disappointment, for it was devastating.

"Don't you want some good sex after all these years?" she had asked me when I told her I had agreed to marry Leo. And I did. I really had re-fallen in love with Leo and I meant what I had told her about loving the feeling of being a real woman with him now, no longer a frightened little girl. But just how important *was* sex in the whole scheme of things? He would gratify me and like doing that, but did I want this to be all we had? It might be different if we had had a long and vigorous history together, had raised our children, and then he had subsided and wanted to do this for me. I could see us sailing this way into the sunset across Golden Pond. But I was still young and I did want more, finally, tardily.

I had never told Beth my secret hope that I would become pregnant after I married Leo. I could hear her explode: "Good God! An old man to look out for, a disturbed little boy, working full time, and then a baby? Dearest, dearest, dearest, what am I going to do with you?"

Having to abandon that hope now was the reason my disappointment was so devastating. I could still be sexually active with someone else for years to come, but on my next birthday I would be forty-five and I knew now that like Aunt Carrie I would never have a child.

"Oh, Dorothy!" she cried out. "Can't I have one of yours?"

But in a way she had had one of Dorothy's, and with a family of her own she might never have been able to give so much of her loving self to me.

How ironic this thing was. I remembered that night in the dawn of my relationship with Leo when I was lying between him and his beautiful wife and how frightened I had been of his potent organ, and later, when he and I were a couple, how I had clung to my virginity because I needed so desperately to be my mother's good child and to have her love. I cried quietly for a while in that narrow single bed before finally falling asleep.

When I woke the next morning with the sun moving through the bare shade-less, curtainless window and across my bed, I lay there, letting the bits and pieces of this unfolding drama come back into consciousness. My dream of what it would be like up here with Leo had been shattered. Was what was left enough? If I decided to honor my commitment to him what would my life be up here? What would I have? No children of my own, an impotent husband, rocky finances, a disturbed stepchild and a disturbing, puzzling relationship between him and his father, but also, a charming, accomplished, cozy, affectionate and intellectually stimulating companion.

What Leo and Émile *both* needed, I now realized, as Beth's friends had feared, was a mother, a mistress of this house, a resident therapist, and a breadwinner. I could be all these things. Émile would be a challenge, but he would probably come around in time, especially if I made his father happy so that he wouldn't need Émile so much. But how irrevocably were they entwined?

The assignment was formidable. I had grave doubts about taking it on but found myself cruelly torn, knowing what these two needed and that I was unencumbered and a perfect fit for the part. I knew, too, what I would have to give up. I did not want to go back to a full-time job, but I would have to until I could get licensed and professionally known and could build up a private practice. We would of course have to go on living in this dreary little house and I would have to give up my dream of buying a farm and living day by day with the cycles and rhythms of the natural world. Leo was an urban man and did not share this passion of mine, thus my life with these two would be mostly an indoor life, moving back and forth between an office somewhere and this homely interior with a few moments snatched now and then to tend the needy little garden. Perhaps, as Beth had warned me, I *had* become too set in my ways to make this massive adjustment. Perhaps other things I had come to hold dear had become too precious for me to part with.

"If I truly loved this man," I told myself, echoing Beth, "I would want to make sacrifices. I would want more than anything to make him and his little boy happy. I would not be lying here paralyzed with indecision, but getting up, throwing on my clothes and hurrying down where kitchen sounds were telling me that he had started our breakfast. He would be standing in front of the stove in his apron not hearing me coming, and I would tiptoe up behind him, put my arms around him and lean my head against his stooped and weary old back.

But I still could not move.

I had wanted a man so different from my father and once thought those many, many years ago that I had found him in Leo. Now I realized that I had again been seduced by his charm, his warmth, his attentiveness and his coziness, but that underneath those appealing characteristics was hidden another, self-gratifying man. Leo had this amazing way of making me feel that I was his one-and-only, but I knew that I was as easily replaceable as I had been before. What made this different and why I could not hard-heartedly walk away from it was that Leo was older now and beginning to be spent, and that replacements for me would not be lining up outside his door.

I had to get up, but I still did not know what I was going to do. It would just have to play itself out like a novel that was writing itself.

I left him happy, assuming that all we were waiting for was his divorce. I let him enjoy my being there, helped him unpack his books that were still in cartons, and concealed the anxiety that was gnawing like a rat at my insides. It had never occurred to me to tell him that I was running scared and to ask him to be patient while I sorted it out. As before, his response, depending on whether it was kind or harsh, might have tipped the balance of my conflict, but we had never had that kind of openness. If I had told him when he re-proposed that I did not know, as Beth had suggested, it would have been painful for him to have my ultimate answer be no, but fair in the game of love. Now he was riding so high that I did not have the courage to tell him I was having serious doubts. So I temporized throughout the rest of my visit. I let him take me out to dinner and show me off, and at bedtime turned in early, pleading the threadbare excuse of fatigue.

"If it was just the sex," Beth said after I came home, "and you wanted the rest of it, you could find a lover up there."

Even though I was in such an upset state I had to laugh. The idea tickled me that Beth thought such an emotionally retarded romantic could make the leap into this sophisticated arrangement.

"Dorothy wouldn't like that," I said.

Beth laughed. "What changed your mind, do you think? You were so sure it was what you wanted when you went up. It has to be something more than the sex." She got up and came back with two glasses of ginger ale. "I'm really trying," she said. "It's easier not to want it when you're here. So why do you think you changed your mind?"

"I honestly don't know. I know what I like about it and what I don't, but it's not just that the bad outweighs the good. It goes deeper in some way. The morning after that awful first night I remember standing with my hand on the doorknob, knowing he was waiting for me to come down and tell him how happy I was we were going to be together, and I could feel two firm hands gripping my arms from behind, holding me back. I don't know whose hands they were. They weren't my parents. They could almost have been yours, but I think you see more possibilities in this thing than I do. I think they had to be mine, coming from some deep fear of being trapped without love. But Leo's the most demonstrative person I've ever known except you."

"Being demonstrative and being loving aren't necessarily the same thing. You have to trust what you feel."

"Maybe the love I'd be trapped without is my own, my own for the other person. Maybe I'm not capable of loving anyone enough. Ma always made me feel I was cold and heartless."

"Now don't start getting into that garbage! You know it isn't true. You'd have be a saint to want to take all that on with an impotent husband. When are you going back? You still have the ordeal of telling him."

"I told him I'd come up next weekend."

"I'll be praying for you," she said.

"And by the way, Salomé didn't eat her supper tonight, and she left some yesterday. She hasn't been her old self. If she doesn't pick up maybe you should take her to the vet before you leave."

To make what lay ahead more difficult I was going to have to say an anguished goodbye to Salomé before I left and would be alone when I came back. She had been on a special diet for a kidney problem and when I took her to the vet he said that her kidneys were finally giving out and that she would become more and more miserable. The sooner I could face it, the better it would be for her. I knew he was right but was unprepared for the depth of my grief. She had been my family for almost ten years, always cheerful, always glad to see me. She rescued me from loneliness after breaking up with Natalie. I had missed her in Italy but knew that she was happy with Beth and the children, maybe happier than with me when she had to spend so much time alone.

Knowing on that last day that everything was our last made it harder to bear —our last morning greeting with her tail thumping on the floor, our last walk together, her last lunge at a passing squirrel, and her last eagerness to get into my car for that fateful trip. Beth came with us and the vet was able to administer the meds in the car. We brought her back to Beth's house and she helped me dig a grave in a far corner of their yard. When we had finished burying her Beth said a prayer, asking that Salomé run freely and forever in animal heaven, never be hungry and without shelter, and always find a clear, cool stream where she could drink.

When I walked into Leo's house for the second time I found him in the front hall in his apron vacuuming the rug with the long, narrow crevice attachment. Did he not know that there were others? He turned off the machine and stood with the hose in his hand. "I've turned into an old woman," he said, giggling.

We embraced. This was the kind of moment that made him so lovable and my conflict so painful. His androgyny had always been a big part of his appeal. I could hear Beth saying, "So, you'd have ended up in a same sex relationship after all!"

Then a door opened upstairs and a shoe was thrown down into the hall. A second followed and I had to duck to avoid being hit.

"Émile!" Leo screamed. He flung down the hose and hobbled up the stairs as fast as his old legs would carry him. When he reached the top a door slammed, was opened, slammed again. Voices and fury rose and fell, the door opened, closed again, and Leo came down. We went into the kitchen and sat down at the table. Leo put his head in his hands.

If I had still been planning to move up with them, I would have seen what just happened as progress. I would have seen the thrown objects as a communication, not necessarily saying, "Get out of here," but "Take notice of me. I'm here too. I'm readier now for something." I would have replied to his communication, perhaps by bringing him his supper if he was still refusing to come down. I might have remarked on something in his room that interested me, but asked no questions. I felt sure that with time the resident therapist could have done it and done it well, and again this made my conflict more painful. I had so much to give these two.

"You aren't going to want to come up now with Émile behaving like this," Leo said, putting on the long face. "He's just ruining it."

How easy it would have been to jump on that escape, for I was dreading his rage and the scorn and anger of other people in his life when they learned that I had changed my mind and was not going to undertake the rescue. Leo, of course, had told everyone that we were to be married.

"At least he opened the door this time," I said.

No time is the right time to knowingly inflict pain, and I had kept putting it off until shortly before I had to leave. We had another congenial visit, shopping at the market, walking around his old campus and taking our drinks at happy hour out into the abandoned garden. He had finally found a neighbor's boy to cut the grass. We were in the kitchen again, he snacking on a yogurt and I fixing a sandwich to take on my trip. When was I coming back, he wanted to know. When I hesitated, he snapped, "You aren't going to be moving up with me, are you?"

"No, I'm not."

He flung down his spoon and exploded out of his chair, tipping it over and knocking the yogurt carton on the floor. "This will happen to you someday!" he screamed. "You belong in a nunnery! Get out of my house!" He stormed out of the kitchen, then stormed back in.

"You want a younger man, don't you?"

"Yes, I do."

"I would have given you that."

I got a paper towel and started wiping the yogurt off the floor.

"Why wouldn't that work?" He picked up the fallen chair and dropped into it.

"I shouldn't have given you hope in the first place," I said, "but it was so extraordinary our running into each other that way. And then you worked your old magic on me. I didn't know until I came up last week that I can't do it. It isn't Émile. It's me. I'm not even sure what it is that holds me back. I probably do belong in a nunnery."

I began to cry and went back to making the sandwich, throwing it together, wrapping it up, putting it in a paper bag. Then I went over to him and crawled into his lap and put my head on his shoulder.

"I'm sorry," I sobbed. "I'm so terribly sorry."

"I knew you'd back out," he said. His arms were limp.

"Please don't punish me. Don't make it any harder for me than it already is."

I stayed in his lap a while longer and he remained motionless.

"Well," I said, getting up. "It's a long trip. I should be going. Would you like me to visit again? We always have good times together. I just can't marry you."

"I don't care what you do."

"I can't believe I've done this again, saying yes and then saying no. We're playing the very same scene."

"We're what? I don't know what you mean."

"Never mind. It's not important. I should be leaving now. Do you want me to come up again?"

"You can do whatever you want. What I want never seems to matter, does it?"

"I wouldn't say that's altogether true." I put my hand on his shoulder. "I'll come back just as soon as I can."

Beth was sweet when I returned, kinder to me than I was to myself. She was mostly silent, letting me crash. She held me tightly.

"You should probably think about getting a puppy one of these days," she said. "I'll go with you when you're ready."

I had been home for several weeks when Martha called. She had stopped on her way down from her summer in the mountains to visit a friend who worked at the college where Leo taught. Her friend told her that Leo was back and was seen with an attractive blond woman. "Was that you?" she asked. "I thought it had to be. I was worried about you getting involved again." She had called Leo and he invited her for lunch. To her amazement he asked her to marry him. Although they had been in touch when she sent him her compositions for a critique, she had not seen him in years. She told Leo that she was not interested in marrying anyone at this point and was quite content with her children and grandchildren and her music. Leo told her nothing about our aborted plans and before my dream collapsed I had not let Martha know about them either. I had not wanted to hear her cautionary advice, but now I was relieved to be able to pour out the whole saga to her, even telling her about my crazy pregnancy fantasy. I found her far from reproachful.

"I know just why you wanted to do it," she said. "And I certainly can understand the child thing. After all I've had five of my own. And he can be so seductive. But I'm awfully glad you didn't. His little boy sounds like quite a handful."

After I had given myself time to settle back into my single life, I decided to call Leo and invite myself up for a visit. I knew that he had to be lonely, and I missed him. His proposal to Martha had not upset me —I saw it as the desperate flailing of a drowning man —but I was touched by the sadness of his not knowing that he was no longer irresistible. He was cool at first, still punishing me a bit, but he agreed to my coming up the following weekend.

While we were both cautious at first, we quickly fell into a pattern of easy and congenial asexual cohabitation. During the following year I went up to see him as often as I could. Even though Leo and I were not married, we *were* married in a way and I could enjoy being with him without my morbid fear of entrapment.

For a while his household was functioning fairly smoothly. Émile was doing well in school and having regular visits with his therapist. Leo had been asked to be the director of a community chorus and he was occupied with preparing them for their concert. I went to rehearsals when I was there, and as I re-experienced his impeccable musicianship I remembered how thrilling it had been when I was a young student to be preparing beautiful choral works under his direction and performing them for New York audiences. I had forgotten how skillful he was in shaping a group of amateur voices into a single sensitive instrument and pulling out of us such a moving reading of whatever work we were preparing.

The concert went well and Leo was elated, but in the months that followed there was a steady decline from that high, with his household becoming increasingly disorganized. Émile had been growing more and more defiant towards his father. Leo was becoming a weaker, more incompetent parent, swinging from enraged outbursts to helpless despair. He talked occasionally with Émile's therapist but had no counselor of his own to help deal with Émile's growing independence. I tried to fill that role, tried coaching him not to rise to Émile's bait, but when I was absent tensions built alarmingly. Once in a fit of anger Émile smashed all the glasses in the kitchen cabinet. I was sufficiently troubled by these developments to telephone his therapist and Leo's son who lived nearby with his fiancée, and found them equally concerned. They had been trying without success to find a live-in housekeeper. I offered to take some vacation time so that I could make a longer visit and try to settle things down a bit until a housekeeper could be found. At least I could set the house to rights and diffuse the tension between the two antagonists. For some time Émile had been leaving his door open when I was there and coming to meals. He still would not make eye contact and rarely spoke in my presence, but I sensed that he was grateful for a calming presence in the house.

Throwing myself into the role of mistress of the house, a role I had always seen myself in before I slid into a professional career I did not want, I straightened, cleaned, did loads of piled-up laundry. Leo and I cooked the meals. He and I shopped daily at the market and he loved that outing. We always had to be sure that we had treats for the "happy hour" that he loved. One day I had a naughty image of him: I was pushing the cart and Leo was sitting in the child seat reaching out his child's arm for the Camembert and anchovies that were his favorites.

In the afternoons when he liked to take long naps, I recharged my batteries weeding the overgrown garden. One evening he persuaded me to try singing some Schumann songs. In making this lovely music together he and I experienced a union that was perhaps more deeply satisfying than the one that had eluded us upstairs in this house many months before. Music had, after all, been where it all began.

Leo always helped me clean up the kitchen after supper. Then he would go to bed with Émile, leaving me with one of the novels I had brought which usually lay open on my lap unread while my mind wandered. Many years before, when I looked through the window of that house in Princeton on a snowy evening before Christmas and saw a mother and a boy and a girl and their cat, I had wanted to be that mother's little girl. In time I had found a mother in Beth, but I had also wanted to be the mother of that little girl and her brother. If I looked at myself now through the window of a small gray house in New England I would see a mother sitting with a book in her lap, dozing off, weary from the ceaseless activities of her day. Her two children were upstairs, fast asleep.

On the night before I left after this longer visit, Leo and I went out to dinner. He usually loved going out, but now he was gloomy, giving me the long face treatment that I knew was punishment for my leaving the next day. He wanted to know why I couldn't stay longer. I explained that I had started working part-time for a Catholic Counseling Service and needed to get back to that commitment. His face clouded. He hadn't known that I had become a Catholic. I told him I hadn't and that the Counseling Service often hired non-Catholics to do counseling, and that seemed to satisfy him. Leo carried little cash, paying for most everything by check, and when it came time for him to pay for our dinner he took out his checkbook and then looked bewildered. "I don't know what I'm supposed to do," he said. I filled in the check for him and he was able to sign it. He did not seem particularly upset by this lapse, but I was. I had learned a great deal about dementia from Ma. As we walked out of the restaurant he said again, shaking his head, "I never thought you would become a Catholic." I told him again that I hadn't. I kept wondering why he was so upset about this until I remembered that the students in music school had gossiped about his having to marry a Catholic girl before he came to America. Remarkably, he and I had never talked about his family and his life before he came to America. He managed to change the subject whenever I tried to bring it up.

When I came into the kitchen the next morning there was no greeting. No smiling face, no bear hug, no breakfast on the table. His face was the longest and darkest I had ever seen it.

"You have brought evil into this house," he said, speaking quietly, ominously, "and everyone is throwing me out." I did not know what he meant but learned later that he had not been reappointed as director of the chorus. Then he accused me of having brought a Catholic priest up to my room the night before and having sex with him. I told him that was ridiculous.

"Yes, you did," he said. "You did. I saw you." He glared at me threateningly and I was afraid he was about to strike me.

"And when I went into the bathroom this morning he came out of the toilet and smiled at me. I flushed him down." Then he burst out laughing at the absurdity of what he had just said.

That awful threatening moment was behind us, but as we went on to make breakfast together I was filled with apprehension. He's really losing it, I thought, first the check, and now this. I had been planning to start out after breakfast but decided I should not leave without letting people know what had happened. Émile had already gone to school, but somebody should be looking in on Leo after he got home. I made an excuse about needing to run an errand and stopped at his son's apartment. He had left for work, but his fiancée was there. I explained what had happened. She said they would check in frequently until they could move over to the house and that they would stay there until Émile's mother returned from abroad and Émile could join her. She would put in a call to Émile's therapist as soon as I left. We agreed that it would probably not be long before Leo would have to be hospitalized.

As I stood on Leo's front porch holding him in a long goodbye embrace I thought, "I know this sad thing about you, dear Leo, that you don't know. You will think people have turned against you and you will be wearing the long face more and more. You will be made to do things you don't want to do and you will get angry and reproach everyone. You won't remember how much you have been loved."

"Please come back soon," he said.

"I will, Leo. Just as soon as I can." But I knew that I would not. This was the last time that I would see him. After his son and his fiancée moved into the house I would not be needed and I wanted to remember our good times. I did not want to be with him as his mind became more confused and he became angrier and angrier and our old connection began to fray.

When I waved at him from my car he stood on the porch waving back. He was still wearing the apron he had on when we were making our last breakfast together. What was it about that apron that made me weep and would not let me stop for miles and miles and miles?

PART IV

Claiming Myself

I did not go out and find a puppy as Beth had suggested, needing to mourn Salomé for a while, but in the early spring a little stray found me. I was eating my lunch at the clinic, sitting out in the back yard of the big old house that had been converted into our offices, when this altogether original, very small dog approached me and asked for my lunch. She had the soft red coat and "feathers" of an Irish setter and the small pricked ears and alert face of a terrier. She was confident, not ingratiating as strays often are, holding her tail high. A clump of hairs on the end of it fanned out over her back like a feather duster. The overall effect except for her tail was of a little fox. She was wearing a collar with an outdated rabies tag, so she had, or once had, a home. Her ribs showed and she did not seem satisfied with as much of my lunch as I was willing to share. She was there again the next day. This called for some phoning.

"Oh, is she gone again?" a tired-sounding woman said against a background of fighting children. "She's always running off. You can have her if you want. I'll just tell the children she's gone for good this time."

When I lifted her into my car I was shocked that she weighed almost nothing. She sat erect in the back seat, a small personage, poised, almost regal, as if she were accustomed to the services of a chauffeur. That night I took her to a vet who updated her shots, instructed me how to worm her, and recommended the extraction of some rotten teeth. She thought that her odd, off-center gait was caused by an untreated fracture. She had probably been hit or kicked. She needed care and I needed a great deal of emotional support after my farewell to Leo. We had come into each other's lives at just the right moment.

I dreaded menopause, that incontestable announcement of the end of fertility. It had sneaked in quietly with missed periods and I had pretended at first that it hadn't arrived. Being jolted awake in the middle of the night by a wave of heat rising in my body followed by a drenching sweat, however, could not be ignored. I had often wondered what a hot flash would be like and now every time I had one I was reminded that I would be ending my days as a barren woman. I hated that word, but now I would have to learn how to live as one. Somewhere in my middle thirties I had decided that if I were not married by the age of fifty I would no longer keep myself on hold waiting for the shared life, although I would always keep the door open. In my reading I had come across a phrase of the novelist Elizabeth Bowen: "Companionship with a beloved person and a base, a home, the vital, warming core of existence." It described the life I had wanted to live, but I could no longer assume that the desired companionship was to be. The time had come to stop postponing my solitary journey and go where my single heart and inclinations wanted to take me. I would have to assume that from then on I would be on my own and would set about trying to enjoy what was perhaps the only compensation of that state —pretty much doing whatever I wanted, whenever and wherever I wanted to do it. I would not be working out those arduous compromises with a husband.

Soon after the little stray came into my life I heard from one of my friends that her daughter, who had been living in a converted hayloft not far from Princeton, would be leaving it in a few months. It was primitive, just one big room with a space heater and a small bathroom and kitchenette, but the property was beautiful. The idea of living there intrigued me, so my friend and I drove out to see it. When we approached the small barn I knew almost without going in that I wanted it. My little stray bounded up the steep staircase and we followed her. The haylofts of my childhood had been dim and dusty and full of cobwebs, and I was surprised when we opened the door to find the space so clean and bright. The original hayloft door had been replaced with a Dutch door that was half open, letting the light flood in. I walked over to it and looked out at a view of fields and woods. A lively stream had been dammed to form a small pond and a larger barn silhouetted itself against a gathering sunset, echoing the Small Paradise. I needed no more than this to know that I would be living in this place. This was the air I had been needing to breathe.

A simple verbal agreement was reached with my landlady-to-be, and as soon as the loft was vacant my little stray and I moved in. It had all the basic amenities and furnishings, and all I needed to bring was my writing table, pictures for the walls, my books, and my loved objects. My only regret was that there was not enough room for my piano. I did not want to part with it and found an older single woman, not unlike myself, who was overjoyed to have it and to care for it until I was ready to reclaim it. Eventually I would want more of a home than this, but wasn't Beth always saying to "live in the now"?

I loved my loft, appreciating its uniqueness after the boring sameness of the apartment units where I had been living. When you live in one high-ceilinged room that has many functions, whatever function is operative at a given time occupies the entire space. Thus, while eating on a card table I could see myself occupying a large formal dining room like the one at Aunt Carrie's. When I was engrossed in a book, I was settled cozily in her library with a warming fire crackling on the hearth. At night, while lying on my built-in-bunk waiting for sleep, I was in a spacious bedroom and could see myself soaring around the rafters like the swallows and bats that had once occupied this barn. I realized after settling in that this was the first time since I had left the Small Paradise that I loved being in my physical surroundings. Although my emotional surroundings were still wanting, I was out of suburbia and city life, probably forever. Living closer to the natural world I was feeling the kind of contentment I imagine a cat feels, sleeping on a sunny windowsill.

It is fortunate that I was living in this nurturing place and not my old apartment when I began sinking lower and lower into what I finally realized was a menopausal depression. I was finding it hard to get to work and began wondering if I was stable enough to be doing therapy. When I started having uncontrollable bouts of crying both at home and at work, even during interviews, I telephoned Bernie, the psychoanalyst I had been consulting about my private work. He and I had developed a warm, congenial relationship. Initially, I had addressed him as Doctor, but the Sixties' revolution had been loosening up the old professional formality and some of my clients had begun calling me Fairlie. One day he said, "Oh, just call me Bernie, for heaven's sake," and I did. The Sixties had also given us permission to greet and part with a hug. Bernie was a Teddy Bear of a man, a bit on the heavy side, with a head of thick, curly graying hair, and his bear hugs reminded me how much I had been missing Leo's.

"It isn't about my cases," I told Bernie, "it's about me. I'm coming apart at the seams. Can I talk to you, or should I be going to someone else?"

"Come in and we'll see."

"I probably should be taking a leave of absence," I said after filling him in, "but that's such a lousy thing to do to my clients." I started to cry. "How long is this thing going to go on?"

"Maybe a year. Maybe longer. Women vary. Some women don't have any trouble at all."

I started sobbing. Big, heaving sobs.

"Aren't you answering your own question?" Bernie asked when I finally stopped. "Let's go over your cases. We'll see who's close to ending, and who'll need reassigning. As for getting help for yourself, that's pretty much up to you. Do you have good support? Do you have close friends you can fall apart with?"

I nodded.

"I'm not happy about your living alone."

"I'm not either, but I have a little dog. She'll look out for me."

"I'm sure, knowing you, that you'll be worrying about your clients, but try to trust that other people will be taking good care of them. And try to enjoy the time you'll have to do things you've been wanting to do and haven't had time for. How about finances? Will you be able to manage?"

"I have some savings and I got a little money when my brother sold some of our family property. I suppose I should begin to think of investing for my retirement. I never thought I'd have to. I was supposed to be married."

"How is it for you going through this and not having had children? You've told me you wanted them."

I started sobbing all over again.

"This is a rough one for you to be dealing with alone. Maybe you should be getting some help. I can refer you to a colleague."

"Not yet. Let's see how it goes."

"Okay. Let's talk again in a month or so, and call me any time, even in the middle of the night. Don't be heroic."

Two things kept me going: My little stray's need for loving care and daily walks, and more time for reading and reflection. It had been hard to squeeze in the time around the edges of my work and daily chores. I also began to watch more television, but having these sedentary hours to reflect on where I was in my life and on the state of the world only deepened my depression. I had just lived through the Sixties with its race riots, assassinations, and the demoralizing war in Vietnam. The world I had grown up in was changing almost beyond recognition. Hippies, feminists, and gays were claiming freedoms I had never thought possible. At first I had found these changes disorienting and disturbing, even though some of them were much needed by my rigid, tradition-bound generation. But some of the hippies' values and their sloppiness were offensive to me. At the same time I could not fault them for scorning the hypocrisy of my generation and our incompetence in running the world. Even though I could tune out what offended me in the hippies' behavior, I could not ignore the rising voice of feminist and gay protest, and I began paying closer attention to what they were saying.

I imagined myself back in Natalie's arms and asked myself if I would I have stayed with her if we had been young when this social revolution was taking place. Was this the life I would have chosen if society had embraced us, not scorned us? "Be honest," I told myself sternly, but I still did not think so. I did not believe that I had been holding out for marriage just because of the stigma of either being single or a lesbian. I *wanted* a relationship with a loving man. I wanted to bear our child and have him love that child and be tender with it. But I had not found such a man. Maybe I had just wanted to re-live my childhood with a different cast of characters. So be it. The feminists were angry with men, very angry, and I decided it was time for me to listen to what they had to say.

When I first tuned into their rhetoric they had turned me off. They were not behaving like the ladies Ma would have approved of, but when I finally let their message get through I was shocked to realize how flawed the system was in giving Pa the power to take what he wanted for himself at the expense of his wife and children. I saw Ma differently now and began hearing a different tune in her litany of complaints. I realized that she had been a victim in a patriarchal society, and while not all men abused the power they had been given, how was a young bride to know the kind of man her husband would become? When I was a growing girl and unaware of how powerless women were in that society, Ma's impotence had exasperated me. Now her life seemed tragic in its needless suffering.

I had always been so sure that I was on the right path, but the painful truth was that I was a victim too. To be sure I was not living with a selfish, abusive husband as so many women were, but like all the girls I grew up with I had been raised to believe that marriage, even a bad one, was the ultimate measure of a woman's worth, and I had not married. I had become immobilized between two fears —my fear of failing as a woman and my fear of suffering a fate like my mother's. Not understanding this trap, I had gone on believing that I would succeed where she had failed —finding the kind of man who had made her weep when she came across him in the romantic novels she had loved to read, and now it was too late. So I'll end up a sweet old maiden lady, I thought, who talks to her plants and has chickadees eating out of her hand. There could be a worse fate.

Who knows how long I might have stayed in this brooding state if I had not been jolted into action by my little stray getting sick? She lay limply on her blanket and barely acknowledged me. She had been sick once before when she got into my landlady's garbage, but had slept that one off. This illness had a different, ominous feel to it. The vet was concerned, too. She gave her a shot of an antibiotic and a sedative and would not let me bring her home, wanting to treat her around the clock and keep her as undisturbed as possible.

I had not realized how deep my attachment to this little being had grown until that first night without her and that first next morning when she was not beside my bed, wagging her funny little fan of a tail, ready and eager to go out. I remembered the day she had disappeared on one of our morning walks and how frantically I had searched for her. I had finally given up, telling myself that she was a wanderer at heart and had been called back to her vocation. That night after I was asleep I heard her short high bark outside the barn and I stumbled, crying, down the staircase in my nightgown to let her in. Who knows where she had been? She was covered with mud, but she had come back to me. She *wanted* to come back.

When I went to visit her the next day she had not improved. I opened her cage and put my hand on her soft red coat, feeling her tiny frame still rising and falling as she struggled to live, hoping that she would feel my love.

Early the next morning the vet called to say that she had died during the night. When I went to fetch her the vet handed her to me in a Pet Tabs carton. We were both in tears. That little being who had given me so much weighed practically nothing. Beth said they would help me bury her in their yard next to Salomé, but I wanted to bury her by myself beside the barn, wanting her near me for as long as I lived there. As with Salomé, it helped to put my grief into fighting the hard clay soil. She was so small she did not need to claim much space from the planet.

Beth was worried about me and wanted me to stay with them for a while, but I needed to be alone. For months I had been going through the profound physical and emotional reorientation that is rightly called "the change," and I wanted to stay where I was until I could recover enough of myself to be able to function normally again. I also wanted privacy to grieve. I assumed that, like my grief for Salomé, it would subside in time. But it didn't.

After a few weeks passed I thought I should call Bernie, but I received an unexpected call from the rector of the Episcopal Church. He had recently received funds to start a counseling service. One of my colleagues at the clinic had given him my name. He was looking for someone to help set up his new service and do screening interviews, and to help him recruit therapists in private practice who would be willing to give some therapy time. He preferred this to hiring a smaller full-time staff, for it would bring in a variety of talent and expertise. I liked his vision, and joining him in realizing it seemed like a golden opportunity to ease back into the work. When I was ready I could start doing therapy again, both there and rebuilding my own practice. The rector and I set up a time to meet.

I put in a call to Bernie to see what he thought.

"I think it's a perfect way for you to get your feet wet," he said. "They'll be lucky to get you. I've been thinking about you. I've been meaning to call you. How's it been going?"

"I was doing better for a while and then my little dog died. I've been taking it pretty hard."

"You should have called me."

"I thought I'd get over it. When my other dog died I finally got used to her being gone, but this one doesn't seem to go away. The sadness just won't go away."

"But you were working then, don't forget. You were occupied, not trying to get through a menopausal depression. Are you sure you shouldn't be seeing someone?"

"Not yet. But if this new job doesn't pull me out of it, then I will have to do something."

The rector and I liked each other and he wanted me to start right away. I was still on leave from my old clinic and had to let the director know that I would not be coming back. This was hard and felt almost like a betrayal. But it was time for me to move on. I would miss him and my co-workers and the feeling of being valued and loved as I worked with them, but I had begun distancing myself when I cut down my hours. These months of separation made it easier for me to make the final break. My new job proved to be good therapy for me. When I was working at the church I was feeling like my old competent self, but when I was back in my loft any reminder of my little stray, like seeing her red leash and collar on a hook by the door, would set me off, and yet I did not want to put it away. It would be like burying her again. I thought maybe I should call Bernie and was surprised when I had a call from him.

"I have an idea," he said. "One of my patients has signed up for a group therapy weekend over in Pennsylvania, one of those Encounter Groups. If they still have space why don't you go? Have you ever thought of doing something like that?"

"I have, as a matter of fact. I've been curious about what those things are like. Even if it doesn't help me I'd find out if it could help some of my clients."

"I've had patients who've been dramatically changed by those groups. Why don't you give them a call?"

They were filled up, of course, but at the last minute I received a phone call. Someone had a death in the family. I was excited, and suddenly very scared. Beth was thrilled. She couldn't wait to hear all about it.

While waiting for Neal I walked into the shade of an old apple tree near the kitchen door of the old farmhouse and leaned against its trunk. How fortunate I had been not to have had this experience in a city somewhere but on this old farm where a dozen strangers and their leader labored to produce a strange new harvest of honesty, trust, and forgiveness. I looked over at the huge red barn where we had done our work and thought of other barns that have been significant in my life —the barn where I was living now and grieving the loss of my little stray and my fertility, the barns at the Small Paradise, the barn on Aunt Carrie's farm that I most loved with its towering silo and the mysterious sounds the wind made whistling around its corners and through its cracks. Aunt Carrie would be bewildered by what was taking place in this barn, but in seeing the love, I felt sure she would be able to place it somewhere in her frame of reference as God's work. Without her love for me, I asked myself, where would I be now?

Neal approached me and we embraced. He was so slender, so slight, I fancied I could lift him up and carry him home where I would let him rest and be nourished as if he were my own prodigal son. It was ironic that with all my uncharitable feelings about hippies, it was a hippie with whom I felt the most powerful connection and from whom my parting would be the most painful.

Neal did not feel this way about me, although he liked me and was grateful to me. He had not connected closely with anyone, partly because he was adrift in his life and because he was clinically depressed, although he did not know that he was. My first interaction with him, however, was devastating.

We had all arrived in time for a congenial supper in the farmhouse and then gone over to the barn, settling ourselves on mattresses and pillows for our first meeting. Sheila, our leader, introduced herself. She was a large presence, clothed in flowing, colorful garments and costume jewelry, and refreshingly different from any woman I had known, including myself. I envied her self-assurance and from the outset knew that I was in good hands. After outlining her program for the weekend and laying down ground rules —no drugs, no smoking in buildings, no fucking —and telling us to take off our watches, she opened the floor for questions and comments. I wanted to get everything I could out of this experience and had given myself a pep talk driving over about my fear of speaking in groups. So without waiting as I normally would for everyone else to have finished talking, I plunged in.

"I've been watching the girl with the bad leg." I said. "I don't know her name."

"I'm Helen," she called out.

"I want to say that I think it's very courageous of her to come to a group like this. I'm not sure I would have had to courage to do it. I admire her."

"I find that a very offensive remark," one of the men said. It was Neal, a young 60's stereotype with sloppy clothes and a long blond pigtail.

I was stung by his rebuke.

"Did you find what I said offensive, Helen?"

"Yes, I did."

"It's patronizing," another man said. "You're saying she's different from the rest of us because she has a disability and you're implying she's inferior because of it."

"I didn't mean that. I was trying to say something nice."

"Stop trying to be nice," Neal said. "And I don't trust the way you smile all the time, looking so put together, so lady-like. I don't see *you* limping. Be real."

"I'm sorry, Helen," I called out. "They're right."

What I had said to her *was* condescending, but what was more upsetting was learning how I came across to people. I realized now that when I was anxious in a new situation I presented myself as a courteous, well brought up "lady" –the way Ma had taught me and presented herself –and that I had adopted her ingratiating smile. If I had presented myself honestly I would have let these people know early on how depressed I was and how scared of their disapproval and dislike. When Neal said that he didn't see *me* limping, I should have told him that I had been limping inside all my life. I should have made clear that I truly admired Helen's courage, if indeed it had taken any for her to come, because I hated my own cowardice. It was I who was the disabled, inferior one. All through the next day I became a passive observer and said nothing in our meetings, letting the others claim time to talk. I did not have to worry about smiling the ingratiating smile. Neal had wiped it off my face and I hoped that it was gone for good.

As time passed Neal became essential to our group, functioning as its conscience. In direct hippie-speak he cut through our rationalizations and challenged our evasions, making most of his comments lying on his back on a mattress, staring into the rafters of the barn. But just before midnight on the second night of our marathon he announced that he was leaving. We had been outside having a short break under a seductively beautiful waxing moon and had returned to our usual places, but Neal had remained standing. He said he was going to get in his car and start driving, probably heading west. He wanted time alone, wanted to think things through by himself.

"You can't do that, Neal!"

It was I who had spoken, jolted out of my silence.

"You're a part of us now. You could have left in the beginning. It's not fair now. It's like cutting off an arm or a leg. We need you."

"Fairlie's right," Sheila said.

We were silent, watching, waiting. Then Sheila spoke again. "Would you do something for us, Neal?" He nodded. She told him to lie down on his mattress and for the rest of us to get up and put our hands under him and raise him up then rock him as if he were in a cradle. We would know when it was time to lower him down. We did as she asked and when we lowered him to his mattress he was able to talk for the first time about himself, telling us about his alcoholic father and his mother struggling to keep the family going. One night his father cut off his hair when he was asleep. Neal left home the next morning, dropping out of school into drugs, and he lied to evade Vietnam. After his closest friend had gone and been killed, he tried to enlist but failed his physical. He guessed he had come this weekend because of survivor's guilt.

When our meeting ended for the night and we walked out, I felt someone touch my arm. It was Neal. "Thanks," he said over his shoulder and walked away. He might still leave, I thought, but I believed he would stay. I hadn't realized until then how much I needed him to be there when I claimed my time. I had let time get away from me, postponing and postponing, and now I had only the next morning.

I had planned to be the first to talk, but another woman spoke up before I did. She was a friendly, overweight ex-nun who had left her convent after Vatican II. She hated her job teaching in the noisy, ugly public school world she had found herself in and was trying to decide if she should return to the religious life. She had an appealing way of fending off pain with humor. "I miss my habit," she said. "I used to hide my fat and my bad feelings under it." She wasn't asking for time from us. She planned to find a counselor when she got home. "I'd rather do it that way, but I want to thank you. It's been an education, just being here. I needed a good shaking up. Now there must be someone who needs time more than I do. We don't have that much left."

I leapt in. Normally I rehearsed important things before I said them and I had no idea what I was going to say. "I'm forty-nine," I began. "I'm unmarried and I'm just coming out of a menopausal depression. I'm a psychotherapist and for a while I was too unstable to work. I'd cry at the slightest thing. I always expected to be married and have children, and now I can't. I never will. But the reason I've come is because of my little dog. She died a few months ago and I can't stop grieving for her. When my other dog died I grieved for her, too, but I got over it." Then I found myself spilling out all the rest of it, telling them about Ma and Pa and his selfishness and my fear of being trapped in a bad marriage like Ma, then losing precious reproductive time in my relationships with Natalie and Beth.

"I don't know why I loved that little dog so much. Maybe it was because she was so small. She was much smaller than my other one. I could hold her in my arms."

I looked down and saw her there in her silky red coat with her four little legs in the air and her small head with its perky ears leaning against me.

"She was a baby for you, wasn't she?" Helen said. "She was your baby."

As she spoke I saw my little stray metamorphose into an infant that had just been placed in my arms by a smiling nurse and dissolved into anguished sobbing. The heavy nun struggled to her feet and came over and sat down on the mattress beside me. She took me in her arms and I buried my face in her roomy breasts.

"I dig that girl," a voice said. It was Neal. When I heard what he said I sobbed even harder. No one knew, least of all Neal, that my fresh burst of tears was because he had heard me being real and had forgiven me.

The room remained hushed for a while as it usually did after one of us had tackled the painful work we had come to do, people shifting, recovering from the intensity. Reluctantly I disengaged myself from the nun's comforting arms. "Thank you," I whispered. "Let's be sure to talk before we go. Maybe I can help you find a counselor."

Then Sheila spoke. "Our time is nearly up and I think this is a note I'd like us to end on. There will be lunch at the farmhouse for anyone who wants it. You've been a wonderful group to work with. Take your time saying your good-byes."

One by one we rose from our mattresses and moved quietly out of the barn. The sudden brightness of a noonday sun jolted us into remembering that there were lives out there that we had left and would soon be returning to. Would we be living them better for what we had been through? It was time to be putting our watches back on.

People were finding each other, talking, crying, having long hugs, even two men together. I had never seen that before and it startled and pleased me. I hated good-byes. The only thing that was worse was parting without them. Maybe Neal hated them too. I looked for him, concerned that he might have slipped away, and found him talking to Sheila. "Excuse me for interrupting," I said, approaching them, "but be sure not to leave, Neal, without saying goodbye. I'll be up at the farmhouse." He nodded and I hurried on in search of Helen. Finding her with someone, I waited until she was free.

"I can't thank you enough, Helen. What you said was probably obvious to everyone, but I'd never thought of it. I wish I'd gotten to know you a bit. You never told us about yourself."

"There isn't much to tell. I live with my mother. I have a job. My therapist wanted me to come and get out in the world, get my feet wet. *Both* feet." She smiled, looking down. "It was crushed in a roller coaster accident."

"What I said our first night was so stupid, Helen, so clumsy. Please forgive me."

"Don't worry about it. I'm used to it. People mean well."

Someone was approaching us. Helen waved in recognition, and we parted. As I continued on to the farmhouse I heard my name being called. I turned. It was Sigrid, a lovely blond woman with a Scandinavian accent whom I had admired from a distance. She had rarely spoken and had never claimed time for herself.

"I want to thank you," she said a bit breathlessly.

"For what?"

"You helped me know how much I want to keep this baby." She started to cry and put her hands protectively over her abdomen, although there was still nothing there to see. "It's not my husband's and he'll know it can't be his. We haven't been getting along. I'm going to have to tell him and I don't want to break up our marriage. I have two other children. Maybe this will tell him how unhappy I've been. I have to run now. Someone's waiting to drive me home, but thank you, thank you, thank you!" She opened her arms, sobbing now, and for a few seconds we held each other tightly. Then she pulled away and ran off. Our encounter had been like a sudden gust of wind, swirling in, then swirling out. What an exquisite gift it had brought me.

I hurried on to gather my things and wait for Neal.

"Words may spoil it," I said, as Neal and I drew apart, "but I need to thank you. You did more for me than you can possibly know and I won't try to explain what it was." He was silent. "And I guess it's the mother in me that doesn't want you to leave without knowing that you're more than just sad. You know I've been depressed. I talked about it. It can make you feel hopeless and that nothing's worth bothering with. I don't want it to do that to you. I'm afraid the last thing you'd be willing to do is see someone about it."

"Sheila asked me that, too," he said. "You're nice women. Don't worry about me. I'll do it my way." He started to leave, then turned back. "Get yourself another dog," he said. Then he disappeared so quickly and silently I was almost unsure that he, or even I, had ever been at this place.

I drove home slowly, suspended between two worlds—the life, or what there was of a life that I was returning to, and the physical and emotional space I had been inhabiting with these strangers. We had experienced extraordinary intimacy in the risks we took together. As I drove along they were with me in my car and stayed with me in my loft for days. I kept imagining Neal heading west, destination unknown, hoping that he was safe and wishing I could have been the therapist he would never go to. And I would never see him again.

Beth could tell right away that the experience had been powerful.

"You seem so much more peaceful," she said. "That worried look seems to be gone."

"That's because I'm not anxious for the first time in my life. I suppose this is the way normal people feel. Of course I'll feel it again, but for the moment it's gone."

I had always known what anxiety felt like when it was running high, but I had never realized that it had always been running low until I experienced its total absence. It was a stunning revelation. Beth was disappointed that I could not let her relive the whole weekend with me, but Sheila had asked us to respect one another's privacy. "You're free to tell about your own experiences of course, if you want to," and of course I did.

"What's the most important thing you took away with you?" Beth wanted to know when I finished.

It was a hard question. The anxiety thing had been big, but not the biggest. "I guess the biggest thing was going over there as Dorothy's child, and coming back as myself."

"Oh, I love that!" Beth said.

For several months after being home I thought off and on about Neal's parting advice. I wasn't sure I was ready for another dog, but one day I spotted an ad for German Shepherd puppies in a town nearby and decided to drive over and have a look at them. I liked the idea of having a dog like Salomé again. I asked Beth to come along, hoping it would be a distraction for her. Not long after I had came back from the group, her brother Toby had died from a massive heart attack, and she was shattered by this loss. I could not comfort her, for there was no comfort, but she brightened at the idea of seeing the puppies. I picked her up in my car and several hours later we were driving home with a dove-colored puppy curled in her lap. I had chosen a female because I could see puppies in our future. I decided to name her Spring.

Neal's prescription took immediate effect. As I attended to the needs of this little being I forgot my own woes. She was then about the same size as my little stray and needed cuddling even more. I bought her a crate and trained her to feel safe in her new little den when I was away at work and found a high-school girl who would come over in the afternoons and spend time with her. I felt ready to work seriously now, ready to be a therapist again. Mercifully my menopausal crisis was history, but soon a new crisis appeared.

As I began attending weekly conferences with my colleagues at the counseling service, I found them talking a new therapy language that essentially discredited my way of working. While I had been absent they had fervently espoused "family therapy." I had read about it and attended some workshops before I went on leave. I was in awe of the way the leaders of this new approach could step right into the hornet's nest of family dysfunction and somehow put things to rights. But I was hurt by the fervor and dismissive scorn of some of our new young therapists who spoke disparagingly of the "old child-guidance" approach —"They wouldn't even let the child and his parents be in the same room!"

This new way is the only way was the message I was hearing. Many of the other more senior members of our staff, hearing the same message, were hastily enrolling in family therapy courses. After years of struggle and self-doubt I had finally come to respect my professional expertise. Then menopause struck, and I was feeling like a beginner again —uncertain, clumsy and confused. How could I ever learn to work in this new way? If I didn't, I would be obsolete as a therapist, or so it seemed to me then.

I came back from my weekend in Pennsylvania confident that I could offer a life-changing experience to the troubled people I had met there and was eager to get started again. Was I now supposed to dump the contents of my trusty black bag and start all over? I hadn't opened that little bag for some time. When I did I had to admit that it looked like a bureau drawer that needs straightening and some discarding. Yet it seemed to me there was still a lot of good stuff in there. I had the solid foundation of my training at Smith, followed by the discipline of my first clinic job where I had written one after another of those exhaustive psychosocial evaluations. As new insights and approaches came along, I had always added what worked for me to my therapy bag. Eric Berne, for one, creator of Transactional Analysis, had given me a wonderful tool with his concept of how different parts of ourselves —adult, parent and child —interact with those same parts in others. So why was this new Family Therapy approach so threatening to my self-confidence? Was it because its practitioners were discrediting with such fervor these earlier ways of working? Or was it because it would challenge me to work with *groups?* I had always been intimidated by groups of any kind and usually silenced by them. In dismay I called Bernie.

"What's pushing the panic button?" he asked

"I'm afraid I've become obsolete as a therapist. Everybody's doing family therapy now and I don't want to do it."

"Are you going to get fired if you don't?"

"No. They still need people to work with individuals, but there's a lot of peer pressure to do it and I respect what I'm learning about it."

"Why don't you want to do it?"

"I don't think I'd be good at it. It scares me. What I'm good at is making connections with individuals and then helping them straighten themselves out. We have a two-way mirror now at the counseling service and I've been watching other therapists doing it. You're supposed to restore the health of the whole family and not get too connected to any one family member. That's just the opposite of what I do well. And you try to figure out who has the power and how to empower the others. There's a lot of manipulation in it and I can see it working, but I don't think I could do it. I don't like manipulation. And good family therapists have to be very sure of themselves, which I wouldn't be. I'm much too introverted and timid. I've imagined being in a therapy room with my own family and I see myself crouched in the corner with my face to the wall. It would have been terrifying to have had all that emotion pulled out into the open. I'm afraid if I do try to do it I'll end up in that corner."

Bernie laughed. "If it had been my family I would have locked myself in my room and refused to go. I don't see any reason why you have to do family therapy, but it's good to have a grasp of new ideas and apply what's useful. Professionals don't have to learn every specialty that comes along. If you feel this strongly about it, why force yourself?"

"I'm afraid if I don't do it, I'll feel defeated. I should be able to."

"So here are your old shoulds again, grinning at you. Being introverted, by the way, isn't a bad thing. It's part of what makes you connect so well with individuals. And I don't see you as timid. I think you have a lot of guts."

"So you won't give me a failing grade if I don't do family therapy?"

"I wouldn't be good at it either, but it's given me ideas for my own work. I think what you should do now is build up your private practice again. It's time you got back to doing what you're so good at. If your clients need family therapy you can refer them to family therapists the way you refer to other specialists. You wouldn't run an encounter group either, would you? I'm glad it worked so well for you, by the way. I want to hear more about it some time. Now. Are you ready to hold your ground and not run with the pack?"

"I *think* I am. Thanks Bernie. I'll be getting back to you when I get a practice going again."

But having Bernie's "permission" not to do family therapy didn't get me off the hook. Being my own worst taskmaster I still felt I should be able to do it, but before investing time in a training course I decided to try winging it with a few families. After all hadn't groundbreaking gurus started cold? Freud had. I tiptoed in with the smallest family unit that exists, one parent and one child —in this case a single mother and her "acting out" adolescent daughter. Playing the role of the absent father they never talked about freed the girl to ask her mother festering questions and the mother to cry and reveal the pain she had been hiding from her daughter.

Emboldened, I took on a "real" family with a mother and father and three children. A twelve-year-old boy was the so-called "identified patient." The opener I usually used with individuals and couples —"What brings you here?" —elicited a tirade from the father at his "lazy" son who was throwing his schooling away.

"And you know, Billy, how I had to leave school to help your grandmother support the family!" My attempts to draw the others out brought only "I think his father is too hard on him" from the tired, defeated-looking mother and shrugs from the boy and his younger sisters. Feeling my anger rise at this man who was abusing power like my own father I could sense my objectivity and usefulness to this family slipping away. It was clear that the son was challenging his father with his passivity, but I was unable to stop a scene that probably took place every day in the family's kitchen and ended up in the corner as I had feared. After this failure I could accept Bernie's advice, but its theories intrigued me and of course I thought about how they applied to my own family, particularly the roles we children had played.

The most common roles in the theory are the peacemaker, the rebel, and the scapegoat, although there are others. I immediately saw Mary as our peacemaker. With Pa she had been a little coquette which he clearly liked, and, as she had once told me, she "spent her childhood trying to make our mother smile." Hope, of course, was our family rebel. She declared her independence early when she disappeared through the hedge. Later when she became an adolescent, she challenged, exasperated and defeated Ma. There was not much competition for the role of scapegoat, needless to say, and if I say I *claimed* it, it was not because I wanted it, but because it was a perfect fit. After Little Brother died I became a left-over half without full family membership. Ma's rejection of me inevitably relegated me to the family basement. Finally, needing to find roles for Robert and Little Brother, I decided that Robert was the family's "enabler," giving his sisters a displaced target for their hostility to their parents, his mother a focus for her passion, and his father an excuse to escape from the emotional complications of family life. I saw Little

Brother, who was still very much with us, as the Keeper of the Family Silence. His message was stern as he looked down on us from his portrait, first in the village house and then when he came with us to the Small Paradise: *No important truths that need saying in this family can ever be said because there can be no more unbearable pain.* Until we children were grown, his family rule had been strictly obeyed.

Longing for Home

When lilacs last in the dooryard bloom'd,
And the great star early drooped in the western sky in the night,
I mourned, and yet shall mourn with ever returning spring.

I was sitting in the Princeton Chapel with Beth, listening to Walt Whitman's poem set to music for voice and orchestra by Paul Hindemith.

In the dooryard fronting an old farm-house near the whitewash'd palings,
Stands the lilac-bush tall-growing with heart shaped leaves of rich green,
With many a pointed blossom rising delicate, with the perfume strong I love
With every leaf a miracle —and from this bush in the dooryard,
With delicate-colored blossoms and heart-shaped leaves of rich green,
A sprig with its flower I break.

I found myself slipping lower and lower in the pew, my throat tightening, trying to hold off a rising wave of grief. But then I had to let the grief come, trying to keep it private, quiet, not disturbing. Beth gripped my hand. The poem continued.

In the swamp in secluded recesses,
A shy and hidden bird is warbling a song.

Solitary the thrush,
The hermit withdrawn to himself, avoiding the settlements,
Sings by himself a song

Song of the bleeding throat
Death's outlet song of life...

When intermission came I pulled back into the pew to let people further in edge out past us.

"Let's not go out," I said.

"What is it, sweetheart?"

"I'm not mourning Lincoln, if you're wondering. Not that I *don't* mourn him. No. I'm mourning Long Island. All my losses, I guess. It's all too much. The music is too powerful, and Whitman's imagery. It's our Long Island, his and mine. Our vanished Long Island. I'm going to have to go back. I mean to live, at least for a while. I've seen some beautiful places, but I can't move anywhere else. Not for a while. I've got to go back."

Beth was silent. She took my hand again and held it until people started coming in to take their places.

"Don't *you* die," I whispered. "I'm not ready for that."

Another painful loss had been Aunt Carrie's death. She had started failing mentally a few years before she died, but she was a beautiful as ever, slender and graceful, her lovely, long auburn hair with only a hint of gray. The last time I visited her she was still up and about. She greeted me with her gracious smile, then looked perplexed. "I'm not exactly sure which one you are, dear girl," she said, "but I know you're one of mine."

Gradually she had grown weaker and frailer. In my last image of her she was lying in her four-poster bed with its canopy and ruffles, her two long braids lying beside her on her pillow. One of her maids had brought up her breakfast on a tray. When she finished and the tray was removed, she slid her pale bony legs from the bed and was helped onto a waiting commode. Sitting there in her nightgown with her servant's securing hand resting on her shoulder, she was still the erect, smiling, lovely lady she had always been. But making her small tinkling sound, she became the motherless little girl I had never known and wished could have been mine.

Aunt Carrie's death had marked that transition in people's lives when all the elders are gone and we are on our own. Our lives should be in place by then, our commitments made. I was in my fifties. The loft where I was living had been a half-way house for me, a place where I had been evolving from the person my parents had shaped me to be to a person who was finally comfortable as the person I had evolved to be. I still loved living in this loft, but I had outgrown it. I wanted a home of my own now, a place to put down roots, and so I set about trying to find it. My ambitions were far more modest than Pa's had been when he bought the Small Paradise. All I would need to live out the dream of the simple, self-sufficient life was a modest house and a pretty piece of land.

Unlike my romantic self I was promiscuous in this quest for place and proceeded to have a number of affairs. I would fall hard for a region or a particular property and then find some reason why it wasn't practical to live there. On my first stop in New Hampshire I found a small farm that was for sale and in an instant I was in love, but first I would have to find a job. There was only one clinic within a manageable commute. When I inquired there, I was told they were only interested in hiring *a young family therapist!*

I fell even harder for Nova Scotia where I visited friends who had bought farms on Cape Breton Island. But a job shortage for social workers in Canada meant no hiring of Americans. It was hard to say no to that beautiful part of the world, but when I imagined settling there, I knew I could not be that far away from my family and everyone else I loved. A move to the coast of Maine would have been less drastic, but again I could not find congenial work.

And so it went.

While there had been good reasons for saying no to the many alluring places I had explored, the passionate certainty I had felt at that concert about moving back to Long Island made clear that my need to return there was the real obstacle to my moving anywhere else. Until I did go back and live there for a time, I knew I would always find reasons why another place was not quite right.

In the final section of the Hindemith I closed my eyes and let my mind wander. I imagined myself returning to Long Island and saw myself propelled there like a rocket, soaring from New Jersey over the island of Manhattan then diving into the green depths of the Long Island Sound. Breaking the surface I saw myself swimming to shore, then walking up on that beach that I will always love and standing there, waiting for a shy and hidden bird to start singing the song of the bleeding throat.

"What are *you* doing here?" she asked.

"Old elephants come home to die," I said.

I was standing at the front door of the house of an old friend on Long Island, ringing her bell. I had stopped by to see if she happened to know of a place that I could rent. My blue Beetle, the one I had bought in Germany and brought back with me on the boat, was parked in her driveway. Spring and her adolescent son, Alex, sat alert in the back seat watching intently for developments.

It turned out that a small farmhouse on her mother's property would be vacant in a few months. The bachelor tenant who was leaving had abused the house and neglected the grounds and they would be glad to see him go. She looked at her watch. He was away during the day. There would just be enough time to fetch the key from her mother and have a quick look before he came home.

Just as I had known on sight that I had wanted to live in my loft, as soon as my friend drove us into the old homestead and parked under an apple tree I knew that I must live in this place. The two acres that went with the house sloped gracefully down to marshes along the same river that flowed by our family's Small Paradise about a mile upstream. The house, a small barn and other outbuildings were all painted red like the farm buildings on our property. This place, in miniature, was its clone —a *tiny* paradise.

Originally the farmhouse had been just two small rooms, one up and one down. Over the years it had acquired a small kitchen and bath, a living room, and a second bedroom. A screened-in porch had been added with a view of the river. I stood there with my friend studying the scene, not caring how comfortable the living space would be. Anything would do if I could occupy this beautiful piece of land that bordered the river of my childhood wanderings. There were magnificent old trees on the property, but most powerful of all for me, not far from the dooryard, was an old lilac bush that, come spring, would bear "heart shaped leaves of rich green/ With many a pointed blossom rising delicate." The tears I had fought in the Princeton Chapel listening to Whitman's poem filled my eyes again.

It was time for a tour of the house. One quick look told me that it would take hours and hours of labor to claim this space as mine. The departing tenant had covered the old walnut banister with orange enamel, had painted the kitchen midnight blue with green trim, and the two small bedrooms in shocking pink and purple. But I knew that I would be able to make this place livable and had already begun mentally to restore the house and to recover the neglected grounds. It would be like freeing the potential in an emotionally damaged client. I told my friend that I wanted the place as soon as I could have it, and we drove over to her mother's house for a conference. Since the house was in such poor condition her mother agreed to my taking it as it was for a modest rental. She would replace the leaking roof after the tenant moved out. Then this "handy-woman's-special" would be mine.

A few weeks later the lease came in the mail. I signed it, drove over to the post office, and pushed my envelope through the out of town slot. It was done, legal, a fait accompli. The place was mine. That night I had a dream:

I am on the beach, the loved beach of my childhood to which I will be returning. I am standing with my back to the water. A companion makes me look around and I see a huge tidal wave about to break over me and sweep me away. I awake in a fright.

In reality I was being drawn back irresistibly to the shore of my childhood and was not aware of any apprehension, but the dream seemed to be saying that it was going to be a dangerous place. Then I remembered a full-page picture I had seen as a child in a Victorian children's book. A little girl is sitting on the shore with her back to the water. A tidal wave is cresting behind her and a puppy is tugging at her sleeve. I had been frightened and haunted by that picture. As I pondered the meaning of the dream I saw the sea as the ultimate power, having created life, but also being capable of destroying it and claiming it back. The picture in the book was illustrating the imbalance of power, with the puppy (did it represent love?) being too weak to save the child. This left the child at the mercy of the ultimate power, which in a child's life is the parent. But I was no longer a helpless child. My parents were dead and no longer had power over the direction of my life. Fully awake I could see no danger in this place, but I was still uneasy. If there was nothing to be feared, why had I had this dream?

W here is your home?
Even though I had been living on my own for almost a quarter of a century after leaving my parents' home, I always hesitated when I was asked that question. "I live in such and such a place," I would answer, "but I come from Long Island."

This came to mind when I was standing on the sandy shoulder of the road that went by my new "place of residence" —the first of many of Webster's definitions of "home." I was out there with a post-hole digger and a shovel, preparing to install my new mailbox.

When Hope and Mary had gone off with their husbands into new territory and started their families, they had, in the normal course of things, created new homes, leaving their childhood home behind them. They had established new centers of gravity. My recent search over the northeast for a place to put down my roots as a single woman had been to find a corner of the world that moved me as powerfully as my "place of origin," another of Webster's definitions. But I never did. And now I had returned to it. I loved the new address I had just painted on my mailbox. It was exactly where I wanted to be.

My old community embraced me warmly in a way I had never experienced in the places I had tried to become a part of without the E-Z pass of husband and children. Its social life revolved around a beach club on the Long Island Sound where Ma had taken me as a child and which was perhaps the only place where we had been happy together. Returning to the club, not as the child of my parents but as a member in my own right, was a significant rite of passage, reflecting belief in my worth as an independent adult, even though I was still an unmarried woman. My two sisters experienced that passage when they married. While both those marriages had ended in divorce, they had never lost their status as fully-arrived women. By the old criteria marriage was all a girl needed. Even though I knew that some of the elderly women in our club were probably thinking, "Poor Fairlie never married," I no longer saw mine as a failed life. I could in part thank feminism for this, but I could also give myself high marks for perseverance in my struggle to emancipate myself.

If you were to imagine a film of the new life I was embarking upon, you would see a figure rushing in fast motion from room to room in a small house – scraping, painting, re-plastering, and wallpapering –and then you would see her lock up her house, leap into her car, leave her dogs off at Hope's boarding kennel, and plunge into a sea of moving vehicles, coming at last to rest in her office in New Jersey. In the course of the next two days you would see her usher clients in and out of her office, meet with her students, have conferences with her colleagues. Then you would fast-forward her back to Long Island where the cycle would start again.

But when she took time to luxuriate in her new homestead, the film would be in slow motion. You might see her on her screened-in porch, a cup of tea in hand, watching a family of quail cruising and feeding across her lawn. Or you might see her paddling on the river in her new canoe, or strolling on the beach with her dogs, or swimming her slow, long-distance crawl along the shore.

The slowest film speed of all would find her tending the vegetables and flowers that she was raising in the organic way, having hauled scrap lumber from the beach to make raised beds and a cold frame, and seaweed to nourish the soil. A still photograph would do here as well, for time had a way of stopping altogether when she was in her garden.

In the end she need not have to go all the way to Nova Scotia to find the good, self-sufficient, simple life. She was able to live it for a time in her own nation, Long Island, even while asphalt, hand in hand with suburbia, was creeping stealthily over the land, and a new crop, row after row of tract housing, was being planted in the fields.

I t was always hard to leave my tiny paradise and head out on the punishing, fume-ridden drive to New Jersey, but when I re-entered my other life of clients and colleagues it felt like another kind of homecoming and I was glad to be there. I was an accomplished professional now and relatively free of my old fear of failing. I no longer needed to write time-consuming evaluations to get my bearings and could usually make rapid assessments of each new assignment. I had learned how to hear both the said and the unsaid and to read body language, and I could figure out pretty quickly why my clients were stuck, what needs they had that were not being met, what resources they had, both inner and outer, and whether I had their trust or would have to build it. Although the intense human connection that counseling requires could sometimes be emotionally draining I always welcomed it, for it gave me what I did not have enough of as a single woman.

On one of my trips I had, as usual, left the dogs off at Hope's kennel, and they had both been in high spirits. But when I picked them up Spring was listless and strange. Alex was crying with pleasure, but Spring barely greeted me. When we got home I took her temperature. It was not yet high, but if she were no better in the morning I would have to take her to the vet. Not long after I was asleep, I was awakened by her crying as if she were in severe pain. I found her staggering in circles with her head tilted awkwardly to one side. She finally collapsed, exhausted. I put in a call to the vet's answering service, and before he arrived in the early morning she had had several more episodes. When they were going on her cries of pain were unbearable to hear. Alex, visibly distressed, was keeping his distance in the next room.

When the vet told me it was meningitis and might well be fatal I did not take it in at first. I had thought only people contracted that disease. He said would treat her intensively with antibiotics, but if the disease were viral she would not respond. Even if she did, there was likely to be brain damage. He gave her an injection while we talked. She would need them every four hours and to be sedated. Could I manage this? It would be better not to move her. He showed me how to give her an injection, left prescriptions for the medication and syringes, and said he would be back the next morning.

"How did she get it?" I asked.

"It's carried in bird droppings," he said. "Some dogs like to eat fecal matter."

I remembered shuddering the first time I was aware that she did that. My other dogs hadn't, but human children can have traits you don't care for and you love them anyway. I looked down at her sleeping peacefully now as if she had just come back from a run on the beach. Your little habit may have done you in, I thought, and felt tears starting. But it was time for action.

My pre-med nephew, home on vacation at the Small Paradise, responded to my call for help. He would pick up the prescriptions and stay with me until the next morning. Since he wanted to do the injections I was spared an ordeal I had been dreading. Under sedation Spring was less agitated, but episodes with the painful cries broke through periodically during the night. It was at daybreak the next day when I was sitting on the floor beside her that I knew she would not be coming out of this. It had been a warm night. The door to my porch was open and I could see the beginning of light moving into the eastern sky. Soon the birds would be waking and I would hear robins making the first entrance in the early morning chorus. I put my hand on Spring's side, watching it rise and fall with her last breaths.

Why was this happening? What mysterious forces were at play? Was there some purpose here, some message I should be receiving? Why was my dog dying of the same terrible disease that had taken my twin and suffering as he had suffered? So that I would know? Why was she making the same cries, so unbearable to hear, that Ma had heard, sitting beside her beautiful, promising little boy? She would have had to stay in that room possibly for days until he had finally given up in exhaustion. For the first time in my life I felt overwhelming compassion for her. She had been a young woman then, only thirty-nine —pretty and witty, as Aunt Carrie had so often said —and until tragedy struck she had had a good life in place. She was told by her father that she should go into a nunnery, but she married and brought four lovely children into the world. But after Little Brother's death, Aunt Carrie said she had never been the same. The sadness and worry were always there.

I had not been in the room where Ma had been with my twin during his last days, but as I sat beside Spring with the early light slowly and quietly bringing in a new day I imagined the scene of his dying. I saw him lying on a bed in a corner, a small table and lamp beside the bed, and a chair next to the bed. Ma was sitting on that chair and from time to time wiping his feverish brow with a cool cloth. Then I saw him become agitated and twist and turn and cry like Spring, and all Ma could do was to hold him and try to steady him with all the strength and love that she had. Over and over she had been going through this. When he finally died I imagined her dropping her head on the bed beside him too exhausted to weep. When she was reunited with her three girls, I imagined her looking at them blankly. When she looked at her youngest girl for the first time since her son had died and envisioned her precious boy beside his twin, alive and smiling and holding his twin's hand, she could not bear the image. When the little girl asked, "Where is Brudder? Where is my Brudder?" and kept asking and asking day after day, she could not bear to hear it another time.

Was this how it had been?

Whether fact or fiction, as I imagined this scene it was the first time I understood how my mother could have sent me away, and how, when I was sent back to her and was not wanted back, I existed only as a reminder of the one who *was* wanted and would never come.

After the vet had "put her to sleep," the house was quiet and the sun started climbing the morning sky. In a while my nephew and I would be burying Spring in the orchard at the Small Paradise with our family's other dogs. Throughout his mother's dying Alex had stayed in the next room, but now he appeared and approached her. He put his head down, sniffed her, then walked stiffly away. It was clear that he knew death.

"I can't believe what you're telling me," Beth said. We were having lunch on my first trip to Princeton after Spring's death. "You know what mixed feelings I have about God, but the phrase 'hand of God' keeps coming into my head. Was this his gift to you, this epiphany you had, helping you make peace with Dorothy and to forgive her? And to forgive yourself?"

EXIT BETH

"I absolutely adore it," Beth said.

She had driven back with me from Princeton for her first visit. Eddie finally seemed settled in his new job and she decided to give up hers. We were standing on my porch watching Alex explore the yard.

"I can't get over how beautiful it is," Beth said. "The river out there. That beautiful space over the marshes. It's a poem. Why does it feel like an elegy?"

"You're hearing the bell tolling for Long Island. Where we are is a pocket of *old* Long Island. Old families are still living here, and there's money. What we just came through, driving out, *that's* Long Island, or what it's becoming. It won't take long for it all to be gone. I just shut my eyes and pretend I'm living in the world Whitman loved before there were any cars. Come. Where's your bag? Let's get you settled in."

After a tour of the house we sat on the porch eating lunch and feasting on the view.

"I love what you've done with this little house," Beth said. "I've never seen you so happy. Before you moved you always seemed to be walking through water, pushing against something. The only time I saw you like this was when we drove to the shore from Princeton and found that beach with all those shore birds and you ran like Alex ran just now when you let him out of the car. Do you remember when we came back the next summer and there were all those developers' stakes with the red flags and you pulled them out and threw them in the ocean?"

"That was probably the wickedest thing I've ever done in my life. By the way, your night heron is here. He makes a scary 'quark' sound at night. Maybe you'll hear him. We've got to plan what we're going to do while you're here. I thought we'd have a good long walk on the beach tomorrow. What would you like to do this afternoon?"

"I just want to be here. What I'd like best is to lie down for a while and take a nap. I don't have your incredible energy. Would you mind?"

"Of course I don't mind. I'll be in my garden."

Several hours later I looked up from my weeding and saw Beth standing outside the post and rail fence that enclosed my garden.

"That sleep was blissful," she said.

"If you stand very still you may be able to see him. I have a catbird that takes the grubs I dig up. I put them on the fence. Just be very still and see if he comes."

My friendly catbird obliged, dropping out of an overhanging pear tree and gobbling his snacks. "They're almost my favorites, the catbirds, they're so unafraid. Then I see my screech owl up in that locust —he lives there in that hollow. He'll be coming out pretty soon to look the world over and make his plans for the night. I think I love *him* the best until I hear the Carolina wren singing. I guess it's like children. They're all different and you love them all. And of course they *are* my children. You know that, but I wouldn't say that to anyone else. One of the social workers on our staff was presenting a case once and she was talking about a single woman who had an impoverished life. 'She didn't even have a dog!' she said, and then she said, 'Oh, sorry, Fairlie.'"

We were back on the porch again watching the sun set. Supper was cooking. We were having a drink and eating the delicious cheese she had brought with her. She had also brought a bottle of scotch and I knew she had brought it to be sure she had a supply. I was troubled about her. I saw so little of her on my rushed trips to New Jersey I hadn't noticed how much more weight she had put on and she looked as tired as she said she was. There were deep shadows under her eyes. Not wanting her to be angry with me, I had never confronted her about her drinking, persuading myself that her doctor and her psychiatrist would have done that. If they had, she had not been following their advice. I was thinking about how to broach the subject when she went upstairs and came down with another present for me, *The Diary of Anäis Nin*. We had discussed reading it after hearing Anäis give a talk at the Princeton Library, and I was touched that Beth remembered. This was hardly the time to bring up the subject of her drinking, but two hours later I was steadying her up the narrow staircase to her room and helping her get undressed. It was the first time she had passed out on me. Even though I no longer needed her in the desperate way I once had, I felt abandoned and alarmed. I loved this gentle, gifted woman, and she seemed inescapably on her way to destroying herself.

The next morning she was cheerful and not hung over. She was ready for breakfast and made no reference to the night before. She was looking forward to our walk on the beach and hoped we could read a little from the book. I dreaded having to speak to her about what had happened. Apparently she had no memory of it, and if I brought it up now it might spoil our day. I decided to do it at supper when she was reaching for her first drink, even if it made a horrible scene.

W e awakened that morning to the gold and blue of a clear, breezy autumn day. It was low tide when we reached the beach —not good for swimming, but perfect for strolling along the shore. The sandbars were exposed and Alex raced around on them chasing shorebirds that rose in flocks. The intense blue water beyond the bars was beginning to come in and was breaking in little white ruffles along the sand.

"We become children again, don't we," she said, "when we're on the beach." She reached down and picked up the perfect shell of a tiny horseshoe crab. Then she lagged behind, her head down, studying the tumble of debris on the high-water line.

"Is there always this much garbage?" she called out.

She was kicking at the remains of an old mattress. The Sound had been washing up more and more of our century's manufactured debris.

"What is this little leg?" she asked. She pulled at it and the rest of a body emerged, a naked Barbie doll with the other leg and two arms missing.

"Plastic is the scourge of our time," I said. "Every time the tide comes in it vomits it up on the beach. It's indestructible."

"Isn't that the rock you told me about?" Beth said, pointing ahead.

The rock had towered over me when I was a child and I told Beth about climbing to the top and looking down at the world and tasting a rare feeling of power. When we reached it we leaned against its landward side and looked back at Long Island.

"Do you see the stream coming out of that swamp over there and running down the beach to the water?" I said. "We used to make dams on it when we were children. That swamp could be Whitman's secluded swamp. He lived here for a while, you know."

"It's heaven here," Beth said.

But Alex was getting restless, wanting to keep moving. Beth found a log to sit on and I ran off with him. When I came back I found her asleep in the sand. I lay down quietly beside her, not wanting to disturb her, but Alex licked her face and woke her up.

"I wasn't really asleep," she said, sitting up and wiping her face. "I was mostly dozing and musing and thinking what a magical place this is. Some lines started coming into my head. They haven't for a long time. I thought of the phrase, 'ferocious grace' when you ran off with Alex."

She lay back on the sand and we were quiet for a while, soaking up the warmth. Since her visit began we had been slowly reentering the closeness we had forged together in what seemed now a very distant past. But whenever, over these years, we had been able to take time off the moving platforms of our separate lives, it had never failed to be waiting for us.

I hadn't decided to say anything now, but as I lay beside her on the warm sand a sentence came out of me, breaking our silence.

"I'm worried about your drinking."

The closeness we were reentering had been built on an unfailing honesty between us, and there was something about the setting we were in, so beautiful, so open, and so clean that would not tolerate evasion.

"Now that the children are more independent," she said, "I guess I've just been letting myself enjoy it. I used to drink just enough to get me through those years, but I always wanted to be there for the children, and I think I was. I know Eddie and I are using it now to keep away from each other. I think if he really tried to stop I'd try too, but I'm weak. And now that I don't have to keep going for the children the way I used to, maybe I don't care that much anymore what happens to me. Our parents died when Toby and I were young and he was exactly our father's age when he died. He was always sure it was going to happen. Why should I live my life any longer? It almost makes me feel disloyal to be alive."

"Beth! Don't say that!" I reached over and touched her cheek. It was the first time in months that she had spoken about Toby. "What can I do to help?"

"You can't do anything. Just be the best of yourself that you know how to be. You're beginning to be that now and I love to see it. I have to do this myself, whatever it is I have to do, and I'm not sure that I can. I'm not sure that I want to. Can you understand that?"

"I can, but I can't just ignore it, pretend it isn't happening. Shouldn't you be going to AA?"

"Now don't start being a therapist," Beth said sharply. You've never done that with me. But I don't think therapists can help that much, actually. We've stopped seeing Dr. Carter. He told us to go to AA too. He told us not to come back until we had. He said he was sorry he hadn't told us to do it sooner."

"Are you going?"

"Eddie likes the idea and I suppose we should go at least once and see what it's like. I certainly want him to go. But let's not talk about this anymore. It's so lovely here." She sat up and exclaimed at the sight of a pair of cormorants drying their wings on a distant rock. "Now I know why you nearly kill yourself every week with that awful commute so you can get back here."

"It's been powerful for me being home again. I'm understanding so much more. I had a lovely experience here last week I've been meaning to tell you about. On my long weekends I come down here every day either to walk with Alex or to swim, even when it rains. Ma always loved coming to the beach and we had our best times here. I often think of her swimming back then and how she loved to lie on her back and float. I could never figure out how she did that. Anyway, when I was swimming down here a few weeks ago I saw her floating nearby with a contented smile on her face. 'There's Ma!' I thought, 'She's out there floating the way she used to. She's not inside me anymore!' I called out, 'Hi, Ma!' but she just kept on smiling and didn't say anything. You remember how she was always lying under the ceiling in my analyst's office."

"Of course I do. That's lovely, sweetheart. It's lovely."

Alex was panting, getting restless.

"I guess we should be starting back," I said.

"Does he miss his mother?"

"Who knows, but I think he rather likes being his own person. I didn't realize until she died that he had never barked before. She'd done all the barking for both of them."

"I remember her curled up in my lap that day when we were driving back to the loft. That tiny, frightened little thing. Time races by so, doesn't it?"

"Shall we read a little tonight?" she asked. We were on the porch again.

"If we had another day, but I have to put you on the train in the morning, remember? I'd rather just be together and talk."

I brought out the cheese and a drink for us both, but I left the bottle in the kitchen. I wanted to talk more about her drinking and I wanted her to be sober. I wanted her to know what had happened the night before. In our talk on the beach she had been almost more honest than I was ready to hear. I was always so preoccupied with my own problems I hadn't been aware of the depression that lay behind her drinking. I wasn't afraid of her taking her own life. She would see that as cowardly and she would never knowingly hurt people that she loved. With Toby gone, Tillie getting frailer, the children heading out and my not needing her the way I once had, I could see her letting herself go with it, sinking into that rest. Ever since we came back from the beach I had been wrestling with what to do. When people are losing their will to live it's hard not to want to rush in and try to save them from themselves. But are we always doing this for *them*? I decided that what I needed to do for her was to try to divine what *she* wanted in her deepest being. I would fold my hands and do nothing, if that was what she wanted. I would go on trying to be the best of myself, which is what she had asked for. But I would not be silent tonight about her drinking. She needed to know how far it had gone. Then she could decide what she wanted to do.

As the two of us sat there after we had finished eating, watching the sun set over the marshes, I still did not know what I was going to say.

"I hope we don't have our first bad scene tonight," I started.

She looked up in surprise.

"If we'd been living together we probably would have had lots of them by now. When you don't see enough of someone you care about you don't want to spoil your time with them."

"What *are* you talking about?"

"We need to talk about your drinking."

"I thought we already had."

"Not enough. Do you remember my helping you to bed last night?"

"No."

"You couldn't get up the stairs alone. I had to help you get undressed and into bed. I guess you blacked it all out."

"I don't think I've ever done that before."

"How do you know if you don't remember?"

"I don't, of course, but I think it may have had something to do with being here, being able to let down, not having to worry about anything, not having that feeling of having to keep going."

"That may be true, but I think you need to know that it happened. It could happen again. Has your doctor been scolding you? Do you know what your blood pressure is?"

"He's always scolding me."

"I think you should tell him about the blacking out."

Beth looked uncomfortable.

"I'm always in such a rush when I come over to Princeton," I said, "I barely see you. I haven't been paying enough attention to how you are. I didn't realize you'd stopped seeing Dr. Carter. I always told myself I didn't have to worry about you because you had him and now you don't. Has he refused to see you anymore?"

"It's not that rigid. He just wanted us to know we needed something more for the drinking and that talking to him wasn't enough. He's suggested AA before, but he's never been this strict."

"I don't work with alcoholics myself any more unless they're going to AA. I learned that the hard way."

"Are you calling me an alcoholic?"

"Yes, I am. I'm saying everything tonight that I think needs saying and then I won't talk about it again unless you want to."

"What else do you want to say?"

"Have you ever talked to your children about your drinking?"

"We've talked a lot about their father's drinking, but I didn't think I was drinking enough for it to bother them."

"I think you ought to talk to them now. Ask them to tell you honestly how they feel, how they've felt all these years. If I'm as worried about you as I am, they have to be worried too, and angry. Be prepared for that. But maybe they can help you do whatever it is you have to do —give you a reason to."

"That's scary," Beth said. "But you're right. Of course I should do it. I must."

"I've hated having to say all this," I said and started to cry.

"I know you have, sweetheart." She reached over and took my hand.

After supper I ran a bath for her in the old claw-footed tub in my tiny bathroom, washed the dishes, and took Alex out. When I came upstairs she was propped up in her bed reading Nin's diary.

"Anaïs was a very naughty girl," she said. "I thought I was bad. Come. Lie down for a while. I've missed having real time with you."

I lay down beside her.

"When you moved back here," she said, closing the book, "I was worried that it wouldn't work out for you, but now it seems so right. Do you think you'll stay?"

"For a good while, certainly. I love this little place, being the caretaker, looking out for everything that lives here. I've had an odd feeling lately. You'd probably call it religious. It's a feeling of oneness with everything that lives and that I'm not more important than anything else. We all live here together doing what we're here for and try to keep out of each other's way. Sometimes a bird flies into a window of the house and gets killed and I get terribly upset. I feel it's my fault because it's my window. This spring something happened that still makes me tearful."

"Tell me."

"I love feeding the birds, and last year when the red-winged blackbirds returned one of the males was limping. He could fly, but one leg seemed to be broken and he hopped about awkwardly on the other feeding by himself after the others had gone. This spring when they all came back he was with them. He'd flown all those miles and managed to stay alive. Then after a few days I realized I wasn't seeing him. I thought he might be feeding somewhere else, but when I was on my knees one afternoon weeding my iris bed I noticed the leg of a bird coming out of a chipmunk hole and I knew it had to be my blackbird. I pulled on the leg and the rest of him came out. His fleshy parts and one eye were gone. His broken leg was dangling."

Beth gripped my hand. "Go on."

"That's all, really, except I couldn't part with him. I still can't. I cried and cried. I was almost wailing like some primitive woman. I kept looking at him in my hand. His red epaulet was so beautiful against his black feathers. If I hadn't put the corn on the ground he wouldn't have been feeding there."

"But, dearest, you can't be blaming yourself. Wasn't the chipmunk just doing his thing, like you say?"

"He was. I'm not blaming *him*. I'm blaming me. I set it up for him. I shouldn't be feeding the birds, but I love having them around so much."

I reached over Beth and took a tissue from the box beside her bed.

"I go to a different place inside myself when these things happen," I said.

"What do you mean?"

"It's hard to explain. Something seems to take me over. The first time it happened I was living in the loft. I was out walking with Spring and suddenly she ran after a woodchuck and caught it. When I got closer I saw that it was a nursing mother. It escaped from her and ran down into its den, but it was bleeding. I knew there were babies in there. I started screaming and I couldn't stop. I finally lay down on the ground and kept crying hysterically until it was all out of me. The pain becomes unbearable at those times. When I have these fits I have real physical pain in my chest and the screaming seems to be a way of getting it out."

"What did you do with your blackbird?"

"I'm embarrassed to tell you. I put him in my freezer, or what was left of him. He's still there. Don't tell anyone. He's wrapped in a baggie. I suppose it's like Dorothy keeping a lock of Little Brother's hair in her bureau drawer. Do you think other people do crazy things like this when they're alone that they'd be ashamed to have other people know about?"

"Yes, I do."

We lay quietly for a while.

"It's so nice being together like this," Beth said. "I miss the trips we used to take."

"I think I liked best that time I took you to Maryland. I knew you'd love Aunt Carrie and that she'd love you. It's a huge gift, isn't it, giving someone to another person?"

"I can't remember now who gave you to me."

"We met at the writing course. Remember? Our muses introduced us."

"Of course we did."

We were silent again.

"I'm sorry I gave you such a bad time last night," she said. "It shames me."

"I guess we're both lying here feeling ashamed of ourselves. I can't believe how selfish I've been all these years, just taking and taking from you. You told me in the beginning you were a frail reed and I just kept on taking. I worry sometimes about having hurt your children, taking so much from you. I've never really given them anything myself. They were just there —a unit you looked after that I was jealous of. I always loved seeing you care for them so lovingly."

"Even though I've loved them passionately," Beth said, "I'm afraid I've been a very *bad* mother. I was always so preoccupied, so forgetful, and not loving their father. I hope the drinking hasn't hurt them too badly."

"Maybe loving passionately is enough."

"Loving passionately has always been enough for me. Loving you has been the loveliest experience of my life. Do you remember how anxious you were when we first made love?"

"When was that?"

"Don't you remember? We were up in the Adirondacks, visiting Tillie and the Infant King. I just love that name you gave him. It's so perfect. That was the first time you'd seen him and you were appalled by him. You said he was like a two-year-old, sitting in his high chair and banging his spoon for service, and everyone came running. Don't you remember? You couldn't stand being around him and you took me off on one of your favorite climbs. I remember you running ahead of me like a gazelle and I was plodding along after like a donkey lugging a backpack. I remember asking myself why in the world I was doing this and the answer, of course, was because I adore you. But it was wonderful you took me up there. We claimed a lean-to alongside that beautiful lake, and you dove right in. Then you came out shivering and we built a fire. I warmed you up with a nip of what I'd brought. You got a little tipsy, but that wasn't why it happened."

"Why did it?"

"It was just so beautiful up there, and so far away from all your worries. You knew that Dorothy couldn't barge in and rip off the covers. And it didn't hurt that you were still shivering and climbed into the sleeping bag with me. It just seemed so natural and so right. Your guilt seemed to be gone."

"Of course I remember now. And do you remember when we woke the next morning? It was very early. A fog was hanging over the lake and everything was hushed. Then we heard that bird singing its heart out across the lake."

"You said it was that bird you've told me about that you think sings more beautifully than the nightingale."

"The white-throated sparrow. It's irrational, of course, but I felt he was singing 'Yes' —you know how you're are always preaching that to me —that he was saying 'Yes' to our making love."

"And then after we descended you got all anxious again and worrying about your reproductive time. But we did have a lot of lovely trips together before you went to Italy. I think a lot of your going there was to put an end to us. It was terribly hard losing you even though I wanted to find what you were looking for."

"And I still haven't. Sometimes I wonder if I really want what I say I want and that all I've been doing all these years is trying to prove that I'm normal."

"But, Sweetheart, being married doesn't prove that you're normal, whatever that is. There are hordes of married women who envy your freedom. Not just me."

"But like you, most of them have already had their babies. That's the hard part for me, and it was for Aunt Carrie. I've told you what she said when she first saw Ma carrying her twins, carrying us: 'Oh, Dorothy, can't I have one of them?''

"But in the end she did get one of them. Without her own babies she wouldn't have so much to give you. And that's where your maternal love has been going, loving orphans like me, and loving your patients. When you were commuting to Princeton and staying the night with me, I saw how much you were giving them, worrying about them, worrying if you'd given them the right advice." She reached over and touched my face. "I so love being here with you, being close to you again. And if you can believe it, I haven't been in love with another woman since you, and that's kind of a miracle, don't you think, knowing my addiction to passion. Have you?

"Only to Leo."

Beth laughed.

"He said when I was with him at the end that he'd turned into an old woman. I know it was his mothering of me in those early years that was such a huge part of his appeal, but he was still male enough then to have fathered some babies for me. No, I can't think of any other women I've been attracted to since you. I was drawn to you because I was craving a mother. That's been my hang-up. I remember when I was seeing Dr. Porter and realized that I was a child in Leo's lap, not a woman, and felt such shame."

"Sweetheart, will you ever stop faulting yourself for where your craving for love has taken you? Can't you just be the lovely woman you've evolved to be and go wherever love takes you?"

When I came down the next morning I was surprised to find her sitting out on the porch.

"I've been watching the sun rise," she said, "and hearing the world wake up. I think I may have heard the heron. The ducks have been very vocal."

"You're up early."

"I woke around four full of thoughts and couldn't get back to sleep. I've always been so sure they haven't been using drugs, the girls that is. Now I'm worrying. There's never been any sign of it when they come home on vacation, but how do I know? So many of them are doing it. I'm sure *he* isn't, he's too young. But how do I know? His headmaster said there *is* some of it at his school. Maybe I've just been being naïve. When I went to college we all started right in drinking at our parties. Why would it be any different now? If I talk with the children about my drinking, if I level with them, maybe they'll level with me."

"I'm sure they will. It will mean a lot to them to have you be open about yourself."

"I've often wondered what you'd be like as a therapist," Beth said. "It's interesting how sure you are when you're doing that, and how unsure you've always been about the rest of you. I still wish you'd get back to your writing. You're so good at that. But I know that's a sore subject."

"I wish you'd get back to yours. You'll have more time, now that the fledglings are almost gone."

"No. I don't think I'll be writing anymore. I've never had the drive you've had. You'll have to write now for both of us."

"I have a mental map of all the roads around here," I said as I was driving her to the train. "I could almost drive with my eyes closed. I love knowing I belong here, that it's my place. Your situation is so different. You had an English father and an American mother and you were over there until you were eight. Which do you think you are more? English or American? Where do you feel the pull, the kind of pull I felt when I came back here? Do you feel any? To anywhere?"

"More to England, I think, even though I've never been back. I'm drawn to the Adirondacks, too. Those summers were so peaceful. I suppose if some-one told me to 'go home' the way you tell a stray dog, I'd think of our house in Princeton. But it's never felt like a home. And then I might think of Tillie's apartment, but that wouldn't be home either. Then I'd think of London. I'd like to go back and see if I can find the house where we lived. I'd like to look up those aunts of mine."

"Why don't you? Why don't you go back? They're still alive. They'd prob-ably be thrilled to see you. Why don't you go back?"

"It never entered my mind. Toby and I felt so pushed out when we left. Not wanted there. And I was never free enough to go."

I pulled in beside the old board-and-batten station house with its gingerbread trim that had recently been rescued from demolition by the Historical Society.

"That's an absolutely inspired idea," Beth said. "I would never have thought of it. It makes me weak. We've been so strapped, but he's working now. The children are away most of the time. Why couldn't I go? Why shouldn't I?"

We heard the whistle of the train. I grabbed her bag and walked with her onto the platform as the great beast thundered in, breathing hard.

"I'll let you know," she yelled back, starting up the stairs of the nearest car. Then she stopped and looked back.

"I adore you!" she shouted.

Late that night she called to tell me that she had booked a ticket to London on a special ten-day excursion. She had talked to her aunts and they *were* thrilled. She would wait to have the talk with the children on their Thanksgiving break. Maybe being over there would give her strength and resolve.

Several weeks later a postcard arrived:

It's bliss. They're adorable and naughty and very old and drink like fishes. We laugh and laugh. The house where we lived was bombed in the blitz, but I found the park where we used to play and the statue of Alice. Bless you. Miss you. Let's come here together some time. All my love.

Dearest,

    It's fun being the one writing you from the other side of the world! They've been urging me to stay on longer and say they will help with the added expense, and so of course I'm saying yes! yes! yes! This may be the last time I'll be able to do this. I called Eddie and I think he loves having the house to himself. My plan is to return just before Thanksgiving when the children come home and prepare myself for the dreaded conversation. This is the best thing that's happened to me, except for you. I miss you. Write if you can to the above address. There should be time for a letter to reach me. All Love, Beth

Dear Beth,

    I couldn't be happier for you that you're staying on. I know you don't have a camera, but try to get some pictures to bring back. I'd love to see what the old girls look like. You'll have so much to tell me, but I won't be in Princeton when you first get back. The clinic is closing for a long Thanksgiving break. I will be having Thanksgiving with Robert's family and then staying on longer to face something very painful. You will remember that Alex has been having a lot of trouble walking because of his hip problem. It's been getting worse and the vet thinks its time, so I'm going to do it when my nephew is here and can help me get him up to the orchard and bury him beside his mother. So for the first time in a very long time I will be dogless. I enjoyed so much being able to take him to work after Spring died and some of my clients will miss him as much as I will, but it will make the commute easier. I will be thinking of you when you have the dreaded conversation. Have courage. I feel sure it will go well. Soak it all up while you are still over there and store it for some long conversations. Much, much love, f

Dearest one,

    I'm home, and I got your letter just before I left. I am so terribly sorry about Alex. I hadn't realized it had gotten so bad. The children and I adored him as a puppy, but I only saw him once as a grown-up when I had that lovely visit with you and we walked with him on the beach. This brings back our time with Salomé and how painful that ending was.

    Well, the dreaded conversation is behind me, and you were so right! It all ended up with hugs and tears. They've hated my drinking, but not as much as Eddie's. They decided to confront him by themselves, with me not there, and he cried, too, and then we talked as a family. He and I are going to our first AA meeting this week. Actually they suggested that he go to AA and I go to Alanon. You know all about that. The girls say they've smoked marijuana and don't much like it, but have done nothing worse and I have to believe them, but it's all out in the open now and can be talked about. While we were all being so frank the girls said they've hated the way I've put on weight and let myself go. It was painful to hear, but I'm glad they could say it. Now it's up to me. Will I have the strength to do it? I send you deep love and gratitude for persevering with me and making me face what I had and still have to do. Beth

Dearest,

Another quick letter with another piece of news. The girls have kept after me about losing weight and I've decided to go down to North Carolina and go on the Duke rice diet. You have to stay a month, but you can stay longer if you wish. You get a motel nearby and go in daily to the clinic for I don't yet know what. Actually I look forward to that long retreat and am planning what books to take etc. etc. The Alanon meeting was amazing. I'll have to miss the meetings for a while, but they tell me I can probably find a meeting down there. Eddie's taken to it like catnip —he's been to two meetings and already has a sponsor. I honestly don't think I need this as much as he does and before I get into the rigors of Duke I'm letting myself have sip of wine now and then (do I see a scowl?), but I must lose the weight, and the Duke plan should do it if I'm faithful. As soon as I know more about my plans I will let you know. All love, Beth

Dear Beth,

The Duke plan is inspired! Bless the girls for keeping after you. I remember your telling me about the agreement you had with Eddie when the children were small. When you reached your breaking point you could claim a weekend off and he would take over. Going to Duke is like that only more so. You can lie on your bed eating novels like chocolates and watch the pounds roll off. As soon as you get settled send me your address and let me know how it's going.

News item: I've decided to take an examination to get certified to do counseling in New York State. I'd like the option of setting up a practice here and eventually being able to give up the commute. So I have to knuckle down and start preparing for the exam —a daunting task. Wish me luck! Much Love, dear Beth, J.

Dearest,

What a brilliant idea to take the exam! Of course you'll be able to pass it. But when you stop commuting when will be I be able to see you? You asked how it's going down here and I think this is going to work. I love being here all by myself with no responsibilities, so much so that its easy to pay the price of being on this restricted diet. After this first week I've lost five pounds! I'm pretty sure I'm going to want to stay on longer than the month. I have a room at the Hilton Inn and walk to the clinic every day. The exercise is good for me and part of the regimen. And I've found an Alanon meeting. It sort of interrupts the feeling of being "on vacation," but I know I have to do it. I love having your letters. Write soon again. All my love, Beth

Dear Beth,

It's hard to have you so far away and not be able to talk with you about something that happened yesterday. I'm still shaken by it. Do you remember my telling you how upset I was about the chipmunk killing my black bird and how I had what I guess people call "hysterics" when Spring caught the nursing mother woodchuck? Well, I had another one of those seizures.

When I first moved here I planted a Seckel pear tree like the one Pa planted when we moved to the Small Paradise. Aunt Carrie had also planted one in Maryland on her farm. I guess it was sort of a family thing. She said they had one in the yard of their house in Baltimore. Last year the leaves on my tree began turning black and some branches died. I called the nursery and learned that it was Fire Blight, a bacterial infection that's fatal unless you prune it out, twig by twig, sterilizing your shears between each cut. I did everything I was supposed to do and no new symptoms appeared before winter. This spring all seemed to be well, but last week I saw some more black leaves and I've been frantic, pruning as instructed.

Yesterday I noticed some black leaves that were too high for me to reach and went up on a stepladder. I thought I was on firm ground, but it started to tip and instinctively I grabbed a branch to break my fall and broke it off. It was one of the main branches and it left a big gap, spoiling the beautiful symmetry of the tree. I had fallen on the ground with the branch still in my hand and I lay there sobbing. And then I started to scream, "I didn't mean to do it! I didn't mean to do it!" over and over until I was exhausted. It was like a child trying to explain, when something awful has happened, that it was an accident, not an intentional act. The experience was shattering and the rest of the day sort of disappeared. All I can do now is to keep on pruning if the infection spreads and maybe I can stop it, but I've ruined the beauty of the tree and I am bereft. I loved that little tree.

This "seizure" was so powerful it made me wonder if my anguish about what I did to the tree wasn't some kind of reenactment of how I felt when I killed my rabbit and when I knocked my twin off his tricycle into the fireplace. Well, I'm over it for now, more or less, but I realize, that I may never really be over it. Bernie said once that some things go so deep they can always be stirred up no matter how much therapy we have. But there is also some good news to report. I passed my exam! They almost didn't let me take it because of my not having a degree.

How many more pounds have you lost? What are you reading? I miss you so much, f

Dearest,

Your letter made me want to rush right up and put my arms around you. I wish you hadn't been alone when that happened with your tree, but maybe all that emotion wouldn't have come out if someone had been around. Your Bernie is probably right and this may be a cross you will always have to bear, but it may be that some kind of purging or healing is taking place. Could this be one of the reasons you're back on Long Island? It was so amazing when Spring died and all that came out about your twin and Dorothy.

I came down here with a goal of fifty pounds and I've lost twenty. I'll probably lose another five before I leave. The trick will be to keep it off when I get home. I've decided to stop going to the Alanon meetings down here. They were taking me to a place where I don't want to be right now. I haven't had a drop since I came down. Too many calories. I never realized the connection before with my weight. When I first went to the meetings

I was deeply moved by those women's stories, but then it became depressing hearing them say the same things over and over and their lives changing so little. I've been reading lots of poetry, the Bible, the Bhagavad-Gita, Martin Buber —struggling with him —and detective stories! And, dare I say it? I've tried writing some poems. Never thought I would again, and I'm rusty. Not ready yet for inspection. It will be strange leaving the cocoon of this room. Whatever is to happen next, this time away has been wonderful for me. Much, much love, dearest friend, Beth

Dear Beth,

There's just enough time to get one more letter to you before you leave. The pear tree business was so painful it seemed more than I could bear to find a goldfinch lying under my west window. The setting sun may have been reflected in the glass and blinded him. I burst into tears of course. It seems that I've never stopped crying since you opened that little box. I picked him up and held him in my hand and he was still warm. He was heartbreakingly beautiful in his brilliant yellow and black outfit and wearing his little black cap. These birds are so much tinier than you expect when you hold them in your hand. I looked him up later in my guide and they only weigh 0.46 ounces! I cupped my hands around him to keep him warm and suddenly he stirred and flew out of my hands into the sunset. I could see him disappearing into the western sky in that dipping and rising way goldfinches fly. It felt like a miracle, a gift, almost a kind of forgiveness. I will never forget that image.

It does seem as if this time down there has been wonderfully restoring. Will I recognize the svelte you when I see you again? Don't let it all slip away when you come home. Your f

B ut she did.

Soon after her return from Duke she came over to see me. The change in her was stunning. When I met her at the station the young woman in the photograph on Eddie's bureau stepped off the train. At least her face did. Her body had, after all, birthed and nursed three babies since that picture was taken and the long, glamorous hairstyle of her youth had been cropped well before we met. I was torn between admiration for the angular beauty of this unfamiliar face and a pang of homesickness for my old Beth. But as soon as I heard her saying goodbye to a woman she had met on the train, heard that warm voice with the slight accent she had carried with her from that long-ago English childhood, I knew my old Beth had returned.

This was the last time we were together. She had been spending a great deal of time with Tillie who had had a stroke. I did not know, until her daughter called me, that during these months with Tillie, Beth had let herself go and had started drinking again. Her blood pressure soared and her doctor had put her in the hospital to stabilize her. It was there that she had a fatal heart attack. As I took in this shocking news, I remembered that day when we were lying on the beach talking about her drinking and her saying that she felt almost disloyal to be alive —disloyal to Toby and their parents —and while not quite putting it into words, implying that she felt a pull to join them.

Her funeral was about to begin when I came into the chapel in Princeton. I found a seat near the pew where she and I sat during the Hindemith, wanting to remember her sitting beside me and gripping my hand while I grieved for Long Island. I wanted to bring back that part of her I especially loved —the way she understood things so quickly without their having to be explained. She had given me her blessing that night, even though she knew how much less she would see of me after I left.

As we rose to sing the first hymn that her family had chosen —she was not one to have planned her own funeral —I imagined that she *was* beside me. She had slipped into the pew, taken hold of the hymnal and joined me in the singing. Then the two of us went together through the service for the dead, kneeling and rising, kneeling and rising, and singing more hymns —the two of us, side by side, mourning our parting. "Don't tell the others I was here," she whispered as the service ended, "I wanted to be with you." And then she was gone.

Where was she, this dear person? Where she *wanted* to be? Could I hope for that?

It was strange to be back at that house, full of people now, that on many an evening had been privately ours as she and I began weaving our lives together. Here we all were, the people her life had touched —family and friends, some I knew and strangers she had talked about and I'd looked forward to meeting. All of us stood around attending that strange social gathering that is like a cocktail party, where chatter and canapés and liquor mingle with grief and shared memories. Eddie, smiling, was the genial host, and her children welcoming. They were poised young adults now, warm and outgoing like their mother. We hugged and did not try for words.

As the gathering was thinning out I went off by myself and wandered about for a while, knowing that this was probably the last time I would be in this house. On a table in the living room I came across a piece of sculpture that Beth made when I was in Florence. She called it "The Dying Gull." I re-membered Caroline Gordon talking about the controlling image in a piece of fiction in that writing class where Beth and I had met.

"Death is surely the controlling image in our story," I thought, "Beth's and mine. Do you agree, Beth?"

"Yes, if you could *see* death," she replied, "like snow in that story of Joyce's that we studied, but all we can see are the dead, and be undone by it."

Several months after Beth's funeral I received a note from one of her daughters.

"We've been going through Mummy's papers," it read, "and came across this poem. We thought you'd like to have it. Hope you are okay." At the top of the page Beth had written a note to herself, "Finish revisions and send to F."

> *REMEMBERING A BEGINNING*
> *In your ferocious grace I watched night melt,*
> *Mingle with the moon and disappear,*
> *Drawn by your voice the darkness I had felt*
> *Faded to dawn, deliberate and clear.*
> *And in this light enchanted I did come*
> *A shepherd seeking stars at edge of day,*
> *To learn from you of love the total sum,*
> *If one would love one gives one's love away.*
> *So I accepted this season of my heart*
> *And watched it bud in pale and tender leaf.*

I knew this sudden joy would be a part
Of me through the long winters of my grief.
Whatever route you followed you would be
The sun that warmed the deepest part of me.

I wondered what her girls had made of that beautiful poem. Had they had any intimation of her "long winters of grief?" I was sure they had not.

Beth and I had seen a gull dying when she first visited me on Long Island and was deeply moved by it. She made that sculpture two years later when I was away in Italy. She had not done well that year. I had never thought of myself as a source of strength for her, for I had crawled into her lap, almost on sight of her, as a needy child. But when I read her poem it became clear for the first time that, almost on sight, I had become the reincarnation of her beautiful mother. She was the sun who warmed her in her earlier, tender years — that lovely being who had chased her and Toby around the house for no good reason and had sometimes forgotten to feed them, and then had vanished into the long winters of grief.

"I always thought he was a moon to her sun," Beth said when she was first telling me about her father.

I remembered the night when Beth and I came close to being lovers and she had run her fingers over my face and said, "That was the first thing that attracted me to you, your beauty." It puzzled me then that it was of such importance to her, but now I understood. It was not just I who had found the lost mother sitting in Caroline Gordon's class. Both orphans had.

Back to Work

I had made an appointment with Bernie. I thought I wanted to talk with him about my decision to build up a practice on Long Island and to phase out my work in Princeton. I hoped he would let me consult him by phone, coming over from time to time when I was badly stuck. But when he opened his door and pulled me into a big warm hug I knew that I had come for comfort. As I enjoyed our embrace I remembered the formal handshake at the end of my lengthy analysis with Dr. Gautier, only the second time we had touched in those many years. Bernie was heavier now, and shaggier, and like me had relaxed his style in the decades since we had first met.

I've really lucked out with Bernie, I thought, when he went off to fetch us some coffee. The longer I did my own work the more sure I was that an essential component of the healing in psychotherapy was the warm human connection. Not being my therapist Bernie could be freer with me, but even if he had been my analyst I am sure I would have felt that connection with him. I had felt it with the analyst who referred me to Dr. Gautier and I had only seen him once. But Dr. Gautier had been a trainee, learning new rules, and perhaps had not been experienced enough to know when to bend them a bit and let a human person come through, except, of course, when he shouldn't have.

"What's up with you?" Bernie asked. "I haven't seen you looking so down since you were going through that miserable menopause. Do you have your dog with you? You can bring him in if you want."

"I had to put him to sleep. Just a few weeks ago.

"I remember when that other little dog of yours died and that group you went to was so helpful. How are you dealing with this one?"

"I had to put his mother to sleep, too, several years ago, and my very first dog. It's hard to do, but you end the suffering. It's not as hard as sudden death when you're not expecting it."

I hadn't planned to talk about Beth and I could feel tears starting. "This isn't why I came today," I said.

"It doesn't hurt to talk about it."

Bernie didn't know about Beth. There was no reason why he should.

"My dearest friend just died. She was the most important person in my life. You think I'd be undone by it, but strangely I'm not. I grieve for her. I miss her. But I believe she wanted to die. Her parents and her brother had all died young and she was deeply attached to them. I think she felt a strong pull to join them. She'd struggled to be a good wife and mother, but she wasn't cut out for that and she was worn out. She needed a long, long rest. I'm glad she's where she wanted to be, if she is. If she'd died earlier in our relationship I would have been devastated. I was starving for mothering and she took me on in spite of all the other burdens in her life. I regressed totally in that relationship, but in the years we were together she "grew me up" and helped me to become a reasonably mature adult. After she died I worried that I'd taken too much from her, but I knew that I had to have given her something she needed as much as I needed her."

"What did you give her?" Bernie asked.

"It wasn't until after her death that I knew what it was. I believe I was the incarnation of her beautiful mother. Her mother had died when she was a little girl and Beth had adored her. I believe I recreated that relationship for her, brought her mother back from the dead."

"Close personal relationships can be amazingly powerful," Bernie said, "and every bit as healing as therapy. Often more so. But there has to be a balance of giving and getting. Otherwise one of the two gets burned out. Your relationship with your friend seemed tuned just right, and it answers a question I've had about you. More coffee?"

I shook my head.

"I'll run and get another cup. Be right back."

"You've always been an excellent therapist," Bernie went on, "but when we first started working together you were overly cautious and afraid of making mistakes. Even though your analyst made some bad mistakes with you, you shouldn't have come out of five years of analysis still feeling so unsure of yourself. But gradually you seemed to mature and become bolder and as you know you've reached a place where you really don't need me that much anymore. But you always know when you do. You've always been so insightful about your own hang-ups and when they're getting in the way of your work. I was pleased when I saw those changes in you, but I was puzzled about what had brought it about. So it was your friend Beth."

"When I was seeing my analyst and it wasn't going well I asked him if I could see a woman analyst for a while, then return and finish with him. I knew I needed a close relationship with a woman, but of course the answer was no. I was being resistant. I was supposed to be having a mother transference to him. So Beth became my woman analyst."

"You seem amazingly together as you're telling me all this. You seem almost detached. Are you sure you're all right? It's such a huge loss. Your closest friend, and your dog."

"I'm not detached. Bernie. Believe me. I cry plenty when I'm alone. Do you know Emily Dickenson's poems?"

"A bit."

"I came across this line of hers recently: 'I can wade grief. Whole pools of it —I'm used to that.' But there's another reason I think I'm not more undone about losing her. I think we were brought together for a purpose. Some people might say by a higher power. I believe we came together to fill a void in each other's lives. And we did that. We had done what we came together to do and she was back with her own mother. Our task was finished."

Bernie was silent.

"So now I'm ready to pick up my life and go on. Before she died and I was aware of how burned out she was, I asked her if there was anything I could do to help her. She said, 'Just be the best of yourself you know how to be. Give me that gift.' So that's what I'm going to try to do. Do you remember when I had that mid-career crisis and went to Italy, hoping I could become a published writer?"

"I remember."

"Beth and I were both frustrated writers. We'd met in a writing class. Part of my going over there was to stop being so dependent on her, but a big part of it was her enthusiasm about my writing and her feeding my fantasy that I could be published and stop being a therapist. Well, as you know, I got very depressed there and couldn't do much writing and I was grateful that I had the work to come back to. But Beth was deeply disappointed. I think she may have been living out her frustrations about her own life through me. After she died I decided to try to write something really good as a kind of memorial to her, something that would delight her. So I sat down at my desk with the yellow tablet I write on, and this naked lady psychiatrist appears walking down Nassau Street on a Sunday morning to buy *The New York Times*. A patient of hers is sitting at the window in a restaurant having breakfast and sees her go by. She is both appalled and fascinated. She rushes out, follows her, wanting to protect her from humiliation, maybe even arrest, but is afraid to get too close to her. She keeps glancing at her and looking away. The psychiatrist is making a powerful statement and she is speaking for a part of me that has sometimes felt trapped and burdened by my work. She is saying to hell with being a responsible professional, to hell with ethics. Let my patients fend for themselves!"

"How does it end?" Bernie asked. "Don't leave me there!"

"I never finished it. I was afraid it wouldn't be good enough."

"There you go again, doubting yourself. If you didn't need the money, would you like to give up the work and just write?"

"If I could do some really original writing I might say yes, but there's another big part of me that would miss the work."

"What would you miss?"

I surprised myself by starting to cry. "I'd miss loving my clients, freeing them. Trying to get them to a better place. Being a surrogate mother, I suppose. And I'd miss the intimacy, the depth of the connection. It's unique, as you know. It can be very rich. And there may be something else, too, Bernie. I read an article recently by a psychiatrist. He was talking about restitution. He said when there's an early death in a family, or a family member has some kind of disability, another member of the family often feels compelled to make up for that loss in some way. Maybe I've been doing that in my therapy all these years, trying to create new lives. Beth said something like that. She said that successful therapy is a kind of rebirth. But when I fail with the therapy it feels like another death and then I want to run from it. Maybe that's why I keep on struggling with difficult clients long after it would be reasonable to give up. Do you know what I'm trying to say? Do you understand that I'm really not free to stop the work and probably never will be?"

"I do," Bernie said. "But I hope a time will come when you've created enough new lives and can let yourself rest. Our work is so gratifying when it's successful, but so stressful when it's not. Now about the question you came in with. Of course we can keep our connection going after you move. I'll be here until I drop. I've never been pulled to do something else the way you have. But is there anything more you want to talk about today? Anything more about your friend?"

"There is one more thing, but it's not easy to talk about. Maybe I should be taking it to a therapist."

"Let's see."

"Ok. I had a sex dream recently about one of my women clients. She's been very hostile to me and I dreamed that she burst into my bedroom while I was asleep, flung herself on me, and told me that she loved me passionately. I've never had a sex dream about a client before, male or female, and having this one, and being powerfully aroused by it, made me terribly anxious. It made me wonder if I should be doing this work. As we both know, having sex with a patient is a therapist's cardinal sin. At the very least, I think the dream should make me cautious about taking on women who have mother issues like mine and desperately need to be loved and affirmed by a woman. Beth loved and affirmed me and it was wonderfully healing, but I panicked when our relationship became sexual and I tried to pretend that it never had. I was terrified that we'd be found out. When I was growing up, you literally were a social outcast if you went this route. I'd had a brief relationship with a girl many years before I met Beth and it almost paralyzed me with anxiety worrying about being abnormal. Then my analyst only made it worse, giving me the old psychoanalytic dogma and telling me it was sick. I think now that he was homophobic and really repelled by same sex relationships. At the time, of course, I believed him, or partly did. But in spite of responding so powerfully to Beth, my life plan after I came back from Europe was still to marry and have children. Even though I'm well past child-bearing age, I half think I still want to find a husband, but maybe it's just because I want the approval of my family and community and to prove that I'm a normal woman. Having that sex dream about my client really freaked me out and made me wonder if I'd been unconsciously seductive with that young woman. What do you make of all this, Bernie?"

"As usual you're overreacting and worrying too much. Of course you shouldn't stop doing the work. First of all, it's not unethical to be aroused by patients or to dream about having sex with them. It's what you do with it. Some therapists rationalize having sex for the good of with their patients, and in fairness to therapists, the intimate, private connection between therapist and patient can be extremely provocative. I remember one of my mentors saying that the therapy relationship is always hovering over a drumbeat of sexual possibility. But having a dream about sex with a patient and having sex are very different. Having a dream can alert you that you may be losing your objectivity and that you're getting too emotionally involved, and it can be a signal that you probably should have a consultation about the case. Now if you ultimately decide that you do have a sexual preference for women that doesn't disqualify you as a therapist. It probably deepens your understanding of complicated issues. I'm sorry this gave you such a worry. Do you think dreaming about your client's passionate love for you might have been a response to the death of your friend and the loss of her mothering?"

"That could be. It probably did make me more vulnerable."

"When we get together again, we need to work some more on why you're so hard on yourself and try to free you from that. It wastes such good energy. Now, have we covered everything you need to talk about today?"

"As long as you think I'm not a risk to my clients I'll go ahead with my plans to set up an office on Long Island, and I'll call you when I get a practice going. Wish me luck! And thanks for being so good to me, Bernie. Dare I say that the intimate private connection between supervising analyst and therapist can be extremely provocative?"

Bernie smiled. "You can say that."

I reached in my bag and handed him his check, and in one gesture he took it and tore it up.

"You shouldn't do that, Bernie."

He shook his head. "I don't want it. You can start paying me again when we're working on your cases." He stood up and saw me to the door.

We hugged, lingering a bit.

"Thanks again, Bernie."

"I'm sure you'll find a nice office, and don't be discouraged building up a practice. It takes time."

"I'll have to advertise myself in some way and I'm not good at that. I hate the business part of being a professional."

"You could always rip off your clothes and walk around your town wearing a sign."

"I just might," I said.

FULL CIRCLE

It was amazing. My search for an office had taken me, of all places, to the house next to ours in the village where I had first attended school. It had taken me right into our old school room. After a number of different occupancies over the years, the space was now a busy real estate office. I had come there to meet with one of the agents.

Those many, many years ago I sat at my small desk with the other children. Now it was an office with grown-up desks, the clacking of typewriters, and the ringing of telephones. I stood there, bringing to mind our neat row of little desks and our teacher, Miss Tyler, shy and gentle and patient with her motley collection of "upper class" children ranging in age from me at five to an eight-year-old boy. I was distracted from my reverie by the sound of honking coming from four lanes of irritable traffic moving past the Judge's house. It brought back an unforgettable day when I was sitting at my small desk in the same room, when the traffic of old-fashioned cars was light and orderly as it moved along what was then called "The Village Street." Each morning when Miss Tyler arrived at our school, she parked her precious newly acquired Model T Ford by the side of the road in front of the Judge's house. One day in the middle of a school morning we heard a crash. Miss Tyler rushed out, leaving the door open behind her. We then heard a cry of anguish. We waited and waited. Then the oldest boy got up and looked out the door. He told us that a car had run into her little Ford and that she was standing beside it talking to some man. We continued waiting until she finally returned, closing the door behind her. Standing there, she reached into her pocket, took out a handkerchief, dabbed at her eyes, and blew her nose. We watched intently. Then she walked back to her teaching place in the front of the room.

"Can one of you tell me what lesson we were learning?" she asked. I don't remember what it was, but we all had learned a lesson that day, not necessarily the same one, and not one she had planned to teach. I believe that I had learned for the first time the enduring lesson of compassion.

"Oh, there you are! The realtor said. "I've been looking for you. I have something to show you." She explained that the Judge's house and adjoining land were now owned by the Historical Society. They had recently rescued an old tavern from the wrecking ball and moved it next to our old house. The downstairs was being used for meetings, but a small room was available on the second floor that the agent thought would be private enough for me. I had noticed an unfamiliar building, standing on the other side of the hedge that I used to squeeze through on my way to school, but there had been so many changes in the town during my decades of absence I had not been particularly curious about it. I *had* been curious about our old house and was shocked the first time I drove by to see that it had been turned into a suite of doctors' offices. Half of our old yard had become a blacktopped parking area, and trees that had been my old friends had been cut down. At first I had been outraged, then sad and resigned. That house was history now. The past was gone.

When I first took possession of my room in the tavern, I paused for a moment to rest after climbing the narrow steep staircase. I'll have to put a railing on these stairs, I thought. I can't have my clients falling off. I always loved shaping a therapy nest, making it attractive and comfortable and a safe haven for my clients. I wondered where I would place my furniture and what pictures to bring. Perhaps as a christening present to myself and my new clients I would buy a pretty new rug. There was only one window in the room, and when I looked through it to see what my view was going to be I could see the same side of the widower's house that had always come into view when I made my passages through the hedge. When I had taken those first steps on my life's journey, that view of his house and of a world beyond had been a powerful, beckoning image. For the past half century I had been out in that world, trying to make my way in it, and here I was back where I had started, looking at that same view as if I had never left.

The issues that people bring into therapy tend to be the same no matter where they live, but I became aware that practicing my profession in the world in which I grew up intensified my relationships with my new clients, for in addition to the therapeutic bond was the bond of attachment to homeland. I do not think that my therapy was any different, but as I brought my skills to the people who lived in my nation I could feel the great divide between my personal and professional selves gradually closing as if two huge sliding doors were moving towards each other and locking together, containing me, finally, as one being.

I felt a special bond with David, a young Long Island native who knew my river and had spent a day canoeing there with his young wife, Cindy, while they were still together. She had been in a "consciousness-raising" group and had gone off to "find herself." David was devastated and close to tears when he was telling me why he had come.

He was referred to me by a psychologist friend of mine whose husband was a biology professor at the new Long Island campus of the State University. David wanted to be a marine biologist and had been his student and had also worked for him in the summers. When my friend and her husband were away one year, David and his young bride had moved into their garage apartment to take care of the property. David was still living there. He had dropped out of college when he and Cindy married. He was now working in a fish hatchery, but he still hoped to finish his degree. He had one more year to go. Cindy had finished hers and was working in a day care center. She would be paying her own way now.

I met with David once and on his next visit he came early and found me struggling to attach the railing I had bought for the steep staircase.

"You need four hands for that job," he said. "You hold the railing and I'll put in the screws." I handed him my screwdriver. "I'm early," he said. "It's good to be useful. I don't know what to do with myself now when I come home from work. You can't just go back to being a bachelor overnight. I could take my boat out, but Cindy used to come with me. I don't like going without her."

There was no one in the tavern who could overhear us, so I let this be where our session was going to begin, with me holding the railing and David putting in the screws and scolding me for not having an electric screwdriver.

"Actually," he said, "I never did have much of a bachelor life we married so young. I think that's one of the reasons she left. She didn't either. She said she wanted the freedom to know what it's like to be on her own."

"Why *did* you marry so young?"

"We were high school sweethearts. We'd talked about marriage then, but we wanted to do college first. We both went to the State University and at the end of our third year her dad got sick. She loved her dad and he adored her. Cindy's a lively, sunny, affectionate girl, but she can be flighty and unpredictable. I think he wanted to see her settled before he died. I guess we did it partly for him, but we'd been wanting to live together anyway, have our first home. He gave us an excuse. It's good that we didn't have kids, but I almost wish we had. I'd still have a little piece of her."

He sounded close to tears again. We finished the job without more talk, then went up to my office. I took more of a history in this session, learning that before he met Cindy he had always been somewhat of a loner. He took after his grandfather who used to sit reading in their house after he retired, rarely going out. He'd been a bay man all his life, fishing for scallops. When David was a boy he loved going out with his grandfather. David's father had been killed in World War II. His mother was a strong no-nonsense woman who had always worked and raised him and his sisters to be self-sufficient and independent.

"You've told me why you love Cindy so much," I said as our session was winding down, "always seeing the bright side of things and pulling you out of your moods. But why did Cindy love you?"

It took him a while to answer. "We liked the same things, I guess, liked doing things together. We never fought. We were very compatible."

"Did you get along sexually?"

"Yes, we did. I know she liked it with me."

"But she could have had all that with another man. What was it about you?"

"She knew I'd take care of her, be a good father when we had our children. I steadied her, made her feel safe. She could always trust me."

"So you were a kind of a parent for her, picking up where her father left off?"

"I guess you could say that."

"Do you think a part of her could have resented that, even though another part of her loved you for taking such good care of her?"

"That's possible. I guess she could have."

"When girls think about marriage and settling down, Dave, you're the kind of man they hope they'll end up with. But before they're ready for that sometimes they want a little fun. Do you think Cindy's wings got clipped too soon?"

"I've thought about that."

"We're running out of time now, Dave. Would you like to go on having these talks?"

He nodded.

"Then I'll see you again next week. Thanks for helping me with the railing."

The following week he didn't show up. I was troubled. He was my last appointment of the day and after waiting a reasonable time I was getting ready to leave when I heard him come in and run up the stairs.

"I could have killed him," he said, dropping into a chair "whoever the hell he was. I'm late. I know. I'm sorry." He got up and started pacing in my small room. "She looked happy. She was laughing. I could have smashed right into them."

"Slow down a minute, Dave. Slow down. What are you talking about? Did you see Cindy with someone?"

He collapsed again into the chair. "I saw her with this guy. They were in a convertible with the top down. Her red hair was flying. I knew it was her. I've never felt so angry in my life. I've imagined it. I've imagined her being with another man, but *seeing* it. *Seeing* it. I keep seeing her face all lit up, looking at him, laughing the way she used to laugh with me. She was the best thing that ever happened to me." He put his head in his hands and started to cry. Then his crying grew into big, heaving sobs. I watched him being undone by his grief and thought of those lines in Beth's poem — *Whatever route you followed you would be the sun that warmed the deepest part of me*. I wanted to take him in my arms, but I knew that I should not, could not even touch him.

"Cindy was the light of your life, wasn't she?" I said when his crying had finally subsided. "You think she's gone forever, but I'm not sure that she has."

"No," he said, shaking his head. "She's gone. She's gone. I know she's gone."

"Maybe she is, and maybe she isn't. I don't want to get your hopes up, but you two seem to have had a lot going for you. Maybe she'll realize that after she's been away from you for a while. I've counseled a lot of couples, Dave. When they come in they're usually very angry and finding fault with each other, but that doesn't seem to be true for the two of you, although I only have your side of it. You said she needed you to steady her, but if she'd let you keep on doing that she might have just gone on being an adorable child that other people like you would want to look out for. She may make some bad mistakes out there on her own, but you're going to have to her let her do what she has to do, and get on with your own life. Both you and Cindy have to learn how to get along without each other. Then you can see if you still *want* to be together. If she wants to come back and you still want her back, it may mean everything in the world to her that you didn't just discard her after she hurt you so badly, and that you were willing to wait for her.

"Are you saying that I've been leaning on her, too? That this thing goes both ways?"

"I am saying that. You need to get that boat out in the bay without her and get used to being alone again. When you're alone you can go in any direction you want, and you need to enjoy that for a while. You need some freedom too. With more time now maybe you can go back and finish school. Shall you and I meet again next week?"

"I'll be here."

I sat down after David left, needing to unwind and collect my thoughts. I could still see him with his head in his hands, mourning his loss of Cindy. I had never experienced a man's grief so closely before. I had seen men cry for the first time in the Encounter Group. But then I remembered something I had totally forgotten —seeing Pa on the steps of our old house crying after his dog Lindy died. But I had never seen him cry again. I studied that memory closely now as if it were a faded photograph. In the many intervening years my little stray had died and I learned how grief for one loss can carry the pain of another. Perhaps Lindy's death had been the first echo of the death of Pa's adored young mother. Pa had coughed up blood when Little Brother died, and again when Ma had her breakdown during World War II. His doctors believed that he was hemorrhaging from stress. Had Pa had his own little tin box, but never found anyone with another key?

I had kept an emotional distance from our old house after moving into my new office, but in reliving that moment of Pa's grief on its front steps, I felt pulled towards it as if I had no will. After writing some notes in David's folder and closing up for the day, I stepped into the parking lot, put my things in my car, and faced our old house, looking at it as intently as I had been avoiding it. The hedge was taller and denser after all these years, but I found a place where my grown self could squeeze through. It was dusk and lights had come on in the house and I could see a figure in a white coat moving about in one of our old rooms. I'm a trespasser now, aren't I, I thought. I hope nobody comes out. I just want to stand here for a few minutes and look around. But when I looked for familiar things almost everything was gone —the garage where Mary and

I had hidden from Hope when we played with our dolls, the tool house in the far corner (we had called it the "puppy house" when Lindy had her puppies there), the grape arbor, and the tree growing beside it where Hope used to climb to get away from us so she could read. Unsightly additions had been put on the back of the house, but our sleeping porch was still there and the brick patio underneath, and a few feet away was the very spot where my rabbit's pen had been. I could see a little girl pushing down on that pen, pushing down on her rabbit, although she did not know she was doing that, and I could see her coming out the next morning to play with it and finding it dead. I could hear her screams, see her running into the patio and the nurse running out and hear the rebuking words, "I thought something was really wrong."

Then I could see her turn from the nurse and walk slowly away.

"Maybe it died for some other reason!" I called out, breaking the evening silence. It was the therapist me speaking, wanting to give her a morsel to cling to. But as soon as the words came out, I knew that she would know it was false hope. Her arms, my arms, would never forget what they had done.

Reliving that agonizing moment was too much to bear. I pushed my way back through the hedge, getting a mean scratch on my cheek, and headed for the safety of my car. I'll stay here a while, I thought, leaning back exhausted against the seat. I don't have to go home. Alex isn't there anymore. He isn't waiting for me. I don't have to be anywhere.

So often when I was experiencing something intensely, I could feel Beth's presence. I imagined telling her now about being in this office next to my old house and knowing how intently she would be listening.

"It's amazing!" I could hear her say. "It's just amazing how it's come around like this. There you were over there needing so desperately for someone to hear you and now you are in a room in that old tavern on the other side of the hedge listening to the pain of your clients. If you put it in a novel no one would believe it. It would seem too contrived."

So Long! It's Been Good To Know You

It is dead low tide, but the tide is about to turn. I am at the beach way out alone in that daily appearing and disappearing realm of the farthest sandbars. I am wading in the warm shallows, then crossing the soft, spongy newly revealed sand and reentering the shallows again, taking care not to step on a scuttling crab. Suddenly I see a huge tidal wave approaching and in a moment I will be inundated. I must move quickly. I do not recall running, but the wave pauses too, as though giving me a head start before the race to save my life.

When I had that other tidal wave dream before moving back to Long Island I had wondered if it was a warning not to return. Was this new dream telling me that it was time now for me to leave? I did not want to think so. Living here in these recent years I had been more content than I had ever been. But Long Island was no longer the beautiful, comforting environment I had grown up in. It had become restless and irritable with an exploding population straining its resources, and it seemed now beyond help. But it was not just Long Island that was changing. The whole world was changing. The human race had stumbled into the first Cold War in recorded history and was waking each morning to the possibility of nuclear annihilation. If the Russians decided to send a nuclear missile our way, they would surely target

New York City, the biggest prize. Long Island would be wiped out, or fatally contaminated. It was an uneasy time. I had come so late to some semblance of maturity it seemed as if my life were just beginning and, greedily, I was not ready for it to be snuffed out under a mushroom cloud. It shamed me to be thinking of running away to save my own life and abandoning Long Island, my beloved nation, to its fate, but if I moved to a place where I could still see stars and hear silence, I could say —and it would be true —that my nation had left me.

In the months that followed I thought often about that dream. I would see myself again on those far out bars with the huge wave cresting behind me, then pausing and waiting. It was so beautiful out there and so clean, washed and re-washed each day by the incoming tides. Standing there looking back at the land, I could believe I was living in Indian times. Perhaps I would be gathering clams to bring back to a settlement where smoke from a cooking fire would be rising with the wind.

But I was living in the twentieth century. Any smoke that I saw would be rising from the stacks of an electric company and there was always the sound of human beings on the move, the slap-slap-slapping of motorboats out in the bay and the droning of planes leaving and returning to the airports of New York. And yet I still could not bear to leave.

"How much longer will you give me, Tsunami?" I asked.

My answer came with the news that my landlady had died and that her estate —her house and grounds and my tiny paradise —was to be sold. Painful though it would be to leave, I knew that the time had come for me to put down roots in new soil. I could explore new places and perhaps it would be easier, now that my long affair with Long Island was coming to an end, to say yes to this new search. It was time to let go of the past and let the dead rest in peace.

I have always loved crossing the Long Island Sound on the Port Jefferson ferry. In my childhood the town of Port Jefferson was associated with pleasure. Ma, a skilled seamstress, was always happy when she drove there with us to look for material in a dry goods store. After she had made her purchases she would buy us ice cream cones.

On the other hand you might think I would dislike that town and that ferry because I made my first crossing just after my twin died. Because she could not bear to hear me calling for him, Ma was sending me away to stay with her brother and his wife. A lady she knew had agreed to look out for me on the voyage. I have no recollection of how I felt, but I have a vivid memory of sitting beside a kind stranger on the starboard deck in the warmth of the eastern sun. I always try to find a seat on the same starboard side when the ferry crosses to Connecticut and I am sitting there now on my way to the North Country to search for a place that I can call home. The morning sun floods in from the east as it did on that first crossing. The water is deep blue and choppy and seagulls are soaring and crying.

As I sit there I recall another journey. This time I am the kind stranger, escorting William, a small black child, to a destination unknown to him. I have been dispatched by the children's home where I work to fetch him from the city in the agency's car. It is a few weeks before Christmas. William sits beside me, mute with fear. The previous night his father had beaten up his mother. She is in the hospital and his father is in jail. A neighbor had rescued William and brought him to a child welfare agency where he waited most of the day while arrangements were made for his care. He had refused to eat or speak or play with the toys offered him and sat rigidly, awaiting his fate. It is nearly dark when we start out on our journey. It has been snowing and the city is lying under a fresh white blanket. I drive out on Park Avenue, the city's widest and most beautiful. On the median a row of Christmas trees extends as far as the eye can see, sparkling with blue lights. Barely high enough to view through the window, William, watches the scene intently. Then I hear him say the word "blue," finally breaking his silence.

I decide to walk back to the stern of the ferry and stand there for a while, watching Long Island disappear. I can see the receding towers of the electric company overlooking the bay where I have spent the most contented hours of my life.

We become children again, don't we, when we are on the beach," Beth had said when we walked there together.

I imagine that beach now, seeing the piles of flotsam brought in by the tide and the big rock I have climbed so many times, and feeling the warmth of the sand on the soles of my feet. Another recent dream comes to mind:

The water in the sound is turbulent. I am swimming in this rough water and see a huge wave approaching. I dive under it and start riding it to shore, but I see a log ahead of me that is being thrown about by the waves. If it hits me it can kill me, but I am able to ride past it and leap safely to the shore.

Perhaps this dream has given me the confidence to make this painful parting, to make the final leap, for here I am on this boat, taking my leave from Whitman's and my beloved island. It will always be my nation. And while I know, as I search for a new place to put down my roots, that I will never again find the passion of first love, I am older now and readier, perhaps, for quieter companionship.

The ferry shudders as it slows into docking mode. I have been lost in reverie and have not realized that the crossing is over.

ENVOI

"I used to live here. May I come in?"

I wake from a dream sobbing, saying those words. I see myself standing on the front steps of our old house on Long Island where Pa cried for Lindy. Someone has answered my knock. Almost twenty years have passed since I left Long Island, so why am I dreaming now about going in? Although I have been working on this memoir and deeply engaged in the reliving of my life's story, that does not seem to be enough to explain the intensity of the crying. Then I remember a movie I have just seen, an adaptation of Michael Cunningham's novel *The Hours*, and I start sobbing again. All the people in that movie were crying. Even the music was crying. I can still hear the score by Philip Glass moving relentlessly behind that unbearable sadness. I had seen myself in the character of Richard, the writer who believes he has failed, and I found the scene of his mother's abandonment when he was a little boy almost too painful to watch.

As I relive that scene now, I imagine another scene that was not in the movie. The grown Richard is standing on the steps of the house where he had lived with his mother and father. He rings the bell and a strange woman opens the door. "I used to live here," he says. "May I come in?" He goes directly to the kitchen and opens one of the cabinets. He is looking for the bowl in which he and his mother mixed a cake for his father's birthday. It is not there. The cabinet is filled with unfamiliar utensils. He runs out of the house. Standing on the steps, he remembers his child self, looking after a car that was carrying his mother away. He covers his eyes.

I must go down into our old house, I say to myself. I must finish my story.

I am standing on the steps of our old house and this is *not* a dream. I have driven to Connecticut from upstate New York where I now live, boarding the ferry in Bridgeport, playing my movie backwards, with the stacks of the electric company coming into view and a graceful curve of Long Island's sandy shore marking the entrance to Port Jefferson harbor. I have driven to the village of Smithtown along the old east-west road, remembering its twists and turns, driven into our old yard and parked in the blacktopped parking lot. A plaque on the front door tells me to walk in and report to the receptionist. I open it, but there is no receptionist in sight. Looking through the doorway into our old living room where I gave Ma the present she didn't want, I can see the mantle where we hung our Christmas stockings and half expect to see the portrait of Little Brother hanging over it. Two sofas are placed on either side of the fireplace, not unlike the ones that we had, and patients are sitting there waiting for their appointments.

The stairs to the second story lead straight up in front of me, just as I remember them. Since there is no receptionist to report to, I boldly march up, for these are my stairs. I know every tread. When I reach the landing, I open a door and look into my parents' bedroom. It seems almost unchanged. It is being used for storage now. Cartons are stacked here and there, and there is that same old radiator under the front window. I remember standing on a chair in front of that window, chopping off my hair with Ma's sewing scissors. She had gone out in the car, and as I cut I watched for her return, reasoning that if I stopped before she came back and put the scissors where I had found them, she would not know that I had done it. ("Why do you dress your little boy like your little girls?" someone had asked her in due course, humiliating her.)

Free thus far to wander, I head towards our old nursery. I want to stand on the steps where Ma had stood, looking down with her frightening face, but find myself instead in a no-man's land. Partitions have been knocked down, the nursery walled off, and this new space has become a file room for patients' records, and a storage area for office supplies. I start to leave when someone appears, wanting to know who I am. I am fortunate that this young woman is friendly and when learning that I once lived here, offers to guide me through the rest of the house. On our way down the stairs she points to a room across the hall from my parents' bedroom and asks me what it was used for. It is empty. It is the room where Little Brother died and where I imagined him lying on a bed in the corner with Ma sitting beside him, wiping his forehead. "I don't know," I lie, as the vision vanishes. "Maybe it was a guest room."

I could go in there now. I could cross that threshold, but I do not want to. I am not supposed to go into that room.

As my guide leads me down the stairs, I realize that what I most urgently want to see is the fireplace in the back hall where Little Brother fell and cut his head. When we enter that hall, I am lost again in another alien world. New partitions have been put in, creating a row of offices, and busy people are moving about, but I know just where that fireplace is. I head for it, but it is not there. It is hidden behind a wall.

"There's a fireplace in there," I say to my guide.

"Somebody told me that. It's been boarded up ever since I've been here."

I can't believe this! I have needed all my life to see that fireplace and it is right there! I want to say, "Tear down this wall!" but it is not my fireplace. It is theirs.

"Why is the floor we are standing on half wood and half brick?" one of the doctors asks, learning who I am.

"Because the room we are in extends out over part of an old patio." I do not add, "*where Hope's nurse and I had that fateful encounter.*"

My guide and I continue our tour and she takes me into our old dining room. It is a clerical office now with humming computers and busy printers. We move on into our old kitchen and there is our cranky old cook with the stiff white hair growing out of her chin. She is sitting at a table with my mother, planning the meals for the day. But the kitchen is a medical laboratory now and the vision vanishes. It is all becoming too much and I tell my guide that I must go. So she leads me out of an unfamiliar door that has been cut through the side of the house, giving access to the parking lot. I thank her for her kindness.

As soon as the door closes, I burst into tears. Some patients are getting out of a car and I don't want to be seen crying. I recover myself, and to avoid them I walk behind the house as if I have some purpose, some right to be here.

"Can I help you?" a voice calls out. A woman in a white coat is leaning out of a window.

"I used to live here," I call back. "I'm just wandering around our old yard for a bit. I'll be leaving soon."

She waves and closes the window.

I look at what's left in our old yard, trying to see some growing thing that is familiar and can find nothing. Ivy that was not there is climbing the trees and marching across our old lawn and some strange vine is strangling the privet hedge, making it impenetrable. There will be no more passages of a small child through that hedge.

And for a moment I am that small child again. I have been sent out to play in our yard and I am alone and lonely. Hope and Mary are in school on the other side of the hedge and I have nothing to do. I wander over to our old horse chestnut tree, long since gone to the whine of a chain saw, and gather some of the shiny brown fruit that has fallen to the ground. I put a few to treasure in my pocket and throw the others at nothing in particular. That day blends with another, and I am sitting by the side of the road in front of the house making mud balls and throwing them at the occasional passing car. One goes into the open window of one of those cars and it slows down and stops. I am frightened and run over to the puppy house where I can hide. I wait and wait. Then my father appears, my young father. He is home from work. He has seen me. There is no point in hiding anymore. He comes and takes me over his knee and starts to spank me, but he is laughing so hard it is not a bad spanking. I am not supposed to see that he is laughing. I learn later that my mud ball landed in a basket of freshly washed laundry that was being delivered by a laundress and her husband in their new little Ford. This is my fondest memory of Pa and one that I want never to forget. Where did that young father go?

I should be leaving, but I am still not ready to go. Instead I walk in the direction of the puppy house, but of course it is no longer there. A locust tree has seeded itself where the puppy house used to be. When I reach that tree, I lean against it, and the tears that had started when I left the house burst out of me again. I cannot understand why this grief goes so deep. Is it because I will never be here again? For I will not. Surely, awful as it is, it is not just because of what has been done to our old house and our yard. I imagine myself back in the house, climbing the stairs, passing my parents' bedroom, finding the nursery gone, then hurrying past the room where my twin lay dying, and following my guide down the stairs. I can feel myself being drawn like a magnet into the back hall and to the fireplace where he fell, and stand there again in front of the wall that is hiding it.

But why is there such urgency to see it? What will that old fireplace tell me? Will seeing it again, just an empty space lined with old bricks, erase the memory of my crowding him to get through the door and his tricycle tipping and his having that terrible fall? Will I be spared remembering him in the lap of the woman I hated, with blood gushing from his forehead and being told to "go away?" No! But I know now that in wanting to see it, I had thought, although not really thought, that in seeing it, I would have seen *him* again. Standing at Anna's knee I could have looked at him and he at me, and I could have said, "I'm sorry, Brudder. I didn't mean to hurt you."

42166447R00166

Made in the USA
Lexington, KY
11 June 2015